How to Hold a
Crocodile

How to Hold a Crocodile

The Diagram Group

FIREFLY BOOKS

A Firefly Book

Published by Firefly Books Ltd. 2003

Copyright © 2003 Diagram Visual Information Limited

First printing

Publisher Cataloging-in-Publication Data (U.S.)
(Library of Congress Standards)

How to hold a crocodile / the Diagram Group. –2nd ed.
[192] p. : col. ill. ; cm.

Originally published: London: Sidgwick and Jackson Ltd, 1981.
Includes index.
Summary: Explains how to do practical and improbable things, such as how to roast an ox, handle a hamster, photograph a fish, play the bagpipes, vanquish a vampire.

ISBN 1-55297-805-2

1. Handbooks, manuals, etc. 2. Curiosities and wonders. I. the Diagram Group.
II. Title.

031/ .02 21   AG105.H853 2003

National Library of Canada Cataloguing in Publication Data

How to hold a crocodile / the Diagram Group.—2nd ed.

Includes index.

ISBN 1-55297-805-2

1. Handbooks, vade-mecums, etc. 2. Amusements. 3. Games.

I. Diagram Group

AG105.H69 2003031.02   C2003-902066-5

Published in the United States in 2003 by
Firefly Books (U.S.) Inc.
P.O. Box 1338, Ellicott Station
Buffalo, New York 14205

Published in Canada in 2003 by
Firefly Books Ltd.
3680 Victoria Park Avenue
Toronto, Ontario, M2H 3K1

A Diagram Book first created by Diagram Visual Information Limited of
195 Kentish Town Road, London NW5 2JU

Cover design: Sari Naworynski
Cover photo: Philip Habib/Getty Images
Printed in Canada

how to...

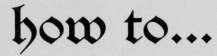

8/ make a bed - handle a hamster - serve port - tell when the Queen of England is at home 9/ keep plants happy - race a crocodile - thread beads easily 10/ make an artesian well - teach a parrot to talk - preserve leaves and flowers 11/ change your name - make a mobius strip - get an audience with the Pope - find a perfect number 12/ make the Moutza sign - play a nose flute - take a pulse 13/ break a thread in a sealed bottle - make Jell-O or jelly set quickly 14/ name the parts of a flag - measure a mile - store wine 15/ become a saint - make a rotten pot - pickle walnuts 16/ make a mummy 17/ leave the earth 18/ wear the toga - tell a centipede from a millipede - cut jade 19/ read music notation 20/ cut a block of ice into one! - photograph fish - store rubber sheeting - peel tomatoes 21/ play Tlachtli - keep the birds at bay - glaze a window 22/ play the bagpipes - classify boxers - identify a diamond - make tanning oil 23/ signal by semaphore - make cottage cheese - make a spanner or wrench smaller - do a headstand 24/ keep flies away - increase your lifting power - get the old cat to accept a new kitten 25/ dry herbs - vanquish a vampire - stop ink smearing in the rain 26-27/ play Hex 28/ personalize a squash - seat an orchestra - go for gold - make candles last longer 29/ peel onions without tears - decode Morse - tell your ass from your hinny 30/ read the secrets of Leonardo DaVinci - improve your diving 31/ make zabaglione - play comb and paper - hold a pigeon 32/ play shove ha'penny - stop a creaking stair - make cawdell cup 33/ cure insect stings - ride a ski tow - play dominoes 34/ escape from quicksand - climb through a playing card - name a horse's gait 35/ make compost 36/ read your palm 37/ bring in the boar's head - bow Japanese style 38/ tie packages tightly - read boustrophedon writing - throw a discus 39/ know the Queen of England's swans - tell a horse's age 40/ know the Olympian gods - tell a crocodile from an alligator 41/ draw a triangle with three right angles 42/ jug a hare - play jacks - get a carp to come when you call 43/ cure a hangover - walk farther - build a sandcastle 44/ measure your head for a wig - copy a picture carved on stone - keep a silver teapot fresh 45/ tell an ape from a monkey - use the binary system - store cheese 46-47/ play Nyout 48/ recognize gold - make a bouquet garni - make a tripod - stop rugs from slipping - take nasty medicine 49/ action paint - measure humidity - remove a tight ring 50/ calculate a birthday - dance the hora - sharpen kitchen scissors 51/ play conkers 52/ tie a clove hitch - protect your cutlery - spot an ectomorph - have four birthdays in a year 53/ crown a soufflé - bottle a whole pear - medicate a cat - prevent facial frostbite 54/ paint a wooden window - crack a coconut - bull your boots 55/ pass a federal law in the US - make Vichyssoise - twist wire 56/ signal at sea 57/ make a brass rubbing - decorate eggs for Easter - tighten a loose screw 58/ make bird's nest soup - clean a saucepan - make your candle fit your candlestick - get rid of a red nose - measure a horse 59/ take a cutting - tame a tarantula 60/ choose fruit trees - prevent string tangling - build a tipi 61/ keep storms away at sea - make a potato print - roast chestnuts 62/ ease toothache by acupressure - tell a zebra from a zubra - improvise an oil lamp - play

135/ pan for gold - ride an ostrich - make Greek or Turkish coffee 136/ hive a swarm of bees - repair a flat bicycle tire 137/ draw an equilateral triangle - pick the apple from the top of the tree - make muesli 138/ find your blind spot - tell the speed of the wind at sea 139/ extract a broken cork - find a coryphee - take the temperature of a cat or dog - tell a cockatrice from a basilisk 140/ ride an elephant - do the lotus - confuse your English 141/ tell the bow from the stern - measure a flea's leap 142/ build a great pyramid - celebrate the Chinese New Year - splint a bird's leg 143/ read an alchemist's formula - dress crab and lobster - make beads from paper 144/ recognize classical columns - catch a cockroach - mount a horse 145/ use a tinderbox - tell a frog from a toad 146-147/ play Pachisi 148/ have a black dinner - get to sleep without pills - name the parts of a gun 149/ be a butler - wear the kilt 150/ get into a life preserver - follow the language of the fan 151/ track a fieldmouse - drink yan - fold a napkin into a fan - remove bags under the eyes 152/ play the spoons - keep a chameleon - cheat fattening squash/vegetable marrows 153/ name your bones 154/ mix concrete - make a daisy chain - know when Easter day will be 155/ understand animal language - split a log - empty bottles quickly 156/ avoid your creditors - feed a panda - know what clouds bring 157/ know your patron saint - climb a rope 158/ repel cavalry - keep an octopus 159/ build a log cabin - recognize comedians and tragedians 160/ mix Chinese ink - throw a lasso - improve your memory - keep a hedgehog happy 161/ measure the flow rate of a river 162/ seat guests at table - raise silkworms 163/ tell a bactrian from a dromedary - avoid the evil eye - tell the sex of an earwig 164/ make a camel dung cigarette lighter - recognize a Greek vase - cross the line 165/ make it rain - clean rusty needles - gain an indulgence - ease backache 166-167/ play Agon 168/ change from the dog to the dragon - polish stone - be a valet 169/ measure the distances of stars and planets - make a hair rinse 170/ calculate volumes - look fat or thin 171/ roast an ox - name the parts of a sword 172/ improve your posture - build an arch - make a square knot or reef knot 173/ make invisible ink - remove a dent from a table tennis ball - carry out resuscitation 174/ drill for oil - be a lady's maid - tell port from starboard - clean stone 175/ milk a goat - determine the new year - play the knicky-knackers 176/ read the tale of the tail - identify the gods of Egypt 177/ improvise a buoyancy aid 178/ identify the apostles and the evangelists - name the "points" of a horse 179/ make pasta - prevent a nail from splitting wood - tell when someone is lying 180/ read Hebrew numerals - be average - move around in space 181/ interpret wine labels - keep flamingo's pink - distil water 182/ make a Zen garden - predict a volcanic eruption 183/ wear the saree - trap slugs 184-185/ play Chinese dominoes 186/ recognize mythical beasts 187/ grow a crystal garden - make a cake for birds - heat a roman villa 188/ hold a crocodile - recognize a member of The Diagram Group.

Included in this book (pp.26-27, 46-47, 66-67, 86-87, 106-107, 126-127, 146-147, 166-2167) are instructions on how to play some interesting and unusual board games. Find or improvise your own playing pieces and use our large illustrations of the boards as a playing area.

How to handle a hamster

An irritable or aggressive hamster can give quite a nip so treat it with respect, and wash the smell of food off your fingers before trying to handle it or a finger might be confused with dinner! You can lift a hamster by the loose skin of the scruff of the neck, but when it is tame it is better to grasp it firmly around the body and support it on the hand. Avoid sudden movements and noise and always handle the animal gently. There should be no need to wear gloves.

How to make a bed

First the foot,
Then the head.
That's the way to
make a bed.

How to serve port

A lot depends on the port: vintage and vintage style (also called "crusted") port are matured in the bottle and produce a heavy sediment. It's essential to decant them carefully into a clear glass decanter. The bottle should be stored with the label uppermost, so keep it that way when pouring. If there is a lot of sediment you may need to run the port through a funnel with filter paper in it. Tawny port, which is matured in wood and then bottled, has much less sediment, and ruby port is a blend of young wines and is usually clear.

Port is best drunk from a port glass as a dessert wine after a meal. At formal dinners the decanter is passed from right to left around the table, and it's considered bad taste to let the decanter "rest" in front of you while others may be thirsty!

How to tell when the Queen of England is at home

Take a look at the flagstaff on the building. If the Royal Standard is flying Her Majesty is in the building. Don't confuse the Royal Standard with the Union Jack, which may be flown for many reasons. The Royal Standard is the Queen's personal flag and the rules covering its usage are strict indeed. It is hoisted only when the Queen is in the building and never when she is passing in procession.

how to keep plants happy

Plants, like human beings, are sensitive to their environment and relate to the temperaments and moods of people. A hostile gardener who ignores his plants will induce wilting and a gardener who is violent in ripping them up will cause fear and shrinking: the picked plants will die sooner; those remaining in the soil will be traumatized and stunted. A gardener who speaks encouragingly and soothingly to his or her plants, who approaches them with real affection, will make them grow and flourish.

It may seem anthropomorphic to use words like mood and emotion about plants but the measurable chemical and electrostatic changes in the plant are as real as similar ones that occur in us when emotional changes take place. Plants are to some extent telepathic and will distinguish between gestures of hostility and those of tending. You *can* speak of keeping your plants happy, and one of the ways to do it is to talk to them as you might to a child or pet. Another way is to play pleasant music: Mozart or Bach or some gentle Schubert seem to have the best effect. Plants' nerves, like those of experimental rats and of some human beings, can, it seems, be jangled by harsh pop music or the more violent sounds of Stockhausen. Whether you are providing an ambience of pop, jazz or classical music make it a mellifluous sound. Our more complex nervous systems and capacity to articulate and rationalize may relish the stimulus of punk rock or a blast of Bartok but the "vibes" they set off may upset your aspidistra.

However, keeping plants happy is not simply a matter of loving. The first principles of gardening come before talking to your roses. Soil and nutrients must be right, the climate good, potting and planting must allow untangled root growth, drainage must be right and there must be a proper balance of sunshine and watering.

How to race a crocodile
Don't fool yourself: if you are ever chased by a crocodile remember that it can run very fast indeed! But fortunately a crocodile cannot make sudden changes of direction. To outwit your pursuer don't run straight, make a series of zig-zags: but make it snappy. If you don't the crocodile will!

HOW TO THREAD BEADS EASILY

DIP THE END OF THE STRING IN NAIL POLISH OR RUB IT WITH SOAP. THIS WILL STIFFEN IT. LAY THE BEADS IN ONE INDENTATION OF A PIECE OF CORRUGATED CARDBOARD AND YOU CAN PUSH THE STRING THROUGH A ROW AT A TIME – THIS ONLY WORKS WITH BEADS OF EQUAL SIZE.

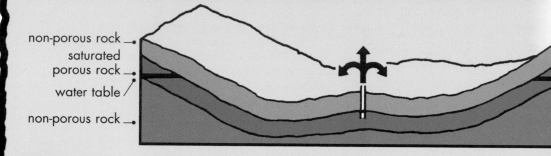

non-porous rock
saturated
porous rock
water table
non-porous rock

HOW TO MAKE AN ARTESIAN WELL

Dig a hole in the right place. Artesian wells may only be sunk in artesian basins. These are areas where a porous layer of rock is sandwiched between non-porous layers in a basin-like geological formation. Rain that falls on the exposed part of the porous rock sinks down through the strata but is prevented from escaping by the non-porous sandwich. The level of saturated porous rock, the water table, is frequently higher than the lowest points in the basin. Sink a well below water table level, and the trapped water will gush out, driven by the pressure of water still within the rock. In some parts of the world the exposed porous strata can be hundreds of miles distant from the location of artesian wells.

How to teach a parrot to talk

The African Gray parrot and the Amazon parrots of South America are among the best mimics of the bird world. Individuals vary in their ability to learn and a great deal depends on the perseverance of their teacher. The higher register of a woman's or child's voice is believed to be easier for most birds to copy. Patient repetition in a darkened room without any distractions is the keynote of success. To save giving up your own time, tape the phrase you wish the bird to copy, and play it for ten minutes a day. Birds also learn to associate words. A telephone ringing may prompt a parrot to say "Hello," or a faucet turned on may be a cue for the bird to make the sound of running water. Attempts to mimic something may at first be very garbled but they become clearer with practice.

How to preserve leaves and flowers

There are three ways to preserve plant material – drying them in air, with a desiccant (drying) powder, or with glycerin. Some plants are better suited to one method than another.

Air-drying Suitable for grasses, seedheads, everlasting flowers, and a few others such as acanthus, goldenrod, mimosa and sea holly. Cut flowers on a warm, dry day, just before they are fully open. Remove leaves. Tie small flowers in bunches with a loop to hang them up. Hang larger flowers separately, or stand them upright in a jar. Average drying time: 1–3 weeks.

Desiccant powder Use, in order of preference, silica gel crystals, borax, sand. Put a layer of crystals or powder in the bottom of a box, lay the flowers on top, and cover with more powder. Average drying time: two days. You can dry and reuse the material. This method suits a wide variety of flowers.

Glycerin About the only method for leaves. Make a mixture of two parts of hot water to one of glycerin and stand the stems of your sprays of leaves in it. In 4–5 days the water in the leaves will be replaced by glycerin, and they will have turned dark.

Muhammad Ali

Irving Berlin

Margot Fonteyn

Greta Garbo

Al Jolson

Marilyn Monroe

Mark Twain

Voltaire

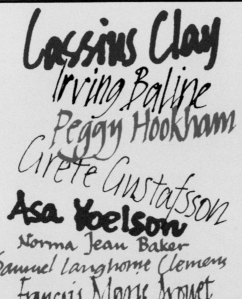

How to change your name

In the United States and the United Kingdom it's simple – you can just do it. An American can establish his or her right to a new name just by using it. But it's advisable to obtain a court order as well, or you may run into problems of legal identity. British citizens can also adopt new names if they wish. But again it's advisable to have some legal proof of the change, either by swearing an affidavit in front of a lawyer, or by a deed poll, a written declaration drawn up by a lawyer. In any case it's helpful to advertise your change of name in your local newspaper. It's just as simple to change your name in some other countries, but in many you have to obtain permission from a government department. Make sure you inform your bank, tax office, insurance companies, etc, that you have changed your name.

HOW TO MAKE A MOBIUS STRIP

CUT A STRIP OF PAPER, TWIST IT ONCE, THEN GLUE THE ENDS TOGETHER (A). YOU HAVE NOW FORMED A STRIP WITH ONLY ONE SURFACE; YOU CAN PROVE THIS BY STARTING AT ANY POINT AND DRAWING A LINE ALONG THE STRIP. IT WILL EVENTUALLY JOIN UP (B).

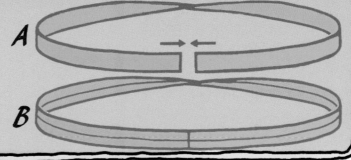

How to get an audience with the Pope

The Master of the Ante-Chamber at the Vatican arranges all audiences with the Pope. You should apply to him, stating your reasons for wishing to see His Holiness. If you are successful in your application you will receive a letter telling you the time and place of the audience, and what you should wear. If you are a Roman Catholic, you may be well advised to ask your bishop to write to the rector of the appropriate national college in Rome, who will make all the arrangements.

HOW TO FIND A PERFECT NUMBER

TO SEE WHETHER A NUMBER IS PERFECT, FIND ALL THE NUMBERS THAT CAN BE EXACTLY DIVIDED INTO IT. ADD THEM TOGETHER; IF THE TOTAL IS THE ORIGINAL NUMBER, THEN THAT NUMBER IS PERFECT. THERE ARE ONLY THREE PERFECT NUMBERS UNDER 500; THEY ARE 6, 28 AND 496.

How to make the Moutza sign

This Greek insult can be made in five different strengths: all mean "go to the devil".

1 Bring the arm forward toward the victim with the thumb and last two fingers folded and the first two in a V-sign.
2 Make the same movement with the palm flat and all fingers spread (=×2).
3 Do it with both hands at once (=×4).
4 Push the sole of your foot at the victim as well (=×6).
5 Push both feet forward and both hands (=×8). This is a very serious insult. Be careful of raising your palm when politely refusing another drink or other offers in Greece: it is easily confused with the *moutza* sign.

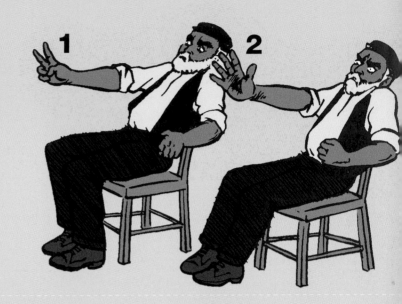

How to play a nose flute
This instrument is sounded by the breath from the nostril instead of from the mouth. It produces a weaker flow of air, but nose breath is thought by some peoples of the Pacific to have special powers. In Polynesia the nose flute is regarded as a national instrument. Most are side-blown, like orchestral flutes, but in Borneo they are blown from the end. There are few finger holes and melodies are characterized by wide leaps between notes. To play a nose flute one nostril is plugged with cloth, or sometimes with tobacco, or pressed closed with a finger. The breath is then directed down the nose and across the breath hole. This sets off a train of eddies within the flute which produces a tone that can be varied in pitch by covering and uncovering the stop holes along its length. The lungs are refilled by breathing through the mouth.

How to take a pulse

The easiest place to take a pulse is at the wrist, whether it's your own or someone else's. The fingers – not the thumb because the ball of the thumb has too strong a pulse of its own – should be lightly but firmly pressed over the radial artery. You'll find it about $1/3$ inch (1cm) in from the thumb side of the wrist. Move your fingers around a little if you can't find it right away; you will soon feel the gentle throbbing. Count the number of beats in 30 seconds, using a watch with a second hand to make sure you time it exactly, then multiply by two. A healthy pulse can be very variable. The average resting adult's rate is 72 per minute but can range from 60–80; children have a higher rate and a baby's may be 140. If active or excited the pulse rate will increase. In cases of accident and loss of blood, especially suspected internal bleeding, take the pulse every five minutes, making a note of time and rate. A rising rate is an indication of continuing loss of blood.

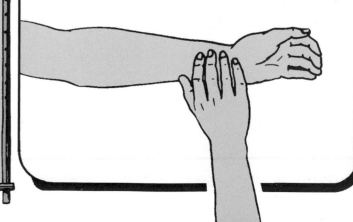

HOW TO BREAK A THREAD IN A SEALED BOTTLE

Take an empty wine bottle, screw a small hook into the base of the cork, and tie to it a thin thread with a small weight attached to the other end. Drop the weight and thread into the bottle, insert the cork and seal with sealing wax or tape. Now challenge your friends to sever the thread without breaking the seal or shaking the bottle. The way to do this is very simple, but not many people will guess how without being told. You can sever the thread without even touching the bottle. Take it out into the sunlight and use a magnifying glass to concentrate the sun's rays until the thread burns through. Of course, you'll look pretty silly if you try this trick on a cloudy day!

How to make Jell-O or jelly set quickly
Do not use the full amount of hot water to dissolve the gelatine. Top up the full measure with cubes of ice and stir them well in. That will bring the temperature down rapidly and speed setting.

©DIAGRAM

How to name the parts of a flag

The part of the flag nearest the flagstaff or pole is the hoist; the part furthest away is the fly. The flag is raised and lowered on a rope called a halyard (haul yard) attached to the flagstaff pole or mast. The round ball usually topping the staff is called a truck. Heraldic terms may be used to describe the flag design: the background color is the field and a cut out section is a canton.

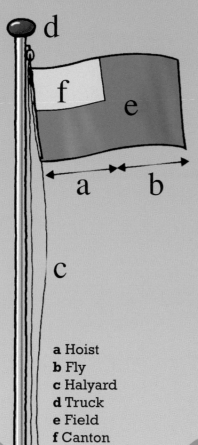

a Hoist
b Fly
c Halyard
d Truck
e Field
f Canton

How to measure a mile

We get our word from the Latin *mille* (one thousand) and it had its origin in the Roman army. The standard pace of the Roman legionnaire was two strides, making a measure of about five feet. When he had taken 1,000 paces he had marched about 5,000 feet, not far off the 5,280 feet of a modern statutory mile. The pace (**A**) was not the only measure based on the human body to provide a rough and ready measure available to everyone. The cubit was the length of a man's forearm from the elbow to the tip of the middle finger, and was divided into palms and digits, and we all know about feet.

Gradually these measurements became standardized. The Romans fixed the cubit at the equivalent of 26.6 inches, and that was divided into 2 feet, each 12 *unciae* long.

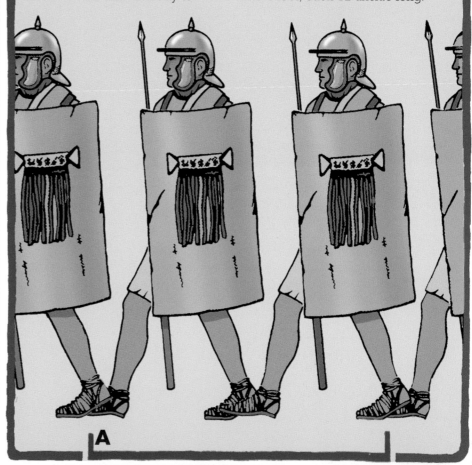

A

How to store wine

Bottled wine should always be stored on its side. That prevents the cork from drying out. Keep it in a cool place with an even temperature.

how to become a saint

To be canonized – that is, officially recognized as a saint – you have to be dead! But everything depends on the holy life you led. Since the 1200s the Roman Catholic Church has strictly controlled canonization, which is now the responsibility of a Vatican department called the Sacred Congregation of Rites. In the Eastern Orthodox Church the process is local: a bishop can proclaim canonization. The Roman Catholic process begins with BEATIFICATION, a declaration that the person concerned is blessed. A local court under a bishop first investigates the person's life. He or she must have shown heroism in following the Christian faith, and the person must have been responsible for at least two miracles either during life or after death. A "promoter of the Faith," commonly called the Devil's Advocate, makes sure that the whole truth about the person is made known, however unfavorable. Then the person's writings are examined, and if all is well the case is passed on to the Sacred Congregation for examination. If this body is satisfied, the Pope orders a ceremony of beatification to be held in St Peter's Basilica in Rome.

After beatification a similar process is carried out before canonization, and proof is needed of at least two more miracles, performed since beatification. The whole process may take many years. For example, Joan of Arc was canonized in 1920, 489 years after her death.

HOW TO MAKE A ROTTEN POT

Pot pourri gets its name from the French *pot putrère* – rotten pot – but is a fragrant mixture of dried petals, scented leaves, herbs and spices. You can make it from a wide variety of scented flowers and plants including bay, borage, camomile, carnations, honeysuckle, jasmine, lavender, marigolds, marjoram, mignonette, pinks, rosemary, roses, stock, thyme, verbena, violets and wallflowers. The quantities of each are not important, providing the resulting medley of smells pleases you.

Dry pot pourri: Lay out the ingredients, cover with a fine net or loosely woven cloth and dry with a hair dryer.

Wet pot pourri: In a large glass jar with a lid or stopper lay dried petals, etc, alternating with layers of half their depth of un-iodized salt (sea salt for example). Alternate until jar is full, pressing down firmly as you proceed. Keep for 6 weeks in a cool, dark place. Keep jar closed when not in use. When the lid is removed the fragrance will permeate the room.

©DIAGRAM

How to pickle walnuts
Use fresh green walnuts. Shell them and prick the walnuts with a steel fork. Soak in strong brine (salt-water) for 7 days, stirring well two or three times daily. Repeat for a second week in fresh brine. Drain and spread walnuts in sun to dry. When black, pack in convenient jars and cover with spiced vinegar. They are delicious served with cheese.

HOW TO MAKE A MUMMY

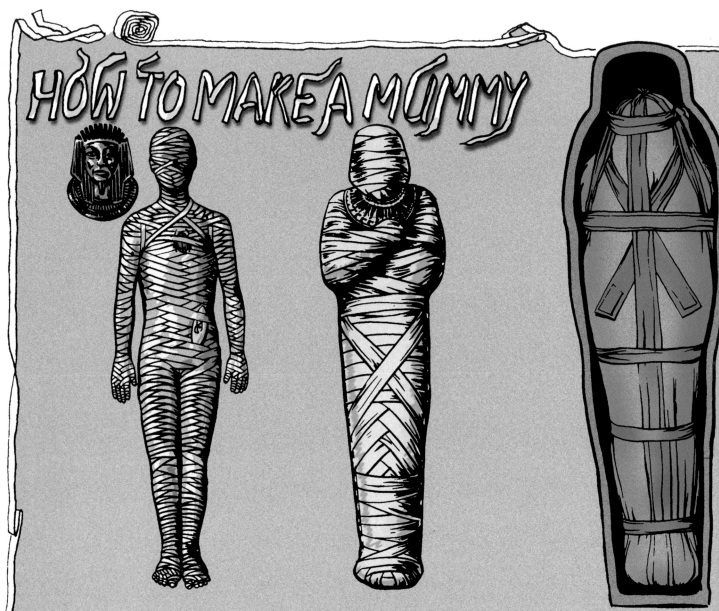

First remove from the body those organs which putrefy most rapidly: the brain and viscera (stomach intestines, lungs, liver, etc). The body organs can be removed by making an incision on the left side of the abdomen. The heart, being the seat of understanding, is usually left in the body. By puncturing a hole in the ethmoid bone of the nose the brain can be drawn out through the nostrils. Anything left in the skull can then be dissolved away with aromatic lotions. The removed body parts are placed in containers with a combination of sodium carbonate and sodium bicarbonate which occurs naturally in Egypt and is known as natron. This dehydrates them. The body is also filled and surrounded by natron which absorbs the moisture

and dissolves the body fats: this may take four weeks or more. The natron and any cloths or other materials used which have absorbed part of the tissues or liquids of the body must be kept for burial close to the final mummy.

When the body is considered sufficiently treated it is washed and carefully dried. The body cavity is now packed with linen to restore a natural shape and if you are following the methods of the most skilled embalmers, the limbs and all parts will be similarly treated to restore a fuller shape to the dehydrated body. The abdominal incision is then stitched and covered with a leather plate decorated with the eye of Horus to protect the body from entry. The eye-sockets are plugged with linen

or set with artificial eyes. Protective unguents, spices and resins can now be poured over and rubbed into the skin. Now begin bandaging. First the fingers and toes, wrapping each separately, then each limb, and finally the whole body. As the bandaging proceeds, place appropriate amulets on the body and among the wrappings. A scarab over the heart is essential. It should be inscribed on its under-surface with an exhortation not to give hostile witness against the deceased. If the deceased was very important and resources are available, a gold mask may be placed over the face, and the hands and feet protected by gold sheaths. Outer layers of bandaging may be completed with larger bandages.

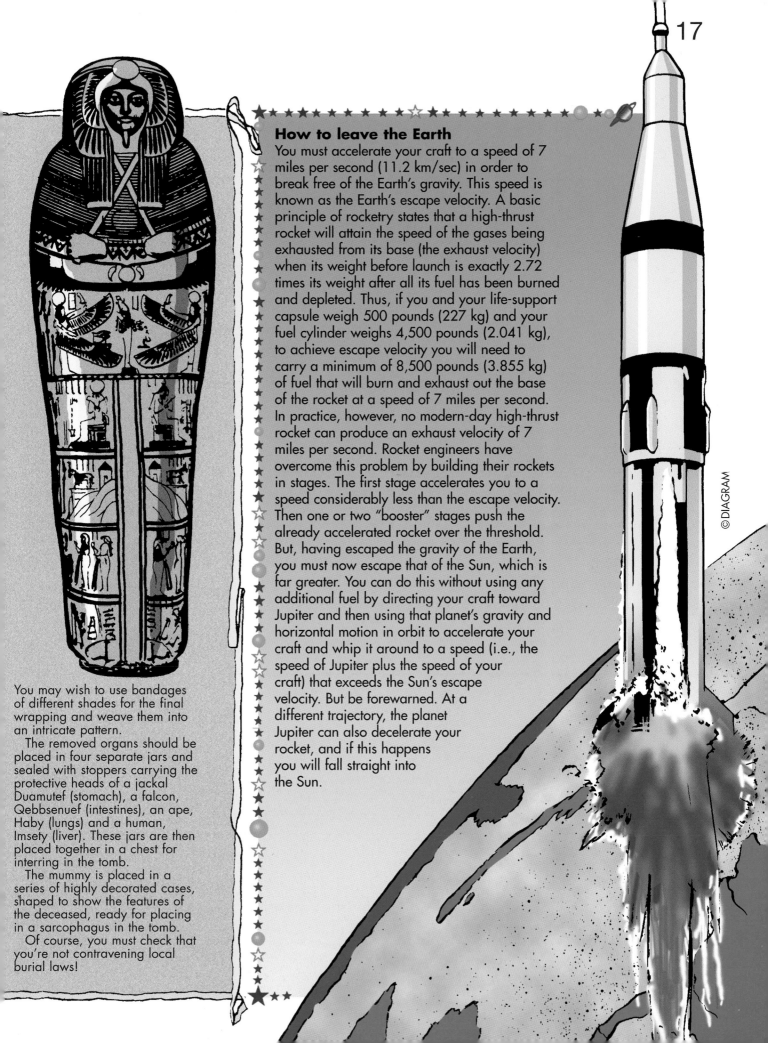

How to leave the Earth

You must accelerate your craft to a speed of 7 miles per second (11.2 km/sec) in order to break free of the Earth's gravity. This speed is known as the Earth's escape velocity. A basic principle of rocketry states that a high-thrust rocket will attain the speed of the gases being exhausted from its base (the exhaust velocity) when its weight before launch is exactly 2.72 times its weight after all its fuel has been burned and depleted. Thus, if you and your life-support capsule weigh 500 pounds (227 kg) and your fuel cylinder weighs 4,500 pounds (2.041 kg), to achieve escape velocity you will need to carry a minimum of 8,500 pounds (3.855 kg) of fuel that will burn and exhaust out the base of the rocket at a speed of 7 miles per second. In practice, however, no modern-day high-thrust rocket can produce an exhaust velocity of 7 miles per second. Rocket engineers have overcome this problem by building their rockets in stages. The first stage accelerates you to a speed considerably less than the escape velocity. Then one or two "booster" stages push the already accelerated rocket over the threshold. But, having escaped the gravity of the Earth, you must now escape that of the Sun, which is far greater. You can do this without using any additional fuel by directing your craft toward Jupiter and then using that planet's gravity and horizontal motion in orbit to accelerate your craft and whip it around to a speed (i.e., the speed of Jupiter plus the speed of your craft) that exceeds the Sun's escape velocity. But be forewarned. At a different trajectory, the planet Jupiter can also decelerate your rocket, and if this happens you will fall straight into the Sun.

You may wish to use bandages of different shades for the final wrapping and weave them into an intricate pattern.

The removed organs should be placed in four separate jars and sealed with stoppers carrying the protective heads of a jackal Duamutef (stomach), a falcon, Qebbsenuef (intestines), an ape, Haby (lungs) and a human, Imsety (liver). These jars are then placed together in a chest for interring in the tomb.

The mummy is placed in a series of highly decorated cases, shaped to show the features of the deceased, ready for placing in a sarcophagus in the tomb.

Of course, you must check that you're not contravening local burial laws!

©DIAGRAM

HOW TO WEAR THE TOGA

THE LOOSE TOGA, WORN BY THE ROMANS AS A SYMBOL OF HONOR, WAS A LARGE CURVED PIECE OF FABRIC WORN OVER CLOSER-FITTING UNDERGARMENTS.

IT WAS DRAPED OVER THE LEFT SHOULDER AND ACROSS THE BACK. THEN BROUGHT UNDER THE RIGHT ARM AND FLUNG OVER THE LEFT ARM AND SHOULDER.

How to tell a centipede from a millipede

The quick way – instead of counting all the legs! – is to look at one of the animal's body segments.

If each segment has two legs it is a centipede; if each segment has four legs it is a millipede.

HOW TO CUT JADE

YOU WILL NEED TO BE VERY RICH FOR THIS. JADE IS VERY HARD, AND CAN ONLY BE CUT WITH SOMETHING STILL HARDER; EMERY AND CARBORUNDUM CAN BE USED, BUT THE MOST EFFECTIVE GRINDING POWDER, POURED OVER THE SAW BLADE AS IT CUTS, IS MADE FROM CRUSHED QUARTZ, GARNET, RUBY OR DIAMOND.

How to read music notation

Music notation tells you two things: how long each note lasts, and its pitch. The length of a note compared with others around it is shown by its shape, as follows:

Whole note ○ = 2 half notes ♩♩ = 4 quarter notes ♩♩♩♩ =

8 eighth notes ♫♫♪ ♫♫♫ = 16 sixteenth notes ♫♫♪ ♫♫♫ ♫♫♫ ♫♫♫ =

32 thirty-second notes ♫♫♪ ♫♫♫ ♫♫♫ ♫♫♫ ♫♫♫ ♫♫♫ ♫♫♫ ♫♫♫

(The British names for these notes are:

○ semibreve; ♩ minim; ♪ crotchet; ♪ quaver; ♪ semiquaver; ♪ demisemiquaver.)

The actual speed of the notes depends on whether you are directed to play the piece quickly or slowly.

The pitch of a note depends on its position on a set of parallel lines called a stave. The notes are named for the first seven letters of the alphabet, after which you hear the same sounds an octave (eight notes) higher. Here is a scale (a series of notes) beginning on C, as you would play them on the white keys of a piano:

D E F G A B C D E F G A B C

Middle C

C D E F G A B C D E F G A B

This scale is said to be in the key of **C**. To play scales in keys of other notes you have to make use of the black notes of the piano. They are at a pitch halfway between the other notes – a halftone – and take the names of the notes either side of them. If they take the name of the notes below they are said to be sharp; if of those above they are said to be flat. A sharp carries this sign before it ♯ and a flat carries this one ♭

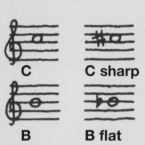

C   **C sharp**

B   **B flat**

Because there are only five parallel lines and there are lot of notes, we have to mark the sets of lines in some way. 𝄞 is the sign for the treble clef (the right hand half of the piano keyboard) and 𝄢 is the sign for the bass clef (the left hand side of the keyboard). Notes above and below the staves are written on short lines (ledger lines). Notes are written either on lines or between them.

To save writing a lot of sharps and flats, music in a particular key is indicated by writing the sharps or flats for it at the beginning of each line. Thus the key of **F** has one flat: while the key of **E** has four sharps:

Music is divided by vertical lines into measures or bars (rhythmic groups of notes). The number of notes in each bar is shown by figures at the beginning of each piece. Thus $^3/_4$=three quarter-notes to a bar, while $^4/_4$ (often marked **C** for common time)=4 quarter-notes.

HOW TO CUT A BLOCK OF ICE INTO ONE!

TAKE A BLOCK OF ICE AND PUT IT ON THE TOP OF A TALL, SOLID OBJECT. THEN TAKE A PIECE OF WIRE WITH A WEIGHT AT EACH END AND HANG IT OVER THE BLOCK. THE WIRE WILL GRADUALLY SINK RIGHT THROUGH THE ICE – BUT YOU WILL STILL END UP WITH A SINGLE BLOCK. THE WIRE ACTUALLY MELTS THE ICE AND THEN THE WATER ABOVE THE WIRE REFREEZES, SEALING THE CUT.

HOW TO PHOTOGRAPH FISH

Photographing a fish you've caught is easy but how do you photograph one that is swimming in an aquarium? To get the best pictures lower a sheet of clear glass (make sure it is really clean and cannot contaminate the water) into the aquarium. Gently move it toward the side through which you want to take your picture. This will restrict the area in which the fish can swim and keep it within your field of focus, but you will still be able to include in your photo the plants and other fish in the background.

How to store rubber sheeting

A rubber sheet is invaluable if you have a visit from the incontinent young or elderly but when they leave after a visit don't fold it up and put it in a drawer. After washing it in warm soapy water, rinsing and allowing to dry naturally – not by heating – take a broom handle and roll the sheet around it. If you don't have a handy broomstick a rolled newspaper will do, although the result will not be so neat. Store in a well-aired and unheated place.

How to peel tomatoes

Place them in a pot of hot water for five minutes. The skin will then lift off easily.

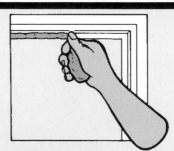

Removing the broken glass

Removing the sprigs

Replacing the putty

Pressing in the putty

How to play tlachtli

This ball game was invented by the Olmec civilization and became an important part of Aztec culture with a playing court in the great temple complex at Tenochtitlán, where Mexico City stands today. This court was shaped like a capital I with the stem 40–50 feet (12–5m) long and 20–30 feet (6–9m) wide with side walls about 9 feet (275cm) high. High on each wall halfway along its length was a stone ring, placed vertically. A goal was scored by sending a hard rubber ball through one of the rings. The players, either teams or single contestants, as in one famous game played by the Emperor Montezuma, could strike the ball only with their elbows, hips or legs and wore padded leather belts over their buttocks. There was a demarcation line across the court between the rings but no one knows its exact purpose. If you would like any additional rules you must invent your own.

How to keep the birds at bay

Birds can be a nuisance and a blessing. They can destroy buds and seedlings and damage fruit but many do eat insects that could attack your plants. An old-fashioned scarecrow will often seep them off: commercial growers sometimes use scaring mechanisms that let off small controlled explosions at intervals. If you have a lot of soft fruit it may be worth investing in commercial fruit cages. To keep birds off seedlings drive pegs at the end of rows and attach criss-crossed cotton thread to make it difficult for them to land.

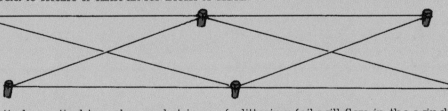

Plastic bags tied to poles and strings of glittering foil will flap in the wind and help frighten birds away. Change methods now and again so the birds do not get too used to them.

For soft fruit, whether low-level strawberries or tall raspberries, use nylon netting stretched over them to give the best protection.

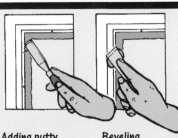

Adding putty over the glass

Beveling the putty

How to glaze a window

Remove every scrap of broken glass, putty and sprigs (the small nails that hold the glass in place) using a hammer, chisel and pliers as necessary. Brush the woodwork to remove any tiny leftover fragments. Make a bed for the new glass with fresh putty, squeeze it around the frame with your thumb and forefinger, and press firmly in all around, pressing on the edges not the center. Push the glass into place. Tap in sprigs 9 inches (23cm) apart to hold the glass in position and then press more putty firmly around the edges of the pane. Using a putty knife (or you could make do with a penknife) produce a neat bevel corresponding to that of neighboring panes. Trim off any excess on the glass and neatly miter the corners. Allow the putty to dry for a week or so and then paint over it.

Metal-frame windows are glazed in the same way but special clips are used instead of sprigs and a special putty must be used. It is also wise to take the opportunity to treat the metal with an anti-rust preparation before putting in the bedding putty.

How to play the bagpipes

This is a very ancient form of instrument and is known in many different forms around the world, but they all use the same principle. It consists of an inflatable bag, originally an animal's skin, into which air can be blown through a mouth pipe. From it also protrude a number of drone pipes which produce sound of a continuous pitch, and one or more pipes with finger stops on which the melody can be played. Squeezing the bag drives air through the pipes to produce the sound, which is not interrupted by the player having to breathe.

How to classify boxers

How to classify boxers

There are eight classes for professional and Olympic boxers, ten for amateurs outside the Olympics. All are based solely on weight – height, reach and other statistics are not taken into account. The weights given are the heaviest for each class.

Boxing class weight limits

	Class	AIBA	WBC/WBA
1	Light flyweight	105.8lb (48kg)	108lb (49.0kg)
2	Flyweight	112.4lb (51kg)	112lb (50.8kg)
3	Bantamweight	119.0lb (54kg)	118lb (53.3kg)
4	Super bantamweight		122lb (55.3kg)
5	Featherweight	125.7lb (57kg)	126lb (57.2kg)
6	Junior lightweight		130lb (59.0kg)
7	Lightweight	132.3lb (60kg)	135lb (61.2kg)
8	Light welterweight	140.0lb (63.5kg)	140lb (63.5kg)
9	Welterweight	147.7lb (67kg)	147lb (66.7kg)
10	Light middleweight	156.5lb (71kg)	154lb (69.9kg)
11	Middleweight	165.3lb (75kg)	160lb (72.6kg)
12	Light heavyweight	178.6lb (81kg)	175lb (79.4kg)
13	Heavyweight	>178.6lb (81kg)	> 175lb (79.4kg)

How to make tanning oil

Add a few drops of tincture of iodine to refined olive oil and shake it well before applying to your skin. It will help you develop a golden tan and keep the skin from drying out.

How to identify a diamond

Diamonds may be a girl's best friend but she'd better make sure they are real ones. There are two quick ways of checking. Breathe on it. If it clouds over then it is almost certainly fake, for most imitation stones have a lower specific heat. Then try dropping it into a glass of water. You may see a join that was previously invisible. The refraction of the light in the water suddenly may reveal that the stone is actually two pieces stuck together – one form of saving money is to stick a real top on a cheap bottom. Diamonds always have sharp corners and facets, the reflections and refractions in the stone being bright and confusing. Hold the stone at arm's length and look at it horizontally; now slowly tilt it. The refraction in the stone should be so strong that you cannot ever see through it. Don't try hitting the stone with a hammer. If it damages the hammer you can be pretty sure you've got a diamond – but if the hammer shatters the stone that doesn't necessarily mean it was fake!

How to signal by semaphore

Semaphore is a visual signaling system using the position of two hand-held flags to indicate the letters of the alphabet.

To send a semaphore message the signaler holds the flags for a moment in the appropriate position for each letter in the message before switching them to the next letter.

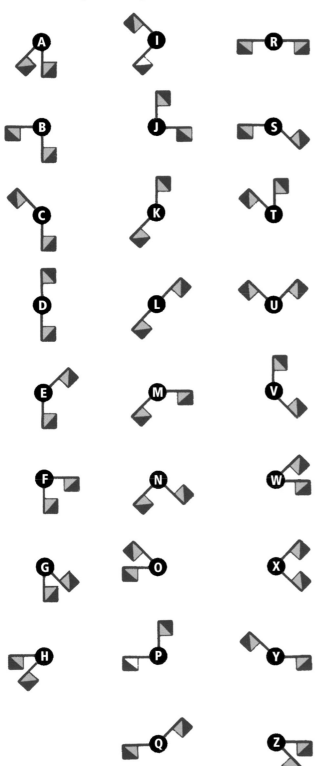

How to make cottage cheese

Put some freshly-made yogurt into a clean square of muslin laid across a strainer. Fold the corners of the muslin over the yogurt and leave it to drain overnight in a cool place. Next day put the drained curds into a bowl, beat in some fresh cream, salt and any flavorings you like.

How to make a spanner or wrench smaller

If a spanner or wrench cannot be adjusted any tighter and is still too big, make it fit by inserting a coin between one jaw of the spanner and the nut you are trying to turn.

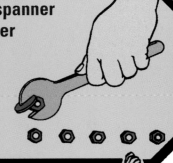

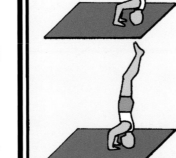

How to do a headstand

To do a headstand, squat and lean forward on your hands. Place your head on the floor, bending your body at the hips. Then push yourself up so that your body is slightly arched, in the headstand position but with your head still on the ground.

How to keep flies away

Grow basil in pots on your window sill and flies will be discouraged from coming in.

HOW TO INCREASE YOUR LIFTING POWER

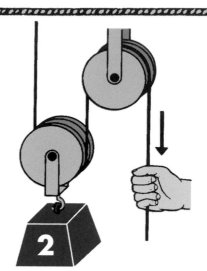

However strong you are there is a limit to the weight you can lift unaided – but over 2,200 years ago the Greek mathematician Archimedes worked out a simple system. By using two pulleys he could raise double the weight, by using four, four times as much – and so on. He demonstrated the method, with his own strength alone, by pulling a ship back into the sea which it had taken many men much effort to haul onto dry land.

A pulley is a variation on the principle of the lever and requires a firm place to which the pulley, or pulleys, can be attached. Each pulley is a pivoted disk around the edge of which runs a groove in which a rope or cable can run with minimum friction. In practice blocks of pulleys are used to dispense with separate fittings and simplify rope runs. These then require a matching pulley block at the point of attachment to the object to be lifted or hauled.

HOW TO GET AN OLD CAT TO ACCEPT A NEW KITTEN

Make the kitten smell like the established cat before they meet. If your cat uses a litter tray rub the kitten with some soiled litter, or rub it with a blanket from the cat's basket or a cushion that the old cat sleeps on, which will be impregnated with its smell. The older cat will then feel that the kitten is part of his or her property and will, if you are lucky, start to wash it.

How to Dry Herbs

Herbs for drying should be gathered in the late morning on a fine day after the dew has dried from the plants. Some herbs should be dried on trays in a warm shady place such as in a linen closet, others should be hung in bunches in a dark place where it is dry, warm and airy. If you want to keep the seeds, hang the bunch head down in a paper bag.

Dry on trays
Bay
Basil
Camomile
Parsley (dry quickly in
    an oven on low)
Marjoram
Rosemary

Dry in bunches
Mint
Sage
Tarragon
Thyme

Difficult to dry
Balm
Borage
Chervil
Chives
Fennel

©DIAGRAM

How to vanquish a vampire

Protect yourself from a vampire by wearing a rosary or a crucifix around your neck. Keep a vampire from your house by hanging garlic and wolfbane in windows and doorways. A circle of holy water sprinkled around you will also give protection. Destroy a vampire by finding the coffin in which its body lies and during daylight, when it is powerless, drive a stake through its heart. Another method is to sever its head and burn the remains.

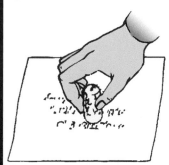

How to stop ink from smearing in the rain
How often have you found the writing on an envelope smudged by rain as you've gone out to mail it? Use old candle ends to avoid this annoyance. Rub the wax over the writing and it will provide a waterproof covering. Don't use this just for letters and parcels, its very useful for garden labels too.

How to play
HEX

Players This game for two players was invented by a Dane. Hex sets are available in some places but the game can also be played with improvised equipment.

The board has a diamond-shaped playing area made up of adjoining hexagons. Two opposite sides of the board are black, the other two are white.

The pieces, all identical in shape, are in two sets of equal number, one set black, the other white. The highest number of pieces that a player can require for a game is 61; usually he will need far fewer.

Objective The first player to place his pieces so that they form a line joining his two sides of the board wins the game.

The line does not have to be straight, but it must be unbroken. Corner hexagons belong to both players and either may use them as hexagons touching his sides of the board.

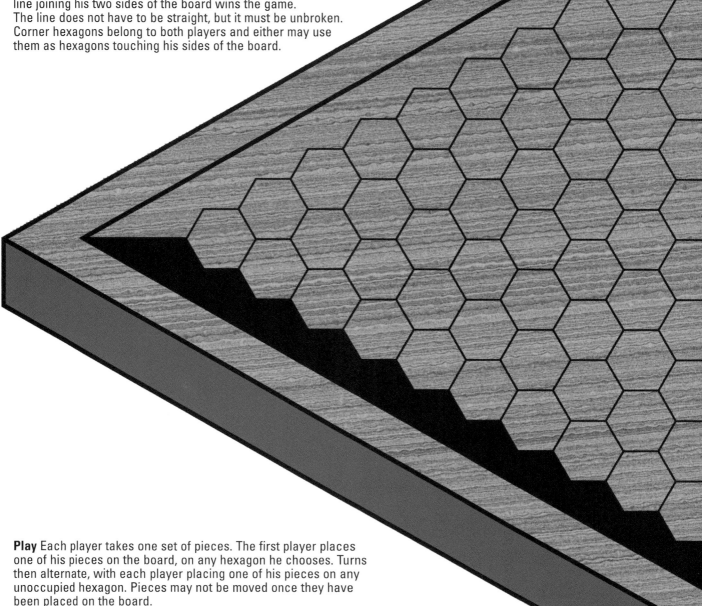

Play Each player takes one set of pieces. The first player places one of his pieces on the board, on any hexagon he chooses. Turns then alternate, with each player placing one of his pieces on any unoccupied hexagon. Pieces may not be moved once they have been placed on the board.

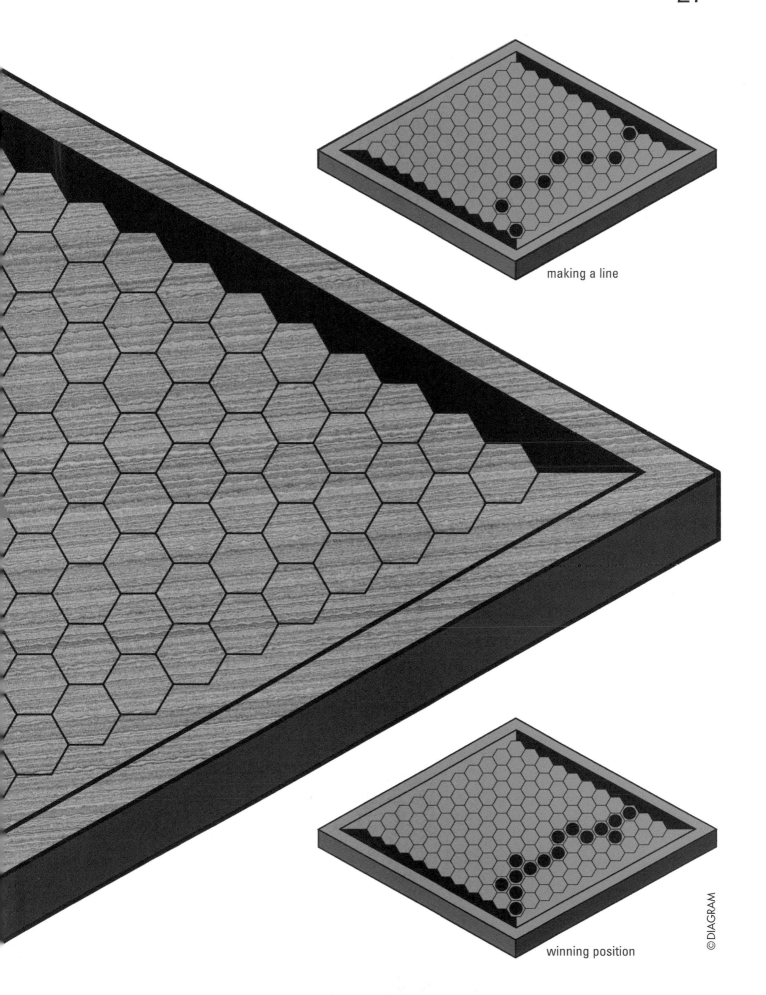

making a line

winning position

HOW TO PERSONALIZE A SQUASH

Delight your friends and relations by presenting them with a squash or similar vegetable bearing their names growing in the skin. The secret is to scratch the name lightly with any sharp-pointed instrument on the skin of the squash or other vegetable when it is first forming. The scar firms and grows as the squash grows and the name will be encrusted in large letters when it is fully grown.

How to seat an orchestra

The players in an orchestra are not seated randomly. The conductor needs the instrumentalists of each type grouped together, so that they can all see the signals he or she gives them, and the groups are placed to give the best sound balance for the work or works being played. Individual concert halls and even specific pieces may require variations on the basic plan but the usual arrangement of the players is as shown here.

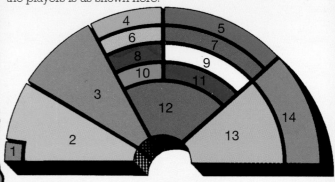

1	Harp	**8**	Clarinets
2	1st Violins		Bass clarinets
3	2nd Violins	**9**	Bassoons
4	Side drum		Contra bassoons
	Bass drum	**10**	Piccolo
	Timpani		Flutes
5	Tam-tam	**11**	Oboe
	Cymbals		Cor anglais
	Xylophone	**12**	Violas
	Glockenspiel	**13**	Cellos
	Tubular bells	**14**	Double basses
6	Horns		
7	Trumpets		
	Trombones		
	Tuba		

If you go in for archery you'll know that the gold is the bull's eye in the center of the target. The standard archery target is made of straw ropes. There are five concentric colored rings on the target, each marked with an inner and outer area. Hits score the points marked for each area.

White outer 1
Inner 2
Black outer 3
Inner 4
Blue outer 5
Inner 6
Red outer 7
Inner 8
Gold outer 9
Inner 10

How to go for gold

HOW TO MAKE CANDLES LAST LONGER

COAT THE OUTSIDE OF THE CANDLE WITH VARNISH. IF YOU HOLD THEM BY THE WICK YOU COULD EVEN DIP THEM IN A CAN. THE VARNISH FORMS A HARD COAT WHICH WILL PREVENT THE WAX FROM RUNNING DOWN THE SIDES.

How to peel onions without tears

Fill the kitchen sink or a basin with water, submerge your hands, and peel the onions under water.

How to decode morse

Morse code enables messages to be sent, letter by letter, using a system of long and short signals, produced by depressing the key of an electric buzzer or any other continuous tone sound source or by flashes of light from a flashlight, or even by puffs of smoke. Make a short pause between words to help the recipient. Dots in the key below represent short signals, dashes long ones.

A .—	N —.	1 .————
B —...	O ———	2 ..———
C —.—.	P .——.	3 ...——
D —..	Q ——.—	4 ....—
E .	R .—.	5 .....
F ..—.	S ...	6 —....
G ——.	T —	7 ——...
H	U ..—	8 ———..
I ..	V ...—	9 ————.
J .———	W .——	0 —————
K —.—	X —..—	
L .—..	Y —.——	
M ——	Z ——..	

comma

semicolon

colon

period

question mark

quotation marks

wait

end of message

error

understand

The two best-known messages to be sent by morse are probably the international distress signal S O S . . . – – – . . . and V for Victory . . . – beamed to occupied Europe by the Allies during World War II, or used musically to introduce broadcasts by them: it appears as the opening notes of Beethoven's Fifth Symphony.

How to tell your ass from your hinny

An ass is a donkey and a hinny is the offspring of a she-ass and a stallion. A hinny is small in size, resembling its father more than its mother and not so strong as the offspring of a jackass father and a horse mother. A mule, looks like both parents with the long ears, short mane and tufted tail of its father and the strength and shapeliness of its mother.

Ass

Hinny

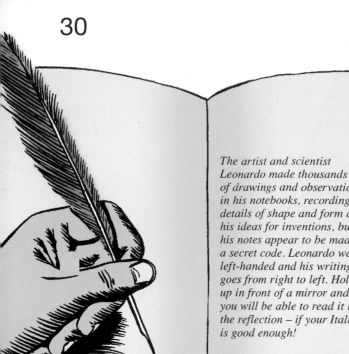

How to read the secrets of LEONARDO DA VINCI

The artist and scientist Leonardo made thousands of drawings and observations in his notebooks, recording details of shape and form and his ideas for inventions, but his notes appear to be made in a secret code. Leonardo was left-handed and his writing goes from right to left. Hold it up in front of a mirror and you will be able to read it in the reflection – if your Italian is good enough!

HOW TO IMPROVE YOUR DIVING

The secret of good diving lies in timing and coordination and the skill is needed on the board and in the air, not after you enter the water. Whether entering at an angle in a plunge or racing dive, or vertically in a dive from a board, the body must enter the water in a single straight line. These exercises will help you to improve body control and to coordinate your movements with the natural springiness of the board.

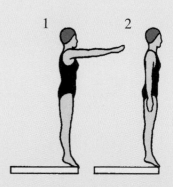

Stand erect, but not stiffly, stomach held in, and imagine you have a book balanced on your head. Walk as smoothly as possible without unnecessary arm or hand movements.

Rise up onto your toes then drop back onto your heels. Now bend your knees so they work with your ankles.

Do this exercise on the board: Rise on your toes, lifting your arms and straightening your ankles at the same time. As the board rises sweep your arms up and rise on your ankles so you bounce into the air.

Practice a standing jump; Stand erect, feet together, toes gripping edge of board, arms extended forward for balance (**1**). Lower arms, maintaining balance (**2**).

How to make zabaglione

A delicious Italian dessert. To make it you need per person:

2 egg yolks
2 tbsp sugar
2 tbsp Marsala wine (or sherry if Marsala is not available)

Method: Beat the yolks and sugar until the mixture is pale and creamy, then slowly add the Marsala. Heat water in the lower part of a double boiler and place mixture in the upper part (or in a bowl over a pan of hot water). Stir slowly until it thickens, about 3–5 minutes; do not overcook or it will curdle. Serve immediately in warmed sherbet glasses. Some people add a little whipped cream and chocolate flakes as a garnish, some even serve it chilled. You may serve *langues de chat* as an accompaniment, or even the delicious Italian amoretti.

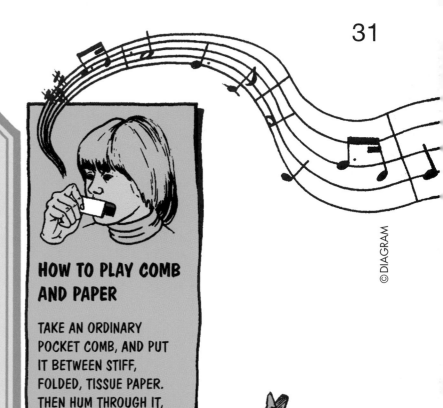

© DIAGRAM

HOW TO PLAY COMB AND PAPER

TAKE AN ORDINARY POCKET COMB, AND PUT IT BETWEEN STIFF, FOLDED, TISSUE PAPER. THEN HUM THROUGH IT, HOLDING IT AGAINST YOUR SLIGHTLY PARTED LIPS.

Sweep arms up and forward, straighten ankles and rise on balls of feet (**3**). Bring arms back and down, bend knees and flex ankles until heels rest on board (**4**). Bring arms up again.

3 4 5 6 7

As this drives board downward, jump off, pushing hard with legs and feet (**5**). Bring arms down to a cross position (**6**), and before you enter water, close arms to sides (**7**) and enter absolutely vertically, feet first.

HOW TO HOLD A PIGEON

Never hold a pigeon by its wings. Place its feet side by side and slip the first and second fingers of one hand on either side of them. Keep the bird's wings folded naturally at its sides and, cupping your hand around the body, use your thumb to cover the primary flight feathers as far as possible. Your other hand can then be placed against the breast to balance the bird.

To hold the bird in one hand pivot its body against your forearm to support its weight and hold it against your body.

How to play Shove Ha'penny

To play Shove Ha'penny you need a board or table top marked out 2 feet x1 foot 2½ inches (60cm x 30cm x 2.5cm) with ten parallel lines at 1¼ inch (3.1cm) intervals and two at right angles along the side edges to mark the limits of the scoring area. Then you need five halfpennies or metal disks of one inch diameter. Two people or two teams can play. Place a coin on the edge of the board and give it a sharp, light tap with the palm or the edge of the hand to drive it up the board. To score it must rest cleanly in one of the "beds," the parallel divisions. If you score this is marked in chalk in the side areas of the board. The winner is the first to get three scores for each bed. Coins can be guided to strike a coin already on the board and knock it into a better position (cannoning or caroming). If any coin fails to reach the nearest line it may be replayed, provided it has not struck another coin, in which case it must be left in position. Any that go wholly or partly over the side or furthest lines are removed from the board. Coins which halt overlapping another coin must be left until the end of the turn. If they still overlap then neither coin counts toward the score. There is no score for a coin lying across a line. After one player has "shoved" five ha'pennies the opponent has a turn. If more than three scores are made on any bed, the extra score may be claimed by the opponent, except that the winning point must be scored from an actual shove.

How to stop a creaking stair

The ghostly creaks and squeaks are probably caused by the top surface of the tread rubbing against the bottom of the riser. A nail or two driven at an angle down through the tread and into the bottom of the riser should stop the movement and silence the creak.

how to make cawdell cup

This recipe for a heartening egg-nog comes from a book of recipes in verse written down in the north of England in the fifteenth century:

Break ten eggs in a cup full fair
Do away with the white without diswayre (*doubt*)
Your string also thou put away
And swing thy yolks with spoon, I thee say;
Then mix them well with good ale,
A cupfull large take thou shall
Set it on fire, stir it, I tell,
Beware therewith that it never welle (*boils*)
If thou cast salt thereto, iwys (*certainly*)
Thou mars all, so I have I blis (*I tell you true*)

HOW TO RIDE A SKI TOW

Position yourself with the tails of your skis located on the checkboard and slightly apart (**1**); reach for the bar as it comes forward. If it is a button tow straddle the bar (**2**); if not, sit to one side. Tuck your poles under your arm, and keep your skis parallel and your knees bent as you are pulled forward (**3**).

©DIAGRAM

How to cure insect stings

Bee and wasp stings are equally annoying, but require opposite treatments. Bee stings are acid and require an alkali to neutralize them; wasp stings are alkali and require an acid. Ammonia and vinegar are readily-available remedies; an easy way to remember which is for which is that a and b (for ammonia and bee) are next to each other in the alphabet, and so are v and w (for vinegar and wasp).

How to play DOMINOES

The usual set of dominoes has 28 pieces. The face of each is divided into two sections, each of which in turn is marked with from one to six dots, or is blank. To begin all pieces are placed face down on the table and the players each take one. The player with the highest number of dots on his piece leads. These pieces are then returned and mixed among the others and each player draws five pieces (or seven if only two people are playing). The lead player lays a piece face upward. The player on his or her left then places a piece next to it with a panel of dots matching one of those on the first piece and so on around the table. Pieces may be added at either end. If players cannot lay down a match they draw from the remaining pool of pieces until they can. The winner is the player who first lays down all his pieces. When no player can go and the game is blocked the winner is the player with the lowest total of dots on his remaining pieces.

How to escape from quicksand
As soon as you feel yourself sinking throw yourself out flat to your full length and then very smoothly, with **no** further sudden movements, either swim or crawl back to where you walked in. Don't give up until you get there. Quicksand holes are often quite small – you are probably only inches from safe ground.

How to climb through a playing card

All you need is to stretch your imagination and, of course, the playing card. Take any card from a deck that is damaged or incomplete. Fold it in half lengthwise and cut a slit along the crease leaving a narrow strip at each end. Keeping it folded, now cut slits at right-angles to the first from the fold almost to the edge, then slits between those from the outer edge almost to the fold. Gently pull the ends apart and you will find the narrow band will open wide enough for you to step through it – and there are still three more suits in the deck into which you can step at will.

cut

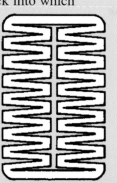

How to name a horse's **Gait**

1

2

HOW TO MAKE COMPOST

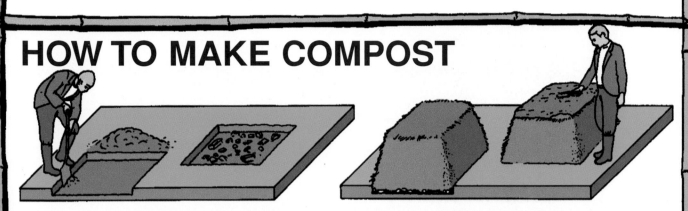

Compost is plant material which has broken down in texture so it can be returned to the soil to enrich it. All vegetable matter will eventually decay on its own, but to speed the process and avoid uncontrolled rotting vegetation, make a compost heap.

You can build a heap directly on the earth or, if there is no room for that make it in a container with a base kept clear of the path or paving on which it stands so air can circulate and the base does not become waterlogged. Special compost containers are available or you can make a simple frame from wire netting and four posts which will be neater than an open pile.

If you are making your heap directly on the earth dig a shallow pit about 6-inch (15cm) deep and about 3 feet (1m) square and fill the bottom with loose stones and bricks to help drainage. Keep the soil you dig out for use in the heap. First build up a 6-inch = (15cm) layer of plant refuse and waste (do not include diseased plants, very woody stems or cuttings from grass which has been treated with weedkiller). Sprinkle the top of the layer with a compost activator or accelerator, available from any garden center, and then cover with a thin (2.5cm) layer of earth. Add another layer of vegetation and include household garbage such as potato peelings – and so on, layer upon layer until it is about 3 feet (1m) high. Cover it all with a thicker layer of soil and leave it to rot. In warm weather it will take 2–3 months for it to become a rich, dark-colored, crumbly compost, rather longer in the cold part of the year. Use it for mulching and generally enriching the soil.

A horse has four natural gaits: the walk, with a speed of about 4mph (6km/h), about that of the average person; the trot, 9mph (14.5km/h); the canter, 10–12mph (16–20 km/h) and the gallop for faster speeds.

1 The walk: The horse raises one foot after the other and puts them down in the same order.

2 The trot: The front leg on one side of the body strikes the ground at the same time as the hind leg on the other side.

3 The canter: Involves three beats: first one forefoot hits the ground, then the other forefoot and the opposite hind leg, then the other hind foot.

4 The gallop: The hind legs are brought forward together and the horse proceeds in leaps, stretching out its forelimbs. Sometimes all hooves are off the ground at the same time.

How to read your palm

1 Girdle of Venus: usually indicates bad character, too influenced by carnality

2 Line of Heart: affection and devotion

3 Mount of Jupiter: ambition and pride

4 will and decision

5 logical power

6 Line of Mars: warlike disposition

7 Mount of Venus: Love, melody, passion

8 Line of Life

9 Bracelets of Life: each represents 30 years

10 Mount of Saturn: fatality

11 Line of Fortune

12 Mount of Apollo: riches or art

13 Line of Brilliance: success in art

14 Mount of Mercury: wit, science

15 Line of Health

16 Mount of Mars: courage

17 Line of Head: reason

18 Via Lascivia: faithlessness and cunning

19 Mount of the Moon: folly or imagination

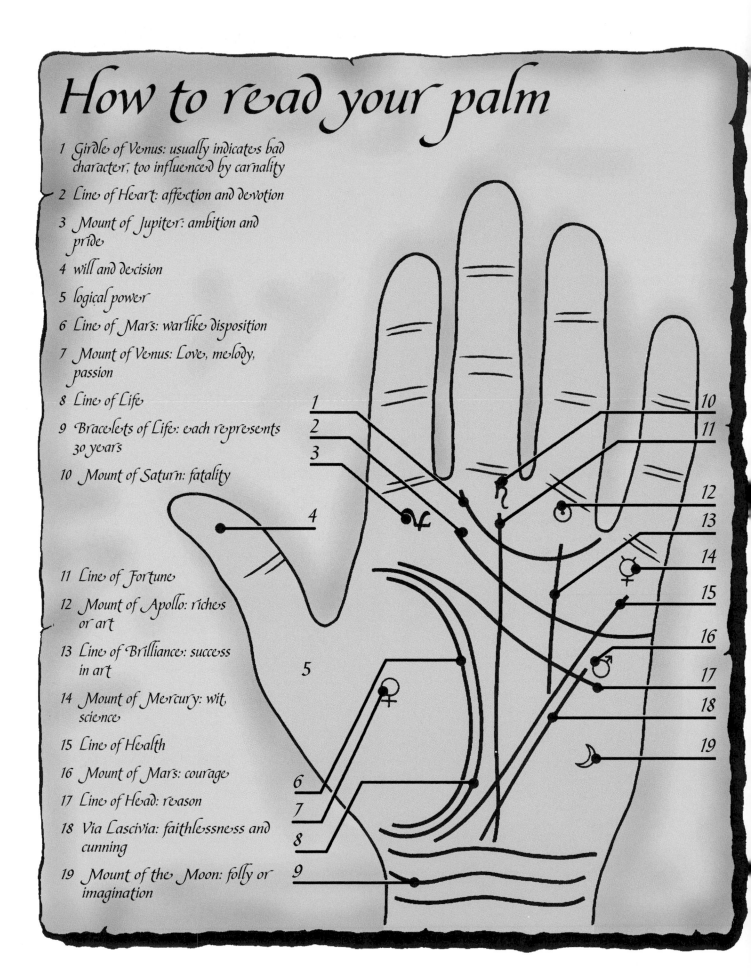

How to bring in the boar's head

Turn that meal into a banquet and serve a boar's head with full medieval pageantry. You can follow the ceremony of Queen's College, Oxford University, where, on Christmas Day, a flourish of trumpets announces the arrival of the boar's head carried around the dining hall on a silver platter while the diners sing this carol:

"The boar's head in hand bear,
Bedecked with bay and rosemary;
And I pray you, my masters, be merry,
Quot estis in convivio. (so many of you as are in the banquet.)
Caput apri defero, (The head of the boar I bear,)
Reddens laudes Domino. (giving praises to God.)"

You'll need a large number of guests to make it worth preparing this impressive dish which can weigh 30 pounds (14kg) with its trimmings: it's worth doing a dress rehearsal with a pig's head for practice. Choose a head with a characterful expression and undamaged ears. Remove the eyes and tongue and bone out the head (easier to ask your butcher to do it), leaving a flap of skin down the neck. Leave the tip of the snout in to help keep the shape. Soak the tongue for two days, then boil in salt-water for about 1 hour, or until you can skin it. Chop up the tongue and add a selection of 5 pounds (2.3kg) of ground meats, chopped onions and herbs. Truffles, pistachio nuts and a splash of brandy are optional extras. Turn your attention back to the head. Singe off the whiskers and scrub it well, especially the ears. Lay it, skinside out, on a large damp cloth, fill with the meat mixture. Fold over the skin and sew together under the chin and around the back of the neck using thread and an upholstery needle. Bind tightly in the cloth and boil gently in a preserving pan for 3–4 hours, adding bones, vegetables and bouquet garnish for extra flavor. When cooked, place it on a board and restore the head shape using pieces of wood and weights to hold it in position. This is the difficult part, for if you do not get it right you will end up with something looking like a haggis with ears! Leave overnight. Next day remove the wrapping.

Traditionally the head was decorated with soot and lard to look like the living beast but today golden breadcrumbs are more favored. You can let your imagination run riot for further decoration. Celery sticks go where the tusks should be, black olives or truffles replace the eyes with hard-boiled egg to make the white, and a shiny red apple or an orange goes in the open mouth.

How to bow Japanese style

Japanese people bow to each other on numerous occasions – at first meetings, when making requests, when expressing gratitude, when saying good-bye. The Japanese bow is an act of self-abasement and humility, and it is probably this more than any peculiarly Japanese body structure that explains why few Westerners are able to perform such a simple motion with genuine grace. The proper bow begins from an erect posture, arms at the side, palms turned inward and resting on the thighs. Bend forward at the waist with a snappy, deliberate motion – not a sag. For a second or two keep your body locked in the bow, eyes down, then return to the vertical. A bow with your upper body 10–20° off the vertical is sufficient for most situations. A bow of 30° is good for making an apology or requesting money. Anything more than that and you are either showing off or in so bad a spot that no amount of groveling can help you.

How to tie packages tightly

Dip the string in warm water before you use it, then tie and knot in the ordinary way. As the string dries it will shrink and tighten up.

How to read boustrophedon writing

Read the lines in alternate directions. One from left to right, the next from right to left. This was the way in which some of the earliest Greek inscriptions were written. The right to left lines also have the letters themselves reading in that direction. No spaces were left between words. Boustrophedon means "turning like an ox when plowing," as the writing does. Among other scripts written in this way is one used in Easter Island.

READ THE LINES IN ALTERNATE
DIRECTIONS ONE FROM LEFT
TO RIGHT THE NEXT FROM RIGHT

How to *throw* a discus

Competitive discus throwing is done from a circular throwing area, like that used for hammer throwing (p.83), into a 40° segment. The discus is made of wood or similar material with a metal rim. For men the discus must weigh at least 4lb 6.5oz (2kg) and for women 2lb 3.2oz (1kg). Discus throwing was popular in classical times both for exercise and in competition, as Greek and Roman statues indicate. The ancient discus was usually made of stone.

Today the thrower may hold and throw the discus in any way he or she likes, but the usual method is to rest the index finger on the rim and to curl the other fingers around the edge with the thumb and palm supporting the discus against the pull of centrifugal force as it is swung by the thrower. To gain momentum the thrower will raise the discus from a low to a high position, twisting the body or even running in a circle, releasing it at the top of its curve and making it spin forward as it leaves the hand.

How to know the Queen of England's swans

Look at their beaks. Do they have small nicks cut in them?
If not then they belong to the British Crown. It was the first
Queen Elizabeth who proclaimed that all swans in England
belonged to the monarch, with two exceptions: two of the
ancient livery companies of the City of London, the Vintners
and the Dyers, are allowed to own swans. Every summer the
ceremony of "swan-upping" takes place along a 36-mile (58km)
stretch of the River Thames from London Bridge to Henley-on-
Thames. Commanded by the Queen's Swan Keeper in scarlet
and feathered cap, two royal boat crews and two from each of
the companies go out to mark the year's new cygnets. One nick
for the Dyers, two for the Vintners.

The English inn sign "The Swan with Two Necks" is actually
a corruption of two nicks, an allusion to the Vintners' mark.

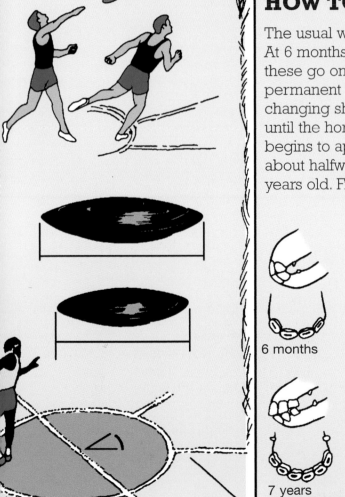

HOW TO TELL A HORSE'S AGE

The usual way to tell the age of a horse is to look at its teeth.
At 6 months it has only 4 incisors, by 2 years it has 6 and
these go on growing until the milk teeth are replaced by
permanent teeth at about 4½ years old. The growth and
changing shape of the teeth are reasonably accurate guides
until the horse is about 9. At 10 a groove on the rear incisors
begins to appear (Galvayne's groove **a**) and this reaches
about halfway down the tooth by the time the horse is 15
years old. From 25–30 the groove slowly disappears.

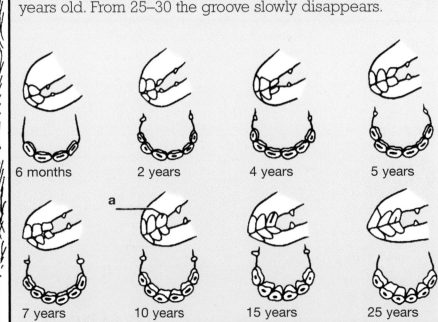

6 months   2 years   4 years   5 years

7 years   10 years   15 years   25 years

©DIAGRAM

HOW TO KNOW THE OLYMPIAN GODS

The Olympians were not the first gods of Greece. First came the Titans, led by Cronos, who ate his children. One of his sons, Zeus, was hidden by his mother, who fed his Father with a

Zeus King of the gods and protector of all Greece; probably originally a weather god, he chastized the wicked and protected the weak. Many tales tell of his amorous exploits and he sometimes appeared in unusual forms to accomplish his seductions: as a bull, a cloud, a swan, a shower of gold, an eagle, a flame, a satyr, even as his daughter Artemis and as a look-alike of one woman's husband. Usually shown as a mature, well-muscled man with thick hair and a curly beard, in early representations often nude, later, richly draped, he wears a crown of oak leaves. In his right hand he brandishes a thunderbolt, he may have a scepter in his left and be accompanied by an eagle. (Roman form Jupiter)

Hera Wife of Zeus; maternal goddess and goddess of marital fidelity. She may be represented as either a young or a mature woman, crowned with a diadem or a high cylindrical crown (the polos). Her scepter is surmounted by a pomegranate and a cuckoo and her sacred bird is a peacock. (Roman form Juno)

Athena, fully-armed and brandishing a javelin, sprang with a cry of victory from Zeus's forehead when Hephaestus split it with an ax to ease a violent headache. She was both a warrior goddess and the goddess of the arts of peace, riding, handicrafts, sculpture and painting. She was the protector of towns and acropolises and goddess of wisdom. She is shown holding a shield and a spear with a war helmet and sometimes a breastplate decorated with serpents and a gorgon's head. On her right palm sometimes stands a figure of a nike (victory). Her emblem is an owl. (Roman form Minerva)

Poseidon God of the sea, of earthquakes and of vegetation and fecundity from the earth. He gave man the horse, and horses and bulls are his animals. Brother of Zeus, he is shown as a mature man with a thick beard and carries a trident. (Roman form Neptune)

Hermes Messenger of the gods; the god of travel, commerce and risk and of eloquence, who escorts mortals to the underworld. In an early form he was shown as a mature bearded man, but more usually appears as an idealized young gymnast wearing winged sandals and carrying a winged staff with snakes twining around it (the caduceus). He may also have a round, winged hat and a cloak draped over his shoulder. (Roman form Mercury)

Aphrodite A fertility goddess in various forms; watcher over pure and ideal love, protectress of marriage and finder of husbands, and goddess of lust and patroness of prostitutes. She also had a warrior form when she would be shown with helmet and arms. Otherwise

How to tell a crocodile from an alligator

Look at its teeth (cautiously!). When a croc shuts its mouth the fourth tooth of the lower jaw is exposed to view – it fits into a slot in the upper jaw. In alligators this tooth fits into a pit in the upper jaw and you can't see it when the mouth is closed. Generally speaking, gators have more rounded snouts than crocodiles. If the snout is very long and thin, you're looking at a gavial.

crocodile

stone instead. When he had grown up he gave his father an emetic so that he would cough up his other children. Zeus became the king of the next generation of gods, who were thought to live on Mt. Olympus. These were the most important:

representations show her in an appropriate form for her particular role. She is often shown accompanied by the winged child Eros who is sometimes thought to be her son. (Roman form Venus)

Hephaestus Son of Zeus and Hera; the blacksmith god, representing the beneficial aspects of fire, and teacher of mechanical arts to man. He was originally seen as a young man but is more traditionally represented as the swarthy smith with beard, heavy neck and hairy chest. He is lame in one leg and wears a short, sleeveless tunic leaving one shoulder bare, and a conical hat, and he holds a hammer and tongs. Husband of Aphrodite. (Roman form Vulcan)

Hestia Eldest sister of Zeus; protector of the hearth and the family (and of the wider family of the town), this chaste goddess played a minor role in Olympian events but was greatly venerated, receiving the first morsels of sacrifices and the first and last libations at festivals. She is not depicted with any characteristic appearance or attributes. (Roman form Vesta)

Apollo Son of Zeus and the Titan Leto; god of light (though not actually a personification of the Sun), of song and divination. He was a shepherd-god and protected crops from mice and locusts; he gave man the lyre and building skills. He is represented as a young man of idealized beauty, with a broad chest and slim hips, smooth-chinned and either nude or with only a chlamys draped over one shoulder. He may carry a bow and quiver, a shepherd's crook or his lyre. (Also adopted as Apollo by the Romans)

Artemis Twin sister of Apollo; goddess of forests and the chase, and of the moon. Although a virgin goddess she is linked with childbirth and in one form, at Ephesus, was a fertility goddess depicted as many-breasted. Shown as a young virgin she wears a short tunic, carries bow and quiver and is usually accompanied by either a hound or a hind. (Roman form Dianal)

Ares Brother of Hephaestus; god of war, brute courage, rage and carnage. Originally depicted as a bearded warrior with a tall-crested helmet and heavy armor, he was later shown as a nude young man, although still with a spear and shield about him. (Roman form Mars)

Hades was brother to Zeus. He did not live on Olympus but in the underworld where he was king of the dead. He received all buried treasure and influenced cultivation through the earth. As Hades he was considered mysterious and terrible but as Pluto he was thought to be a benevolent god. He is sometimes presented as dark skinned. (Roman form Pluto)

alligator

HOW TO DRAW A TRIANGLE WITH THREE RIGHT ANGLES

Everyone is taught in school that a triangle can only have one right angle. However, if you take a sphere, you can draw on it a triangle with three perfect right angles, as shown.

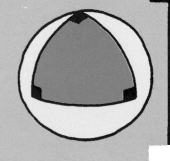

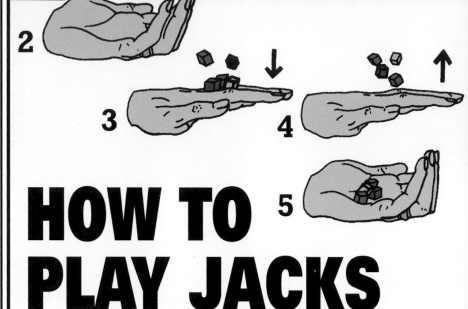

how to jug a hare

This is a recipe you can also use for rabbit, venison or pigeon. You need:

1	hare (or 2lb [1kg] venison,
2	rabbits or 2–3 pigeons)
2tbsp	lard
2	onions, sliced bouquet garni
6	cloves
3	whole allspice
1tsp	pepper
2tsp	salt
1tsp	lemon rind, grated
2tbsp	butter or margarine
4tbsp	flour
1 cup	(250ml) stock
1 cup	(250ml) red wine or beer
1/2 cup	(125ml) vinegar

stuffing balls (bread, parsley, beaten egg and thyme)

Method: Cut the meat into pieces and fry in dripping until brown. Place in a casserole with the onions and the seasoning. Melt the butter or margarine, add the flour. Mix well and stir in all liquids. Continue stirring until it boils then pour over hare. Place in a slow oven (250–300°F, 140–170°C) and cook for 3–4 hours. Serve with fried stuffing balls, boiled potatoes, red currant jelly and fresh vegetables. That is the easy method. A more traditional way is to place the fried hare into a pitcher with the onion, into which the cloves have been stuck, the lemon and seasoning and 3 cups (750ml) of beef stock, thickened with a little flour or arrowroot. Cover the jar tightly and place it in a pan of hot water up to the neck, bring the water to the boil and stew until the hare is tender (3 1/2 hours, or 4 hours if the hare is an old one). Fry or bake the stuffing. Add 1 cup (250 ml) of port wine and the stuffing balls to the jar just before serving.

HOW TO PLAY JACKS

Jacks, fivestones or knucklestones are almost identical games played for thousands of years. They can be a way of amusing yourself or played competitively. You need five small, rounded stones, or small animal knucklebones, or specially made playing pieces of metal or plastic. It's usual to play in a crouching position. Place them all on the palm and toss them in the air (**1, 2**). Turn the hand over and catch them on the back of the hand (**3**). Toss them off the back of the hand and catch them in the palm again (**4, 5**). If you are playing with someone else and drop all the stones your turn ends. If you catch them all, go straight on to the "twos" stage below. If you drop some but not all, leave them on the ground. Transfer all but one of the caught stones to the other hand. Throw that one in the air and with the same hand pick up one of the dropped stones before catching the thrown one. Transfer a stone to the other hand and repeat the maneuver until all stones are picked up.

Now, or if you completed the opening throws successfully, scatter the stones on the ground. Select one and throw it. Pick up two more stones with the same hand before you catch it, pass them to the other hand and pick up the remaining stones in the same way. Follow this with a similar sequence picking up first three stones and then the remaining one and complete it by throwing one stone while picking up the remaining four. Once you have mastered this basic version there are several more complicated variations you could try.

How to get a carp to come when you call

Call your goldfish to the pond edge by ringing a handbell or banging the side of the pond with your palm. These sounds will create stronger vibrations in the water than your voice will. Then drop flake or pellet fishfood on the water in one place only. Do this every day at feeding time, always making the same noise and dropping food in the same place. Soon you will find the fish respond to the signal without waiting for the food to be dropped in the water. Lengthen the time between calling and feeding them and you will have fish coming asking to be fed. They may even come in response to your footsteps as you approach the pond. In the same way, if you have a largish indoor aquarium, you will probably be able to train fish to come to one side of the aquarium when you tap on the glass.

How to walk farther

How do you carry your weight when you are walking? If you shift your weight from the heel to the ball of your foot the weight will be distributed more evenly and naturally. You will be less tired and able to walk farther. It will also make you healthier.

How to build a sandcastle

The design is up to you but there are three basic ways of handling sand.

Simple method Build a form with handfuls of sand, patting it into shape. Fill a bucket with sand, tamp it down with a shovel and turn out to make towers.

Wet method Fill your bucket with sopping wet sand. Scoop it out in the hands and let it drip through your fingers to form fantastic towers, spires and surreal mounds. Not much use for making solid architectural forms, which require compacted sand to stay firm.

Sand sculpture Make mounds of compacted sand – you can create basic forms to work with by filling a large four-sided wooden box with wet sand and pressing on it with shovel and feet until it is compacted and firm enough to turn out as a solid block. Now carve it into shape. Start off with shovels and trowels and then work on with smaller instruments, penknives and nail files!

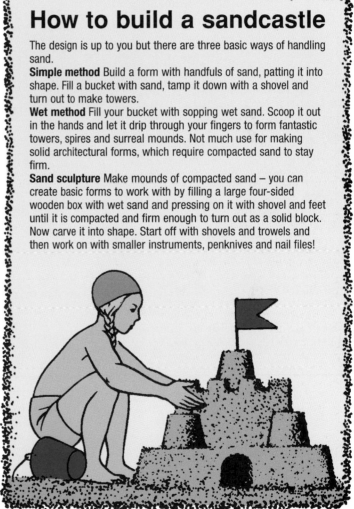

HOW TO CURE A HANGOVER

At its simplest a hangover is a reaction to dehydration: that headache means your brain's environment has been dried out by alcohol, the alcohol that the night before was popping brain cells and giving you that lightheaded feeling. To counteract it take in liquid: water and fruit juice, though fruit juice may upset the stomach. One school of thought recommends milk, which has the virtue of also coating and calming the stomach lining that is temporarily inflamed by alcohol. Coffee gives your brain the extra kick of caffeine; tea will do the same. Analgesic will relieve the pain, but the water you drink with it does more good for your eventual recovery by replacing badly needed fluid.

"Hair of the dog" – having a quick shot of what ever it was you were on last night – works temporarily because of the liquid content of even the strongest drinks as well as the euphoria initially induced by the alcohol, but you are increasing the dehydration when the alcohol gets into your system so it's a bad idea and no cure for a hangover.

If you've been drinking heavily take a large glass of water before you go to bed to help to reduce the strength of the hangover when you wake up in the morning.

HOW TO MEASURE YOUR HEAD FOR A WIG

Five measurements should be supplied to order a wig:
1 Circumference of head: across forehead, behind ears and around back of neck.
2 Forehead to nape of neck over top of head.
3 Ear to ear across forehead.
4 Ear to ear over top of head.
5 Temple to temple around back of head (horizontally).

How to copy a picture carved on stone

A stone rubbing can be made in a similar way to brass rubbing (see p.57) but an alternative method is to make a dabbing. Mix powdered graphite with linseed oil into a paste on a board (**a**). Make a pad from fine cloth wrapped around a ball of cotton (**b**). Dip the pad in the paste (**c**), remove surplus and apply it with moderate pressure to the surface of the paper (**d**). Very little friction is created by this method so much thinner paper, even tissue paper, can be used. This method also works well for very intricate brasses.

How to keep a silver pot fresh

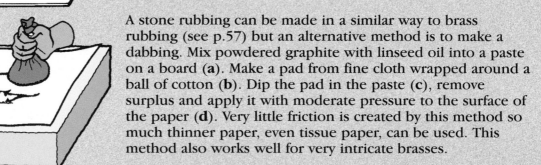

If you have a silver pot which you use only on special occasions it may become musty while tucked away in a cupboard. Try grandma's method of leaving a couple of cubes of sugar in the pot to keep it fresh.

HOW TO TELL AN APE FROM A MONKEY

Apes have arms that are longer than their legs, have no visible tail, and are larger than monkeys. Apes are not indigenous to the New World, but monkeys are, and are found also in Asia and Africa.

How to use the binary system

In the binary system, you count in twos instead of tens. It has only two symbols, 0 and 1. You count from 0 to 1, and then start with a new place – just as in the decimal system you count from 0 to 9, and then start with a new place. You use an additional place for each power of two. It's the ideal system for computers, which can have either an electrical impulse or none – the equivalent of 1 and 0. The table below shows binary numbers up to five places – equivalent to the number 16 in decimal notation.

Binary notation	Decimal notation	
0	0	
1	1	
10	2	$=2^1$
11	3	
100	4	$=2^2$
101	5	
110	6	
111	7	
1000	8	$=2^3$
1001	9	
1010	10	
1011	11	
1100	12	
1101	13	
1110	14	
1111	15	
10000	16	$=2^4$

How to store
CHEESE

Wrap cheese in plastic or a cloth and keep it in a cool place. Stored in the refrigerator, it needs to be taken out at least one hour before eating, or the cold lump will be tasteless. Hard cheese can be frozen, well wrapped in small packages, for up to eight months, but it needs to be at the right stage of ripeness before it is put in the freezer, and defrosted for 3–4 hours before eating.

Potted cheese lasts a long time. Pound or crumble hard cheese and beat it with about one third of its weight of butter, a splash of white wine and herbs or spices. Press it into a pot and pour some melted butter over it to keep out the air. You can pot blue-veined cheese like this, using red wine.

How to play
NYOUT

Players This Korean race game, which is thought to date back some 1000 years, can be played by any number of players, although the usual number is four – two players sometimes playing in partnership against the other two.

The board is laid out as a ring of 20 circles enclosing a cross of nine other circles. The central circle and the four circles at the cardinal points are larger than the others.

The pieces are known as "horses" and are traditionally of carved wood or ivory, but can be any board-game counters or pieces provided that each player's pieces are easily distinguishable from those of his opponents. Each player has the same agreed number of horses, usually two, three or four.

Dice A single die is used to score; the highest score is 5 – players rethrow when a 6 shows.

Objective of the game is for players to race each other to be first to get their horses round the board.

Play Players throw the die to determine their starting order, the player throwing the highest number starting first. Each player in turn throws the die, advancing one of his horses the appropriate number of circles, and counting the "start" circle as 1. Horses are moved around the board in a counterclockwise direction, leaving the ring at the "exit" circle. Players may have more than one of their horses in the ring at any time. In partnership play, a player may move either his own or his partner's horses.

Alternative routes Whenever a horse lands on one of the large circles, it is allowed to take the alternative route along the horizontal and/or the vertical arms of the cross. Routes (1) and (2) provide a short cut; route (3) can be a useful means of evading rival horses on the circles leading to the exit. Players need not take the alternative routes if for strategic reasons they consider it imprudent to do so.

Taking If a horse lands on a circle occupied by an opponent's horse, the opponent's horse is "taken" and returned to the start. The taker is then allowed another throw.

Double pieces If a horse lands on a circle already occupied by one of his own or his partner's horses, the horses may be moved together as a double piece in subsequent moves.

start circle

exit circle

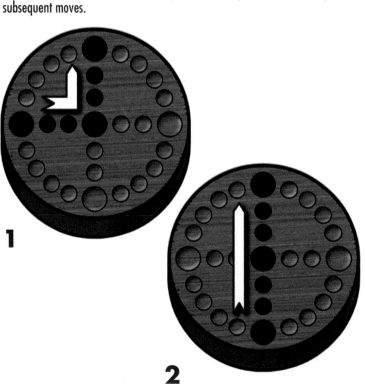

1

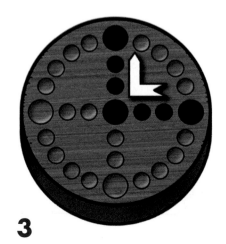

2

3

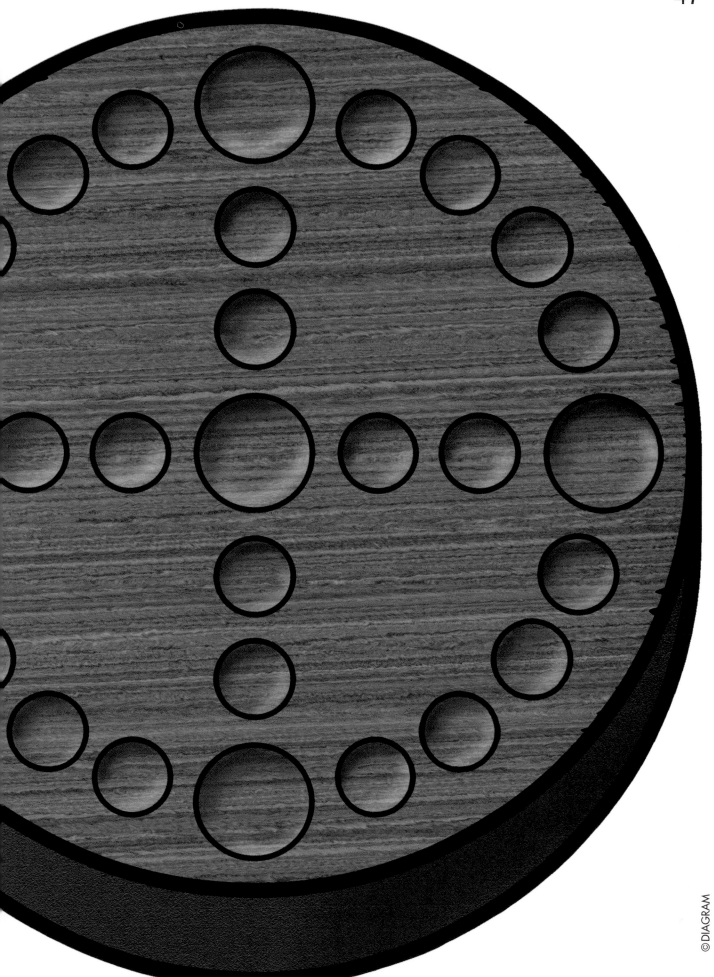

How to recognize gold

Gold stays bright forever: it does not tarnish or corrode when treated with normal chemicals. It is very soft and rarely used without the admixture of other metals, although as gold leaf it can be beaten very thin and so is not too expensive to use. It is assessed either in parts per thousand of pure gold or in carats (24 carats would be pure): 916 (22 carats), 750 (18 carats) and 375 (9 carats) are some of the proportions frequently used. In Britain 9 carats is the lowest grade permitted, in the U.S. it is 10 carats and in many countries it is 14 carats.

Ancient European and Asian gold usually contains small quantities of iridium which the Greeks and Romans could not remove (its absence is one way of recognizing fake gold antiquities). Precolumbian peoples used to mix their gold with copper to make an alloy called tumbago, a reddish gold.

The easiest way of identifying gold is to look for a hallmark – but not all gold is hallmarked. Viewing under a spectroscope will give an accurate analysis of what you see but may fail to detect that the gold is only a thin surface plating. A third way is to take a tiny shaving and either subject it to tests with nitric and sulfuric acid or heat it until it melts and all the impurities disappear and only the gold remains. You can then measure the proportion of pure gold that is left.

How to make a *bouquet garni*

The basic bouquet used by French cooks consists of a sprig of parsley, a sprig of thyme and a bay leaf. Tie them together and add them to dishes while they cook, removing them before serving. Some cooks prefer to take a piece of muslin and tie their herbs inside it. Just cut a 4 inch (10cm) square of cloth, place your herbs in the middle, pull the edges together and tie a twist or two of thread around them. You can use dried herbs off the twig for this method. Individual cooks have their own additions to the bouquet.

HOW TO MAKE A TRIPOD

To prevent a hot plate from marking your table top, make an instant stand from readily-available items. Put three forks, the backs of the prongs facing upward, through a napkin ring; spread the handles out so that they are equidistant, and you have a tripod on which to rest the plate.

How to stop rugs from slipping

One neat, simple and cheap way is to sew a rubber ring, like the one used on preserve jars, on the underside of the rug at each corner.

HOW TO TAKE NASTY MEDICINE

Horrid taste? Forget about trying to mix it with something nice. Eat a very strong peppermint immediately before taking it or suck an ice cube. They will cause such a strong reaction in the taste cells that they won't even register the medicine as you gulp it down.

How to action paint

Jackson Pollock, whose action paintings drew attention to the technique in the late 1940s, favored a large canvas, but you can use any size canvas, card, paper or cloth. Place it on a bench, prop it at a steep angle or lay it on a table or the floor. You must be able to approach it from any angle and work from above. Then, having chosen your paints or colorings, walk around the canvas, away from it, into it, dribbling and pouring paint from a can or a dipped stick. The marks left on the canvas record your motion or action – how you approached from different sides, turned your wrists above the surface, flung your arms about and so on. The choice of colors and patterns is expressive of your deepest esthetic urges and reactions, built up as you study and respond to what is happening to the ever-enriched canvas.

That is the way Pollock worked. His method of action painting was relatively sedate and disciplined. The results were almost invariably graceful. He was the first of a number of artists who sought to develop a new art by founding a painting method that was styleless, profound, iconoclastic, intensely personal in feeling and technique and that resonated from the formless chaos of the Jungian unconscious.

Many young artists who came after Pollock let their expressiveness run wild over the canvas – and you can do the same. You can apply your paint by throwing it, riding a bicycle through it, roller skating on it or bursting paint-filled bags by shooting at them. In 1960 a French artist, Yves Klein, painted naked women blue and had them imprint their bodies on vertical and horizontal cloth and canvas. He even pulled them across his paintings, using them as human paint brushes. Another action painting trick you can try derives from Max Ernst: knock perforations in a can, suspend it on a cord or wire, fill it with paint and swing it like a pendulum, running lines of paint onto the canvas.

A final caution. Action painting can make a terrible mess so do it where you don't mind the over spill and wear old clothes for they will probably end up an action painting themselves.

How to measure humidity

Human hair gets longer in moist air. So one way of measuring humidity is to fasten a long human hair between two points. If the humidity falls, and the air gets drier, the hair will snap. If it becomes loose then the air has become more humid. The greater the humidity of the air the more likely it is to rain.

How to remove a tight ring
Wet the finger in cold water, rub it with soap, working it under the ring, and then push the ring over the joint, twisting it at the same time.

How to calculate a birthday

Well, it is easy enough if you know when conception took place – expect a baby nine months later (assuming the parents are human beings, that is). Every mammal species has its own period of gestation but if you think how hard it is to know exactly when a human baby was conceived think how much more difficult it would be to know when the magic moment occurred in an animal whose delivery date you want to know – unless, of course, you brought the parents together and arranged the mating. It can range from only 18–21 days for a house mouse to 20–22 months for an elephant. Here are some more:

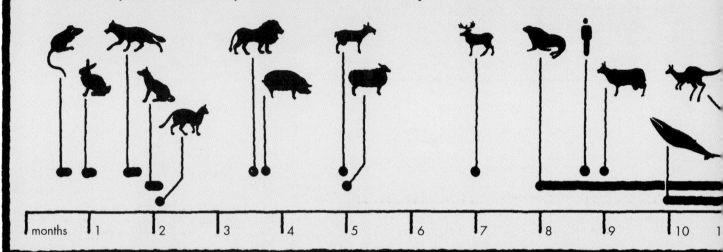

| months | 1 | 2 | 3 | 4 | 5 | 6 | 7 | 8 | 9 | 10 | 1 |

How to dance the hora

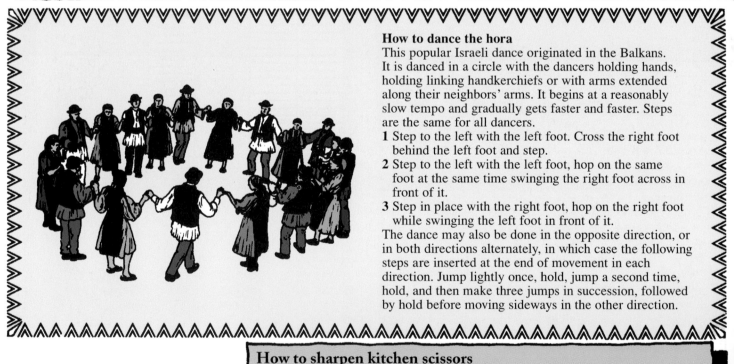

This popular Israeli dance originated in the Balkans. It is danced in a circle with the dancers holding hands, holding linking handkerchiefs or with arms extended along their neighbors' arms. It begins at a reasonably slow tempo and gradually gets faster and faster. Steps are the same for all dancers.

1 Step to the left with the left foot. Cross the right foot behind the left foot and step.
2 Step to the left with the left foot, hop on the same foot at the same time swinging the right foot across in front of it.
3 Step in place with the right foot, hop on the right foot while swinging the left foot in front of it.

The dance may also be done in the opposite direction, or in both directions alternately, in which case the following steps are inserted at the end of movement in each direction. Jump lightly once, hold, jump a second time, hold, and then make three jumps in succession, followed by hold before moving sideways in the other direction.

How to sharpen kitchen scissors

Cut up sandpaper with them and you will soon put an edge back on the blades.

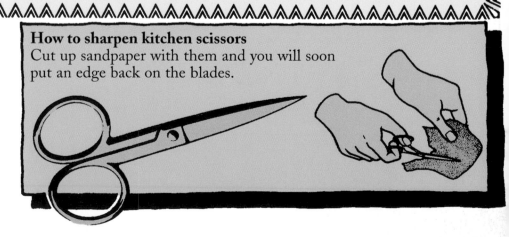

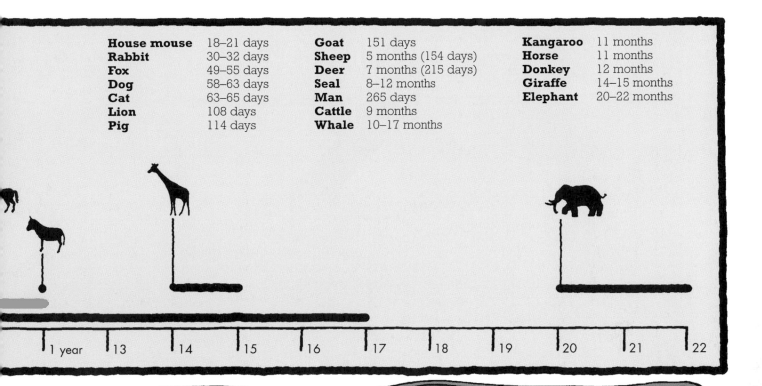

House mouse	18–21 days	Goat	151 days	Kangaroo	11 months
Rabbit	30–32 days	Sheep	5 months (154 days)	Horse	11 months
Fox	49–55 days	Deer	7 months (215 days)	Donkey	12 months
Dog	58–63 days	Seal	8–12 months	Giraffe	14–15 months
Cat	63–65 days	Man	265 days	Elephant	20–22 months
Lion	108 days	Cattle	9 months		
Pig	114 days	Whale	10–17 months		

HOW TO PLAY CONKERS

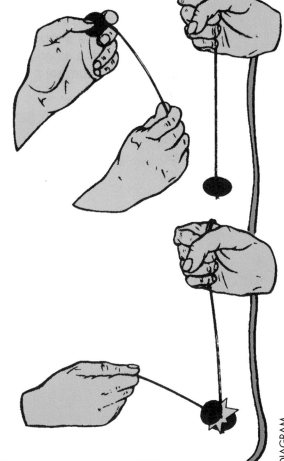

Conkers are the nuts of the horse chestnut tree. Each conker is pierced with a sharp instrument and a string threaded through it and knotted at one end. The string should be long enough to wrap once or twice around the hand and then hang down about 9 inches (23cm). One player allows his conker to dangle while the other takes his conker in one hand and, holding the other end of the string in the other hand, draws back the conker and releases it in a swinging downward blow to strike his opponent's conker and break it. The striker is allowed three attempts to make a hit and if the two strings tangle may call "strings" and claim an extra shot. The other player then has his chance to strike and the game continues until one or other conker is destroyed. A victorious conker is then described according to the number of others it has vanquished and for this purpose adds on the victories claimed for the defeated conker. Thus a conker that has had one victory against a first-time contestant and then beats another with four victories becomes a "sixer" (1+1+4). To make conkers less vulnerable players prepare them by soaking them in vinegar or in salt water and by baking them for about a half hour. Storing them in the dark for a year is also said to make them tougher.

©DIAGRAM

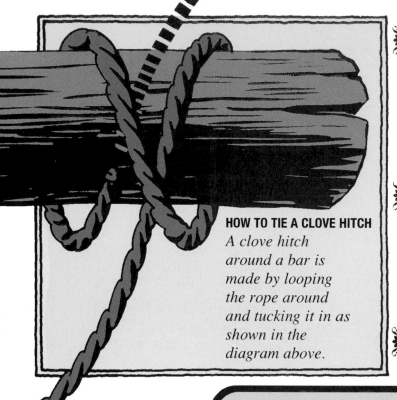

HOW TO TIE A CLOVE HITCH

A clove hitch around a bar is made by looping the rope around and tucking it in as shown in the diagram above.

How to protect your cutlery

The combination of salt, very hot water and certain detergents can cause corrosion and pitting even to stainless steel. Don't take the risk: carefully scrape salt from dirty plates before immersing them in dishwater – or better still, wash cutlery separately. Cutlery that is not often used will stay fresh and shiny if, before you put it into store, you rub it with a cloth impregnated with a little olive oil.

How to spot an ectomorph

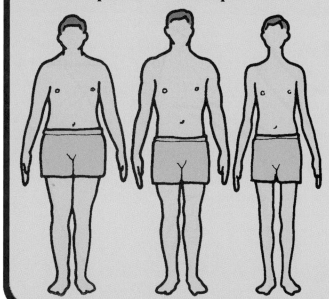

Despite their alarming titles, endomorphs, ectomorphs and mesomorphs can be really very ordinary people – in fact they *are* ordinary people. The names are ways of classifying the human body: endos have a soft roundness with short body and limbs, mesos have wide shoulders and muscular limbs while ectos are tall. spare and rangy.

HOW TO HAVE FOUR BIRTHDAYS IN A YEAR

This one is easier said than done! "All" you have to do is fly to the planet Mercury, where a year – the time the planet takes to revolve around the sun – consists of only 88 earth days. Your birthday will therefore occur four times in every Earth year of 365 days.

HOW TO CROWN A SOUFFLÉ

To give your soufflé that professional touch give it a crown. Before you pop it in the oven smooth the top of the mixture then take a teaspoon and with the bowl draw a shallow circle a little way in from the sides of the dish. When it is cooked the crust breaks around the circle and the center part rises higher than the rest. As well as looking good this helps the soufflé to rise evenly.

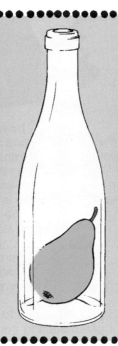

HOW TO BOTTLE A WHOLE PEAR

As a piece of gamesmanship, produce after dinner a bottle of pear-flavored brandy, with a full-sized pear mysteriously intact inside the small-necked bottle. The secret lies in tying an empty bottle to a branch of a pear tree so that it encloses a blossom; with luck this will set into a fruit that will grow and ripen. When ripe, break the pear off at the stem and fill up the bottle with brandy; leave it for some months to mingle flavors.

©DIAGRAM

How to medicate a cat

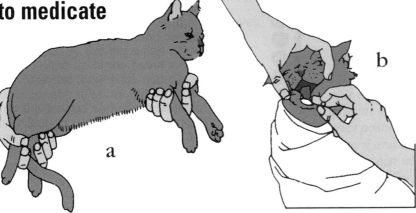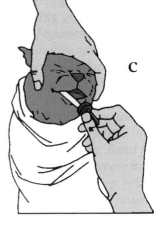

If your cat becomes ill it may be necessary to medicate it at home; here are instructions to make it as trouble-free as possible. Two people may be needed; one to hold the cat, the other to give the medicine. To prevent scratching, restrain the cat as shown (**a**) or by wrapping in a towel. Place pills at the back of the cat's throat (**b**) and stroke the throat to encourage swallowing. Pour liquid medicine into the side of the cat's mouth from a dropper (**c**). Hold the cat's mouth shut until the medicine has been swallowed.

HOW TO PREVENT FROSTBITE

Frostbite on the face can be prevented for a short time at least by stretching and wriggling the face into grimaces and grins, so increasing the blood supply.

HOW TO PAINT A WOODEN WINDOW

1 2 3 4 5

1 2 3

How to crack a coconut

Pierce the eyes with a screwdriver and drain out the milk. Put the coconut in the oven at a temperature of 325°F (170°C) and leave it for a half hour. Let it cool. It may crack on its own - if it doesn't, tap it lightly with a hammer.

How to bull your boots

You need a cloth, boot polish, spit and plenty of energy. With the cloth apply a generous layer of polish to the boots, spit on them and rub spit and polish well into the leather – hence the expression "spit and polish". Some people spit into the polish can instead, and others cheat and melt polish over their boots and burnish it with a smooth bone, the handle of a toothbrush or a spoon. Bull is British army slang for polishing, cleaning and ceremonial drill. Bulling your boots to put a shine on the toecaps you can see to shave in looms large in the life of a new recruit, but by burnishing away the natural grain of the leather it can damage the leather and shorten the life of the boots so it is actually discouraged in wartime.

Use a special metal protector to prevent paint getting on the glass, or do the same job by laying masking tape on the glass right up against the edge of the woodwork. Naturally you will make sure the woodwork has been properly prepared.

Casement windows Paint (1) the places where glass and wood meet, (2) horizontal and upright cross bars, (3) top and bottom rails, (4) sides, (5) window frame.

Sash windows Pull the top sash down and the bottom up. Paint (1) the meeting rail, some way up the sides and the underside of the bottom sash, (2) the inside of the frame at the top and the exposed runners – avoid getting paint on the sash cords, (3) almost close the window and proceed to paint the rest in the same order as for a casement window.

How to make vichyssoise

This refreshing soup can either be served hot or chilled.
To serve 4 you need:
3 medium-sized potatoes
4 large leeks
2 cups (.5 liter) chicken stock
7 oz (.2 liter) double cream
salt
black pepper
grated nutmeg
chives
butter
Peel and thinly slice potatoes. Add to chicken stock. Cut white parts of leeks into short pieces, discarding rest, sautée gently in 3 tablespoons butter for 5 minutes without browning. Add to stock together with salt, ground pepper and grated nutmeg to taste. Simmer until all vegetables are cooked. Press through a strainer or blender until smooth. Chill in refrigerator if to be served cold. Before serving stir in double cream (chilled if serving cold), sprinkle with chopped chives and more pepper if desired. Because of its delicate color vichyssoise looks more attractive served in dark colored bowls.

HOW TO PASS A FEDERAL LAW IN THE US

A senator or representative must introduce a bill by sending it to the clerk of his house, who gives it a number and title. This is the *first reading*. The bill is then referred to a committee.

If the committee decides the bill is unwise or unnecessary they *table* it – which kills it at once (tabling a bill means something quite different in Britain). If they decide the bill is worthwhile, they have hearings and invite experts and interested persons. They then debate the bill, perhaps offer amendments, then take a vote; if that is favorable, the bill goes back to the floor of its house, is read sentence by sentence by the clerk (the *second reading*) and then debated. (In the House of Representatives there is a *cloture rule* to limit the time for the debate. This is not so in the Senate except by 2/3 vote for cloture, hence the possibility of a *filibuster* in which one or more opponents hold the floor endlessly to defeat the bill.) The *third reading* is by title alone; the bill is then voted on. If it is passed it goes to the other house of Congress where it may be defeated and die. If it is passed with amendments, a joint congressional committee must be appointed by both houses to iron out the differences.

If the bill is passed by both houses, it is sent to the president. If he vetoes the bill it goes back to the house of origin for further debate and vote. The bill must now get a 2/3 majority or it dies. If it is passed again, it goes to the other house for a vote. If that house also passes it, the president's veto is overruled and it becomes law. If the president has no objections when he gets the bill the first time, he signs it and it becomes law. If the president gets a bill he wishes neither to sign nor to veto, he may retain it for 10 days (Sundays excluded) and it becomes law automatically. If Congress has adjourned in those 10 days, however, the bill is killed.

How to twist wire

A strand of wire will twist evenly if one end is held in a vice while the other is fixed in the chuck of a hand drill; turn the drill handle slowly to control the extent of the twist.

©DIAGRAM

How to signal at sea

Signals at sea are sent by many methods, including morse code, signal lamps, radio and semaphore, but flags have long been used to identify a ship's nationality and to convey clear messages. Flags of different patterns and colors form an internationally recognized code for the letters of the alphabet and each also has a meaning of its own when flown individually. Among the best known are the Blue Peter, a white rectangle with a blue border which signifies "I am about to sail" and the plain yellow flag which indicates that a ship is in quarantine. They are also the international code flags for P and Q.

N & C flying together means "In distress: need immediate assistance"

R & Y flown together from masthead mean "Crew has mutinied"

INTERNATIONAL CODE

A: I am undergoing speed trials.
B: I have explosives on board.
C: Yes.
D: Keep clear, I am in difficulties.
E: I am altering course to starboard.
F: I am disabled.
G: I require a pilot.
H: Pilot is on board.
I: I am altering course to port.
J: I am sending a message by semaphore.
K: Stop at once.
L: Stop, I wish to communicate with you.
M: A doctor is on board.
N: No.
O: Man overboard.
P: (The Blue Peter): I am about to sail.
Q: Quarantine flag.
R: I have stopped.
S: I am going astern.
T: Do not pass ahead of me.
U: You are in danger.
V: I need help.
W: Send a doctor.
X: Stop, and watch for my signals.
Y: I am carrying mail.
Z: I am calling a shore station.

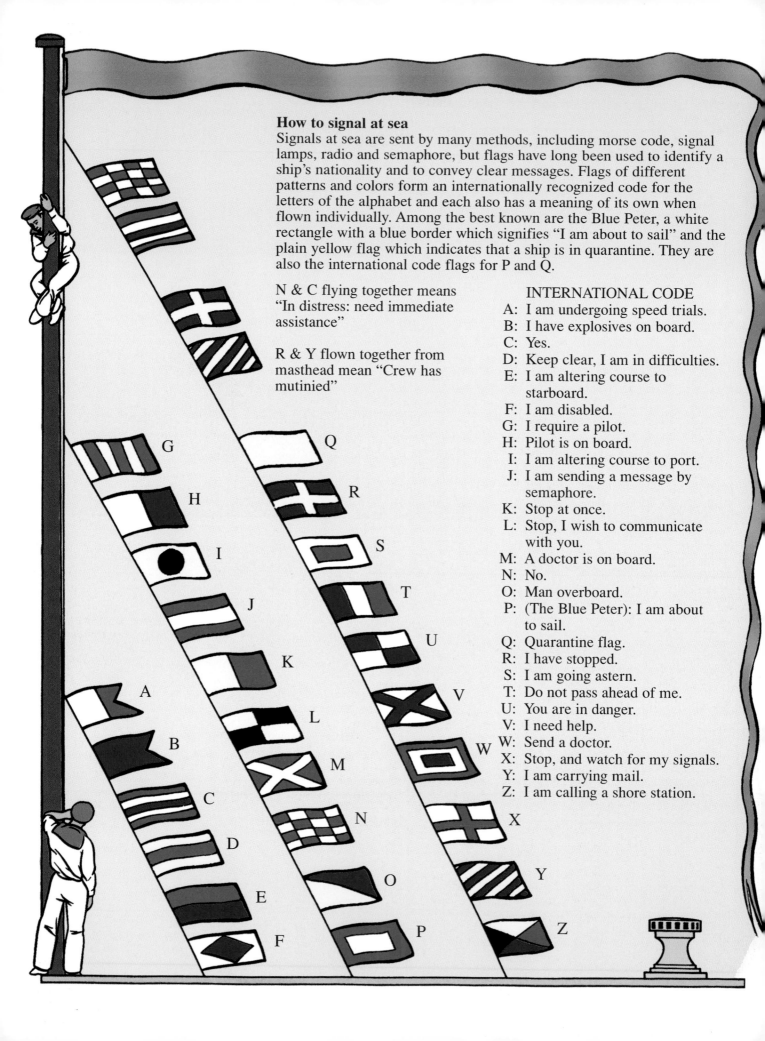

how to make brass rubbing

You will need:

- Architect's or draftsman's detail paper (preferably) or decorator's lining paper.
- Stick of heelball (originally produced for cobblers, it is a compound of beeswax, tallow and lampblack).
- Weights or masking tape.

First obtain permission from the owner, or the clergyman or caretaker if the brass you wish to make a rubbing of is in a church or public building. Ensure that your paper is wide enough to cover all the brass to be rubbed (you can join the paper but it makes rubbing more difficult). Clean the brass with a duster and soft brush to remove grit and dust which may tear the paper, and then carefully position the paper. If the brass is on the floor, weight the corners to prevent the paper moving. On some surfaces masking tape may be used to stretch and hold the paper in position but beware – it may damage soft plaster or stone. If it is not possible to secure the paper, great care must be taken that it does not move during rubbing. An assistant to hold it will help. If the brass is an outline shape remember its position. With a firm and even movement rub the heelball over the area of the brass and an image will appear. You can either restrict your rubbing to the brass itself – with practice you will be able to follow the edge of the metal quite easily – or rub across the whole slab of stone on which it is mounted. The latter method will enable you to record the position of missing pieces of brass as well. Use only a moderate pressure over such areas and a circular action. Before removing the paper make sure you have not omitted any details.

©DIAGRAM

HOW TO DECORATE EGGS FOR EASTER

You can boil them and then paint the shell, or draw on them with felt-tip pens. You can add food coloring to the water in which you boil them to give an overall color.

If you want to produce a pattern, take the egg from the water as soon as it is cooked, stick patterned shapes onto the shell, then add coloring to the water and return the egg.

In Greece, where visitors are always offered colored eggs on Easter morning it is the custom to hold the egg firmly in the hand and bring it down onto another's egg, the victor being the egg which survives this and other successive encounters.

HOW TO TIGHTEN A LOOSE SCREW

WRAP STEEL WOOL AROUND THE THREAD, THEN SCREW IT ALL THE WAY IN. IT SHOULD HOLD TIGHTLY.

How to make bird's nest soup

Not any nest will do. This traditional Chinese dish demands the nest of a particular swift of the Collocalia genus. These birds stick hairs, grasses and bits of fish together with their saliva to form small concave platforms which project from caves in southeastern Asia. The whitest nests are the most prized, those in which the swifts have raised a family are the poorest quality. You don't have to go east to gather nests – bird's nest soup comes in cans from oriental food stores or you can buy a boxed cake of the dry brittle powder ground from whole nests to make your own. It is very simple to make: allow 1oz (30g) of nest to four servings. Boil in plenty of water (it will absorb quite a lot) for one hour. Cool.

Since the flavor is not strong you may like to strengthen it with chicken stock, diced cooked chicken, Chinese roast pork, bamboo shoots and mushrooms. Boil until the mushrooms are cooked, add soy sauce, sesame oil, salt and pepper. Serve as the Chinese do – at the end of your meal.

HOW TO CLEAN A SAUCEPAN

Fill it with cold water into which you have put a tablespoonful of vinegar, and boil for 5 minutes. This should deal with minor burning.

How to make your candle fit your candlestick.

Don't burn it at both ends. If it is a little too large or too loose dip the bottom end for about one inch into a bowl of very hot water for a couple of minutes. This will soften the wax and as you press the candle into the holder it will adapt itself to the space available.

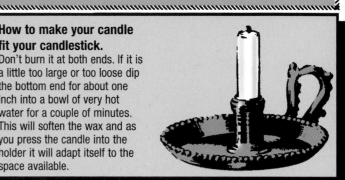

HOW TO GET RID OF A RED NOSE

Rub your ears briskly with your hands. This makes the blood rush to your ears, reducing the amount in the nose. It works if the red nose is caused by being engorged with blood, which is usually accompanied by a mild burning sensation.

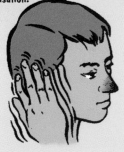

HOW TO MEASURE A HORSE

The size of a horse is given by its height at the withers, the highest point on its back at the base of its neck. It is expressed in "hands" – a unit based on the width of a human hand – in practice considered to be a measure of 4 inches (10cm). The height is given to the nearest inch so that a pony measuring 50 inches (127cm) is said to measure 12.2 hands (12 hands plus 2 inches).

How to take a cutting

Hardwood cuttings (gooseberries, currants, forsythia, roses, etc) Take cuttings in early autumn. Select a mature side shoot, about 12 inches (30cm) long and low on the plant. Pull it from the stem so that a "heel" is left. Remove buds and leaves from the lower 4 inches (10cm), dip the heel in hormone powder, and plant the cutting firmly in a pot or trench. Keep well watered.

Softwood cuttings (carnations, geraniums, delphiniums, chrysanthemums, etc) Take cuttings in summer. Choose a young shoot up to 5 inches (12.5cm) long according to the size of the plant. Cut off below a leaf joint. Trim off lower leaves and buds to leave 3 to 5 pairs of leaves at the top. Dip the end in hormone powder and plant in a pot or propagation box. Softwood cuttings need a damp, close atmosphere.

How to tame a tarantula

Despite its reputation a tarantula spider is generally no more dangerous than a wasp or bee. It is best kept in a covered container in case it escapes and frightens people; an aquarium tank with airholes is ideal. A dish of water with a sponge in it will be needed for it to brush its mouth against for moisture – spiders do not drink in the way we do. Or you could spray a fine mist of water onto the sides of the tank.

Feed it on insects or even small mice. If you have problems with cockroaches or other insect pests you could let your spider out on a leash – one spider enthusiast cleared his apartment of cockroaches in a matter of days. Just in case you are one of those rare people to whom a tarantula bite could prove very dangerous, avoid touching it and handle it carefully with tongs if necessary.

How to choose fruit trees

When buying fruit trees, check whether they are self-fertilizing or cross-pollinating. Cross-pollinating types need another variety of the same type of fruit nearby so that pollen can be exchanged.

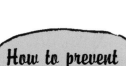

How to prevent string tangling

Put your ball of string into an ordinary plastic funnel. The kind used for putting liquids into bottles, or gasoline into cans. Select one large enough to hold your string. Nail it to the wall or fix it on a bracket at a convenient height. Thread the loose end of the string through and let the ball rest in the funnel mouth.

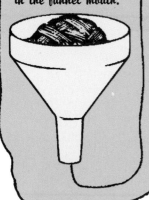

How to build a tipi

You need wood poles, a crescent shape of buffalo hide or bark fabric, and plenty of rope to make the traditional shelter of the Sioux Indians. A ceremonial tipi (or tepee) 20 feet (6m) high and 30 feet (9m) across requires about 50 buffalo skins, a small one only a few. All need three main poles plus lesser ones according to size. Sew hides or bark fabric together to form an open-topped cone, but sew only the top of the final seam, leaving about 7 feet (2m) open for an entrance flap. Sew thongs either side of this flap to tie it shut and attach a long rope to the edge of the cone. Lay three main poles on the ground, lay the cover over them and raise the poles at the center. Flick the rope attached to the cover around the tops of the poles and pull it taut while the poles are adjusted into a stable position. Bring lighter poles under the cover, put their top ends through the center space to rest against the main poles, and their lower ends as far out as possible in an equidistant circle. These support the covering. Peg the bottom of the cover to the ground making use of pre-cut slits, or weight with stones. By careful juggling of the poles the wind can be prevented from blowing straight down the opening at the top. With a very large tipi the covering could be made in sections, laced together around the already erected poles and then hauled into position.

How to keep storms away at sea

Have a tortoiseshell cat on your boat. Japanese sailors used to believe that tortoiseshell cats, good luck bringers at any time, could foretell the approach of storms and if sent to the top of the mast could frighten the storm demons away.

How to make a potato print

Take a potato large enough to grip easily and cut it in half. Draw a pattern or picture on the cut surface with a felt-tip pen. With a scalpel or penknife cut vertically down into the potato following your pattern, scoop out areas that are to be left blank and trim unwanted areas from the edge. You'll find it easier to cut out the right pieces if you fill in the image you want with solid marks and then you'll know they must not be cut away. Mix some poster, oil or acrylic paint in a saucer. Dip the cut surface of the potato into it so it becomes covered with paint. Press the potato onto paper, cloth or whatever surface you want to decorate. Simple shapes work best. They are easier to cut and to ink cleanly.

How to roast chestnuts

The ideal way is to have a special chestnut roasting pan with a perforated bowl and long handle which you can hold over an open fire or stove, but you can place them on the bars of a fire grate or in the embers of a campfire. If you want to cook them in the kitchen shake them in a pan over the stove as if they were popcorn. For a slightly softer nut put them in a heat-proof dish with a little water and roast them in the oven for about 10 minutes.

Whatever method you choose, you must prepare them first, or they may explode and whizz around like bullets. This may sound fun but it leaves you with the contents all over the place and empty skins. Many people puncture the skin of the nut with a fork but a better way to make sure they do not explode is to cut a ring around the domed surface of each nut. And don't forget to salt them before you eat them!

HOW TO IMPROVISE AN OIL LAMP

Cut a slice off a cork. Pierce a hole in its center and thread a thin piece of string through it, leaving about 1 inch (25mm) to stick out at either side. Fill a glass about two-thirds full of water, then very slowly pour some cooking oil on top to make a layer about 1 inch (25mm) deep.

Gently float the cork on the oil. Allow a few moments for the wick to absorb oil and light it. If you haven't got any string twist a dozen strands of sewing thread together to form a single, thick strand. Tie knots along its length to keep the threads in position and use that instead – if you have more patience you can braid them.

How to ease toothache by acupressure

Acupressure is a treatment of ailments by the pressure of the fingertips or finger nails at specific parts of the body. Pressure should be firm and a slightly rotary or boring movement applied at the same time. A treatment time of half a minute to four minutes is usually sufficient to bring results. Toothache can be treated by pressure on the point known as *Chang-lang*, at the root of the nail of the first (index) finger, close to the thumb-side corner, or at the *Kroun-Loun* point between the outer ankle and the Achilles tendon, the pressure being applied down onto the heel bone.

How to tell a Zebra from a Zubra

It's easy – and a problem that you are only likely to encounter at the zoo. While the familiar, striped, horse-like zebra comes from Africa the zubra comes from Poland and Russia – it's another name for the very different European Bison.

How to play rock, paper, scissors

This is an ancient game for two players based on the facts that scissors (or a knife in very early versions) can cut paper, paper can wrap rock and rock can blunt scissors. Each of the players hides a hand behind his back and adopts one of the finger positions to indicate an object (see illustration). They take turns to call "one, two, three" and on three both show their hand. The winner of each turn is the player displaying the object which can overcome the other. If both show the same sign it is a tie. It is usual to play for the highest score in a predetermined number of turns.

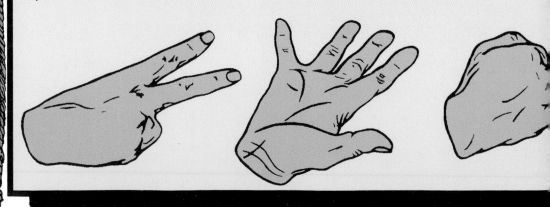

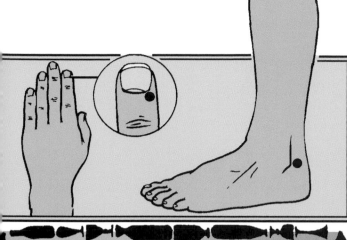

How to clean patent leather

Rub gently with a cloth dipped in almond oil. Polish with a soft, dry cloth.

How to make dandelion wine

You need:

1 U.S. gallon	(3.7 liters) dandelion flowers
1 U.S. gallon	(3.7 liters) boiling water
3lb	(1.3kg) sugar
	orange peel
	lemon peel
	root ginger
	yeast
	piece of toast

Place the flowers in a large pan, pour boiling water over them and stir well. Cover and leave standing for 3 days, stirring occasionally. Strain off liquid into pan, add sugar, peel and ginger root (bruised). Boil for ½ hour, allow to cool and add a little yeast on a piece of toast. Cover and leave to stand for 2 days, allowing yeast to work, then bottle. Leave bottles corked for several months before drinking.

How to recognize a vampire
Don't wait to see the vampire's fangs appear. Vampires have no reflection – so look into a mirror.

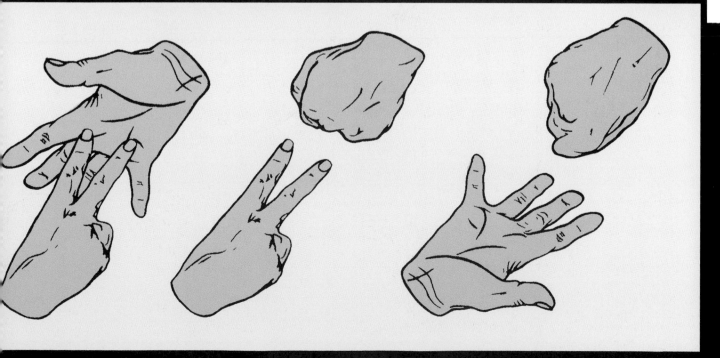

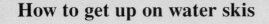

HOW TO MAKE A WORMERY

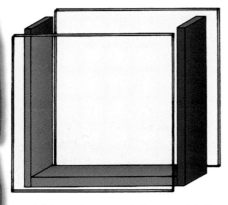

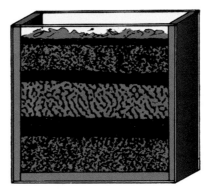

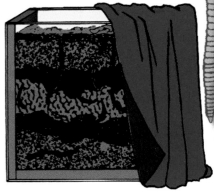

Although you might not think so, worms can make interesting pets. Furthermore they are easy to find and cost nothing to keep. In order to make a wormery like the one shown you will need two rigid squares of transparent plastic about 1 foot (30cm) square. Screw or glue these squares to wood battens so that they are about 1 inch (25cm) apart. Fill the wormery with layers of different kinds of soil and then water thoroughly but do not waterlog the soil. Then introduce about a dozen worms from the garden to their new home, taking care not to expose them to bright light. Scatter a thin layer of gravel on top and cover this with some grass clippings or dead leaves for the worms to eat. Finally put the wormery in a cool place and cover it with a light-proof cloth as worms can be harmed by direct light.

Leave the wormery for a few days and then take a look. You will see how the worms have made many tunnels and have ploughed up and mixed the different layers as they mix the soil in the garden. You will also see how the worms will have taken the dead leaves down from the surface. If you cover the wormery again and take a look every few days you can learn a lot about the way worms live, eat, breed and react to noise and vibrations.

How to make a paper fish swim

Cut a fish shape from a sheet of ordinary writing paper. Make it 4–5 inches (10–12.5cm) long and if you decorate it use colors that will not run off in water. In the center of the body cut a small circle and then cut a very narrow slit from the tail to the circle. Now, keeping its surface dry, gently lay the fish on the surface of a bath or large bowl of water and carefully place a few drops of cooking oil into the central hole. The oil will then expand down the slit and drive the fish though the water.

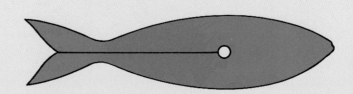

Make sure the skis are properly fitted. Grasp the tow rope and lean slightly backward, but with the head forward and the knees bent under your body. The tips of the skis should be protruding above the surface of the water. As the boat moves away, and the slack of the rope is taken up, move from crouching to an upright position. Keep your arms straight and do not let the boat pull you forward. Resist its pull with the muscles in your back and legs. Don't worry if you do not succeed first time. Getting started is probably the hardest part of water-skiing. If you fall – and everyone does at some time or other – let go of the tow rope immediately, tuck your head in and bring your knees up to your chest so you roll into a ball, and fall backward if you can. When you've recovered you can release the skis if you find it difficult maneuvering with them in the water.

How to cook in the earth

Dig a hole, line it with large stones, then light a fire inside it. Prepare your food and then, when you are ready to cook, scrape out most of the fire. Wrap pieces of meat and vegetables in banana leaves, or in burlap (canvas) soaked in salad oil if you don't have banana leaves or their equivalent handy, and place on top of the hot stones and remaining ash. Pile the hot coals back on top and seal carefully with soil. There should not be any steam or smoke escaping. Leave for six or seven hours – it may take less time to cook but once opened the oven cannot be sealed again – and dig out your meal. Variations on this kind of oven are used in Papua, Hawaii, Madagascar, Mexico and many other parts of the world.

HOW TO HIT A NAIL ON THE HEAD

Hold the hammer at the end, rather than in the middle, and keep your eye on the nail. Tap the nail gently at first so it stands on its own, then, from the elbow, deliver firm strokes, keeping the wrist straight. Keep the surface of the hammer head clean and polish it with a duster. Grease on the hammer head is often the reason why it glances off the nail and strikes your thumb!

How to make a syllabub

This is a traditional English dessert going back to Tudor times. There are versions made with cider and milk but this recipe is delicious, though it dates from a later century.

To serve 8 people you need:
1/2 pt (280ml) cream
1/4 pt (140ml) sherry
1/8 pt (70ml) brandy
3oz (85g) pounded sugar
juice of 1 lemon
a little grated nutmeg

Pound the sugar to a powder with a pestle and mortar. Whip the cream and add the sugar. Mix the lemon juice, the sherry and the brandy together and slowly add to the cream while still beating it. Pour into glasses. Grate a little nutmeg on the top of each. Chill if you wish. Serve with *langues de chat*.

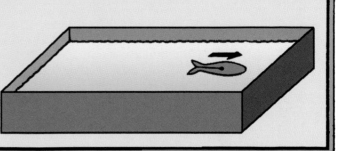

© DIAGRAM

How to play
FOX AND GEESE

Players European fox and geese, which has its origins in Scandinavia, is a battle of wits between two players.

The board Fox and geese can be played on several different layouts. The layout shown in illustration (**1**) probably gives both players the most even chances of winning. Two alternative layouts are shown (**2, 3**) which give the geese an advantage over the fox.

Pieces Any suitable pieces such as checkers, counters, or stones may be used. One of the pieces, representing the fox, must be distinguishable from the pieces representing the geese.

Play The pieces are put into position according to the layout preferred, with the geese at the top of the board and the fox usually in the center (although it may be placed on any vacant point that the player chooses). Players take alternate turns to move, with the fox starting first. The fox may move in any direction along connecting lines, moving one point at each turn (**a**). It may "kill" a goose by jumping over it to an adjacent vacant point; the goose is then removed from the board. The fox may make two or more jumps in one move (killing each goose that it jumps over), provided there is an empty point for it to land on next to each goose that it kills (**b**). The fox is obliged to jump if there is no alternative move, even if it puts itself in a vulnerable position by doing so.

Geese may move along connecting lines in any direction except toward the top of the board (**c**). One goose moves one point in a turn. Geese may not jump over and capture the fox; their aim is to surround the fox so that it cannot move.

Result The fox wins if it: a) kills so many geese that those remaining are not sufficient in number to trap it; or b) manages to evade the geese so as to give it a clear path to the top of the board (where the geese cannot chase it). The geese win if they can immobilize the fox by surrounding it or crowding it into a corner.

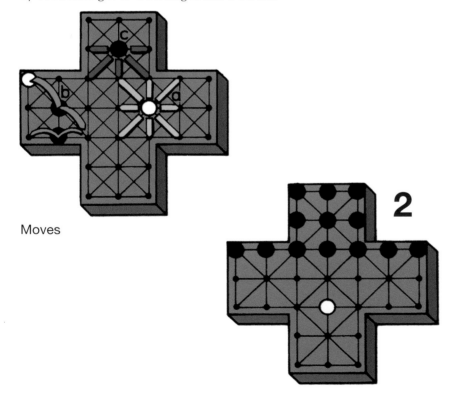

Moves

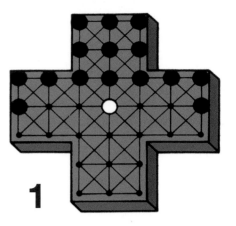

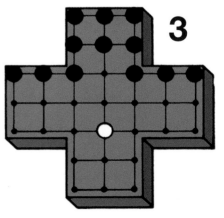

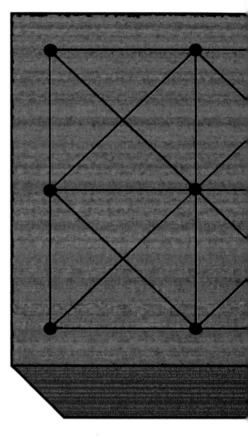

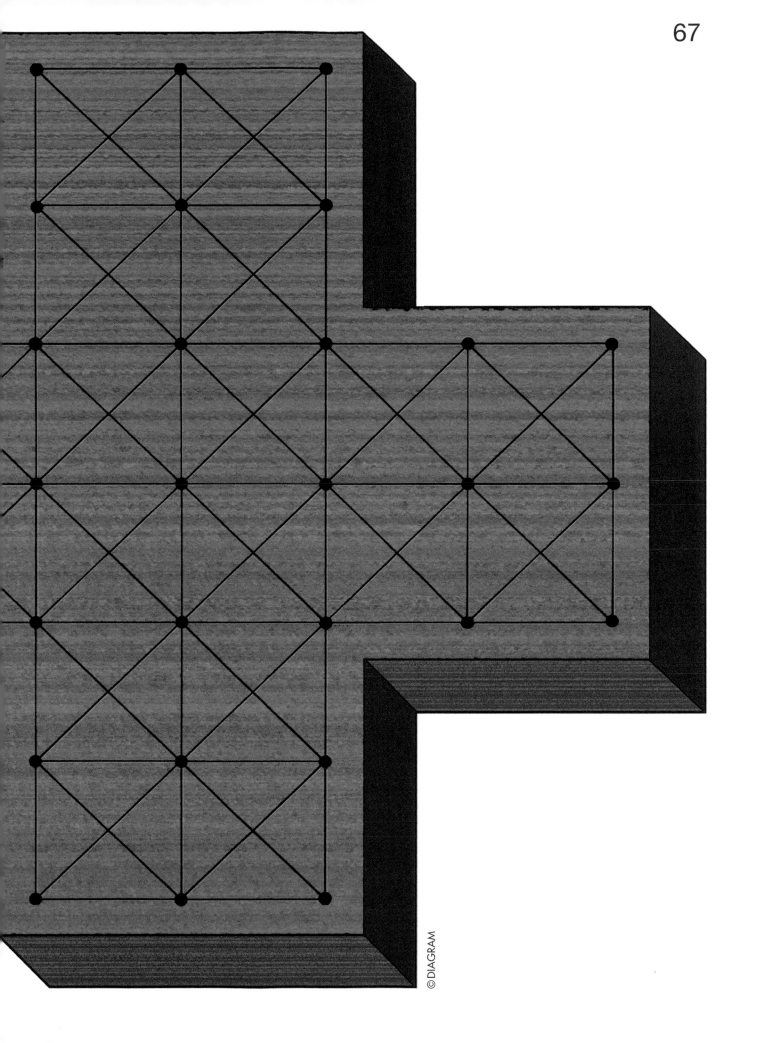

HOW TO CARE FOR A BONSAI TREE

A **bonsai** tree is dwarfed in size by rigorous pruning of both roots and branches. Its cultivation is an ancient Japanese art which aims to produce aesthetically pleasing shapes. Pots or bowls are carefully chosen to form part of the final design. Every twig counts, for a single branch out of place is enough to throw the entire "composition" off balance.

Bonsai trees can be bought from a specialist nursery or can be trained from naturally dwarfed trees found growing in the wild. In the long-term you can even grow from seed. With a nursery tree, you get a preshaped specimen that needs only daily care and periodic pruning and repotting – its general form can be left intact. With a wild specimen you must shape it on your own and with a seedling you shape and prune it from the start. Among coniferous trees, pines, junipers, and spruces are good varieties for bonsai. Maples, elms, and birches are examples of good deciduous bonsai. A conifer's needles will not get smaller to match the dwarfed trunk, but a deciduous tree's leaves will.

Remember that a bonsai is artificially, not genetically, stunted. If not cared for it will grow, and its seed will always produce offspring of normal size. A bonsai should be kept out of doors in its natural element and brought inside to display for only brief periods of time.

Pruning

Pruning not only shapes the tree; it makes it healthier. Starting with a naturally dwarfed tree you have found growing in the wild, look at it carefully to determine its front and a possible configuration for training. Remove: all dead and diseased branches; branches that interfere with the desired shape; branches projecting out to the front from the bottom half of the tree; branches that cross other branches; all branches but one radiating from a single point around the trunk.

Prune twigs in a similar fashion. A common shape to aim for when visualizing the tree as a whole is a triangle with unequal sides; foliage should be thicker at the top (the upper vertex of the triangle) than at the base, and the branches that remain after pruning should be staggered so that they spiral upward around the trunk from the base.

Prune the main branches at the end of winter. Prune leaves, shoots, and buds throughout the growing season. Snip off or cut back leaves on deciduous trees in early summer; new leaf buds will then appear, and these will produce smaller leaves to match the dwarfed size of the trunk and branches.

Use protective paint over all large pruning scars. Make sure each scar is hollowed out so that it does not project from the trunk or branch.

Shaping

The decision as to which branches to prune depends on the shape you want to give the bonsai. A bonsai can be upright, leaning slightly to one side, slanted at 45°, "windswept" and horizontal, or even directed downward like a waterfall (see the examples on this page). These forms are all derived from the forms of trees as they appear in nature, so it is important not to give, say, an elm or maple configuration to a pine, or vice versa.

Wire the tree into the desired shape with copper wire; the thickness of the wire you use depends upon the degree to which the branch resists bending. Wire coniferous trees in winter; remove the wires after a year or so. Wire deciduous trees in early summer; remove these wires in the fall of the same year.

How to pluck poultry and game

It is easiest to pluck a bird soon after it is killed. Start on the breast and underside. Grip the feathers by the handful, jerking them out, but not so violently that you tear the skin. You'll be surprised how many feathers there are – and small ones, in particular, will float away on the slightest breath of wind so make sure that you are away from drafts and don't move about so

rapidly that you create any. Have a large container by you to put the feathers into as soon as they are plucked.

After the underside is done, turn the bird and pluck its sides, leaving the wings and thighs until last. With the wings it will probably be necessary to pull the strong quills out one by one, holding the wing firmly in the other hand.

Repotting

Repot your bonsai every two or three years in early spring. Use a pot of roughly the same size as the old one or slightly larger. Be careful not to damage the roots near the main trunk as you remove the bonsai from the pot. Cut the lower roots back by about half. Put the bonsai in its new pot and fix it in place with wire. Add new soil – a mixture of loam, sand, and peat – and water it thoroughly. Keep the repotted bonsai sheltered for a few weeks until the roots take hold.

General care

- Bonsai need a lot of water in summer – at least once a day – but may require watering in winter only once every other week. Use an organic fertilizer in spring and summer once every week and a half to two weeks.
- Spray occasionally with an insecticide to control insect pests.
- Do not keep the bonsai indoors for extended periods. But do protect delicate varieties from frost, heavy rain, and wind.
- Make sure the bonsai has plenty of nourishment, good soil, air, and light – in short, all the conditions that any plant heeds to thrive.
- Make pruning of leaves and twigs part of your daily routine.
- With proper care, your bonsai will outlive its wild cousins, and probably you as well. Many fine books on this art are available, and you should consult them for detailed information on shapes, soil composition, wiring, maintenance, and pruning techniques.

How to make buttons stay on longer

Paint nail polish over the crossed threads of buttons, both front and back

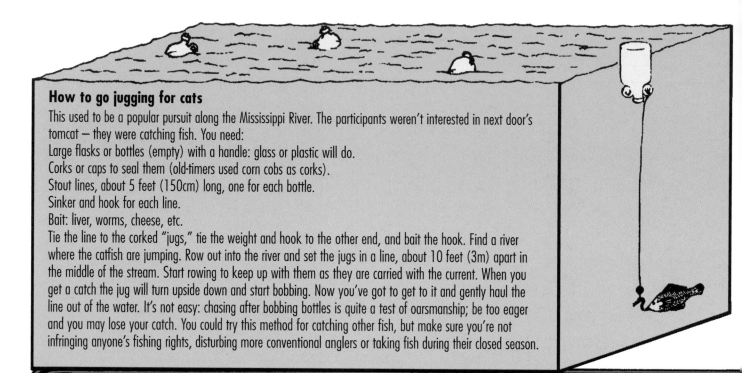

How to go jugging for cats

This used to be a popular pursuit along the Mississippi River. The participants weren't interested in next door's tomcat — they were catching fish. You need:

Large flasks or bottles (empty) with a handle: glass or plastic will do.

Corks or caps to seal them (old-timers used corn cobs as corks).

Stout lines, about 5 feet (150cm) long, one for each bottle.

Sinker and hook for each line.

Bait: liver, worms, cheese, etc.

Tie the line to the corked "jugs," tie the weight and hook to the other end, and bait the hook. Find a river where the catfish are jumping. Row out into the river and set the jugs in a line, about 10 feet (3m) apart in the middle of the stream. Start rowing to keep up with them as they are carried with the current. When you get a catch the jug will turn upside down and start bobbing. Now you've got to get to it and gently haul the line out of the water. It's not easy: chasing after bobbing bottles is quite a test of oarsmanship; be too eager and you may lose your catch. You could try this method for catching other fish, but make sure you're not infringing anyone's fishing rights, disturbing more conventional anglers or taking fish during their closed season.

How to choose the appropriate glass

Glasses must be chosen both to be an appropriate size and to add to our enjoyment of what we are drinking. Long drinks need long glasses, so mixes served with ice are best in tall glasses, but spirits and wines need to be savored and their aroma held in glasses which have been evolved to match their character. Lagers, ales and ciders are usually served in thicker glasses and many people claim they taste even better from silver tankards.

1 **Champagne glass** Shows the color of the wine and retains the bubbles. Champagne should not be served in shallow bowls like sundae dishes; they allow the bubbles to disperse too quickly.

2 **Copita** Traditional glass for sherry; funnels the scent. Half fill only.

3 **White wine glass** in style of Anjou. Slightly sloping sides concentrates bouquet; stem prevents hand warming wine.

4 **White wine glass** in style of Alsace. Usually with a green stem which is reflected in the glass.

HOW TO HOLD A RABBIT

Don't pick the rabbit up by its ears or you may hurt it. You can lift it by the skin at the back of the neck but immediately support its weight from beneath with your other hand. You can rest its body on your hand and your forearm.

HOW TO OPEN ASPARAGUS CANS
Always open canned asparagus at the bottom – not, as normally, at the top of the can. That way you can slide out the stalks without damaging their delicate tips.

5 **Cordial glass** We don't drink cordials much today but this 18th-century design is ideal for straight vodka and similar spirits. Fill to the brim.
6 **Similar to the copita** this glass is suitable for port, sherry or madeira.
7 **Hock glass** The knobbed stem was fashioned to reflect its color into the wine.
8 **Tulip glass** Suitable for white or red wine and for champagne if no flute glasses are available. The in-turned rim helps to retain the bouquet.

9 **Paris goblet** Ideal for red wine. This fairly large glass should only be filled to about one-third.
10 **Cognac glass** It is easily cupped in the hand to warm the spirit and the vapor is retained in the bowl by the shape. Balloon glasses are not nearly so well matched to brandies.
11 **Tall glasses** are necessary if you have a long drink.
12 **Thicker tumblers** are suitable for beer. In Britain the thick glass "pub" tankard with a handle is traditional.

©DIAGRAM

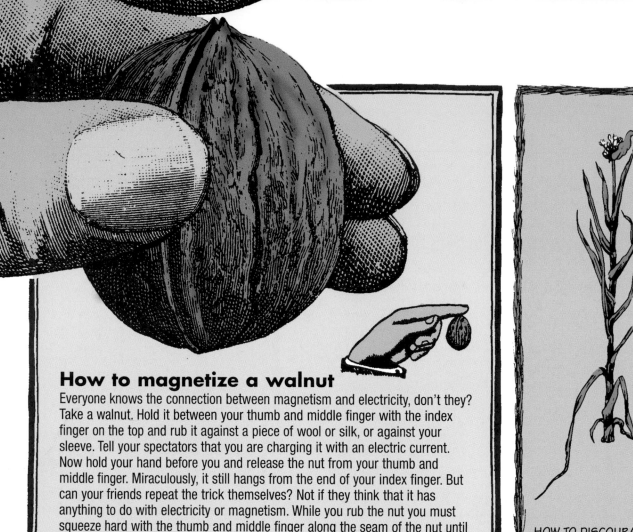

How to magnetize a walnut

Everyone knows the connection between magnetism and electricity, don't they? Take a walnut. Hold it between your thumb and middle finger with the index finger on the top and rub it against a piece of wool or silk, or against your sleeve. Tell your spectators that you are charging it with an electric current. Now hold your hand before you and release the nut from your thumb and middle finger. Miraculously, it still hangs from the end of your index finger. But can your friends repeat the trick themselves? Not if they think that it has anything to do with electricity or magnetism. While you rub the nut you must squeeze hard with the thumb and middle finger along the seam of the nut until it opens at the top. Push down with the index finger and a tiny piece of skin will be trapped in the nut and the nut will cling to your finger when the pressure from the other fingers is released. You can help the nut to open by splitting the seam beforehand with a thin blade.

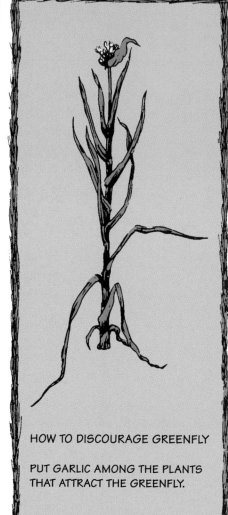

HOW TO DISCOURAGE GREENFLY

PUT GARLIC AMONG THE PLANTS THAT ATTRACT THE GREENFLY.

How to become

King or Queen of England

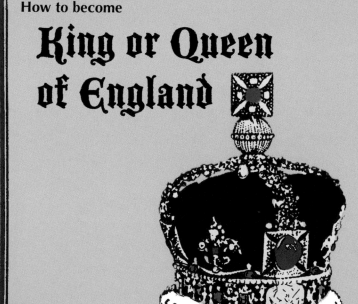

The British crown is hereditary, so first you must be born into the right family. You certainly don't have to be a prince or princess – there must be many people who carry royal blood, though they might have difficulty in tracing their family tree and proving it.

The British succession descends lineally to legitimate offspring of the sovereign, males first, then females. If there are no children it goes next to the brothers and sisters of the preceding sovereign and their descendants and so backwards until a living heir is found. That means that you have to wait until all those with a stronger claim on the throne than your own are dead – in the past some impatient heirs may have hastened their removal but modern security systems are so tight that this could prove difficult unless you could remove large numbers at a single stroke. The British Parliament can upset the order of succession, which could speed things up, but the agreement of all the parliaments of the British Commonwealth would also have to be obtained.

Having removed the competition you would have to show yourself a Christian and a Protestant, for the monarch is the head of the Church. You would have to swear to preserve the established Church of England and the Presbyterian Church of Scotland. At your Coronation, in Westminster Abbey, you would have to be accepted by a shout of acclamation from your subjects – easily arranged if you keep your opponents out, and you would have to take the Coronation Oath in which the monarch swears to rule justly.

HOW TO SHOOT CRAPS

7

11

a Natural throws

2

3

12

b Crap throws

4

5

6

8

9

10

c Point throws

Enormously popular as a gambling game in the United States, and familiar around the world from American gangster movies, craps requires only players and a pair of dice. It is essentially a betting game and methods of betting vary from a game where two or more players place private bets among themselves to open craps, organized with a banker, and bank craps, where a special gaming table is used, which is the way the game is played in casinos.

For the basic game the player ("shooter") shakes the dice in his or her closed hand and throws them on to the playing area. If this area is edged by a wall or backboard it is usual to rule that the dice must rebound from it before coming to rest. This helps defeat controlled throws. The numbers uppermost on the dice are then added together. Any number may play, the first to shoot being by common agreement and turns then going clockwise. New players may join at any point, provided that the others agree, and shooters may leave the game whenever they choose.

Basic play The first throw in a shooter's turn is called a "come out" throw, as is the first throw after each time the dice win or lose. On a come-out throw:

(a) if the shooter throws a "natural" (total of 7 or 11 spots, see illustration) the dice "pass" (win). The dice may be kept for another come-out throw.

(b) if the shooter throws "craps" the dice "crap out" (lose). The dice may be kept for another come-out throw.

(c) if the shooter throws a "point" he must "make a point" to win: i.e. throw the same number again before he throws a 7, no other numbers counting. If he makes the point the dice may be kept for another come-out throw but if the 7 is thrown first the dice "seven out" (lose) and must be passed to the next player.

If the shooter sevens out he must surrender the dice. He may also give them up voluntarily if he has not yet thrown in his turn or if he has just thrown a "decision"—a natural, a craps or a pass on a point.

How to fill a garbage bag
Take an old pail – metal or plastic – and knock out the bottom. Put the pail in the neck of a bag and fix the neck to it with clothes pegs. The rigid open neck will make it much easier to put in garbage and you can even hang the pail from a hook.

HOW TO SAVE ON LEMONS

If you want a drop or two of lemon juice, don't slice into a lemon; pierce it with a skewer and squeeze out the drops you need, then the whole lemon doesn't get dried out.

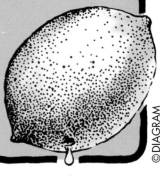

©DIAGRAM

How to keep paint fresh in store

With oil based paints pour a little turpentine over the top to prevent a skin forming. With emulsion paints use a little water.

HOW TO HUNT THE SNARK

"You may seek it with thimbles -
        and seek it with care
You may hunt it with forks
        and hope;
You may threaten its life
        with a railway share;
You may charm it with smiles
        and soap...

"For the Snark's a peculiar creature,
        that won't
Be caught in a commonplace
        way."

IF YOU WANT TO KNOW WHAT A SNARK IS TRY READING LEWIS CARROLL'S THE HUNTING OF THE SNARK.

How to rate a river
These are the scales used by American and European whitewater rafters and kayakers to describe the difficulty in negotiating a river. They are drawn up by experts for experts, so even an easy rating may require more skill than a novice will have.

US Rating	European Rating	
1, 2	I	**Easy** Small waves, clear passages, no serious obstacles
3, 4	II	**Medium difficult** Rapids of moderate difficultly with passages clear. Demands experience and fair outfit and boat
5, 6	III	**Difficult** Numerous waves, high, irregular rocks, eddies, rapids with passages that are clear but narrow. Demands experience in maneuver, prior inspection usually necessary. Needs good operator and boat.
7, 8	IV	**Very difficult** Long rapids, powerful, irregular waves, dangerous rocks, boiling eddies, passages difficult to scout. Reconnoitering essential before first attempt, powerful and exact maneuvering needed. Demands experienced boatman and excellent boat and outfit.
9	V	**Extremely difficult** Very difficult, long and violent rapids that follow each other almost without interruption, riverbed very obstructed, big drops, violent current, very steep gradient, reconnoitering essential but difficult. Demands best man, boat and outfit matched to situation.
10	VI	**Utmost dificulty** All difficulties above carried to the limit of navigability. Any attempt is at the risk of your life. Navigable only by teams of experts when at favorable water levels and after close study. Every precaution must be taken.
U	U	**Unrunnable** Impossible to navigate.

How to use chopsticks

Rest the thicker end of one stick in the saddle of the thumb (the flesh between the base of the thumb and the forefinger) and grip the lower part of that stick between the second and third fingers. Hold the other stick between the thumb and forefinger of the same hand, gripping it halfway or just above halfway along its length (the exact position will depend on what is comfortable for you), and articulate the tip of that stick against the lower one. If you have trouble getting the hang of it use your other hand to shift the upper stick around until you get the right purchase on it. When you can get the upper and lower sticks to pince you are ready to use them for picking up food.

Part of the ritual of using chopsticks is to use a bowl instead of a plate for your food. Make a bed of rice on top of which you can put other foods so their juices flavor the rice. Use small portions and add fresh rice as necessary. Hold the bowl as near your face as you feel etiquette permits – or bend as near to the bowl as you wish — to avoid spilling or dropping food. With less graspable foods, such as rice, you can use the sticks to shovel or flick them into your mouth.

Remember: the principle is to keep the lower stick firmly in place and move the other stick against it.

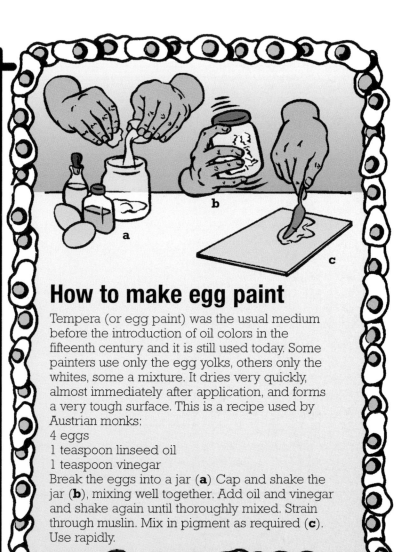

How to make egg paint

Tempera (or egg paint) was the usual medium before the introduction of oil colors in the fifteenth century and it is still used today. Some painters use only the egg yolks, others only the whites, some a mixture. It dries very quickly, almost immediately after application, and forms a very tough surface. This is a recipe used by Austrian monks:

4 eggs
1 teaspoon linseed oil
1 teaspoon vinegar

Break the eggs into a jar (**a**) Cap and shake the jar (**b**), mixing well together. Add oil and vinegar and shake again until thoroughly mixed. Strain through muslin. Mix in pigment as required (**c**). Use rapidly.

HOW TO MAKE A COMPASS

TAKE AN ORDINARY NEEDLE. STROKE IT WITH ONE END OF A MAGNET FROM THE EYE TO THE POINT, AGAIN AND AGAIN. ALWAYS LIFT THE MAGNET CLEAR OF THE NEEDLE AT THE END OF EACH STROKE. CUT A THIN DISK FROM A CORK, PUSH THE NEEDLE THROUGH THE CORK OR GLUE OR TAPE IT TO THE TOP. FLOAT THE CORK IN A SAUCER OF WATER. THE NEEDLE WILL LIE FROM NORTH TO SOUTH. IF YOU STROKE IT WITH THE SOUTH POLE OF THE MAGNET THE POINT WILL POINT NORTH, AND VICE VERSA.

HOW TO COLOR FOOD YELLOW

THE TRADITIONAL METHOD IS SAFFRON, THE GOLD COLORED STIGMAS OF THE SAFFRON CROCUS, BUT THEY ARE EXPENSIVE AND NOT ALWAYS AVAILABLE. YOU CAN ALSO USE THE PETALS OF THE MARIGOLD, WHICH HAVE A DELICATE FLAVOR TOO. USE THEM FRESH OR DRY THEM. IF YOU KEEP THEM SOMEWHERE COOL AND DARK, THEY WILL RETAIN THEIR COLOR FOR A LONG TIME.

HOW TO AVOID NIGHTMARES

According to a medieval herbalist, putting aniseed under your pillow will prevent nightmares.

How to time a watch at sea

The word "watch" comes from the word "wake" and this is nowhere more appropriate than at sea where part of the crew must always keep a wakeful eye while the remainder sleep and rest. That is perhaps why the first of the seven watches into which the day is divided begins at 8pm and ends at midnight.
All the watches except two are of four-hour duration – but if the whole 24 hours were divided equally the same sailors would always be on duty at the same time every day. To avoid this the evening is divided into two watches: the first and second dog watches. Their name has nothing to do with a bark at sea but is a corruption of the word "dodge," for by making each of these watches only two hours long they dodge that awkward repetition.

 First watch
8pm – midnight

 Middle watch
Midnight – 4am

 Morning watch
4am – 8am

 Forenoon watch
8am – noon

 Afternoon watch
Noon – 4pm

 First dog watch
4pm – 6pm

 Second dog watch
6pm – 8pm

How to teach a bear to dance

First, make sure it is not a grizzly bear or some other variety that might have a great propensity to turn mean. North American bears are not usually amenable to training. Your average European bear is a good choice, such as the ones found in Russia. Get your bear *young*. If you bring it up from a cub, it will fixate on you, if you are lucky. Indeed, if you can get a cub at birth and feed it from a bottle (hand-rear it) then you will form a much stronger bond with it and it will be more obedient and eager to please. Once the bear is old enough to stand on its own and cavort a little, you simply play music for it and dance with it. Do this in very short spells and always reward the bear with something that it loves to eat, plus lots of praise and affection. Later on, play it the music and expect it to dance; even demonstrate, but don't support it. If it stares at you in astonishment, put the music on again, and repeat the earlier process. Sooner or later the bear will get up on its hind legs to the sound of the music. Praise it right away and give it a reward. It will get the idea that music means it is going to get fed, but ONLY if it gets up on its hind legs and "dances" first. The method is the one used for training any animal, human or otherwise, a form of *positive conditioning*; as defined by B.F. Skinner, the American behavioral psychologist. Eventually you can stop giving the bear its food reward every time; give it in an irregular pattern. Because it always hopes to be rewarded it will respond when it hears the sound of music in hopes that this will be a time when dancing earns a goodie. It will probably also, from time to time, get up and do a little dance just for the hell of it, music or no, in the hope of earning a reward. Don't respond, for that could lead to persistent pestering.

How to count in roman numerals

The Roman numeral system consists of seven numbers represented by seven capital letters: I = 1, V = 5, X = 10, L = 50, C = 100, D = 500, M = 1000. Most numbers use the principle of addition, for instance XI = 10 + 1 = 11, but 4s and 9s use subtraction, so IV = 5 − 1 = 4, IX = 10 − 1 = 9. So the numbers from 1 to 20 are I, II, III, IV, V, VI, VII, VIII, IX, X, XI, XII, XIII, XIV, XV, XVI, XVII, XVIII, XIX, XX. Working in the same way with the higher numbers, 40 = XL (50 − 10), 60 = LX (50 + 10), 90 = XC (100 − 10), 110 = CX (100 + 10). To write an irregular number, for example 3625, start with MMM (3 x 1000), add DC (500 + 100) and XXV (10 + 10 + 5) and the result is MMMDCXXV. To avoid very large numerals, a bar or *vinculum* drawn over the figure indicates that it is multiplied by 1000, so M̄ M̄ M̄ M̄ M̄ = 5000 x 1000 = 5,000,000.

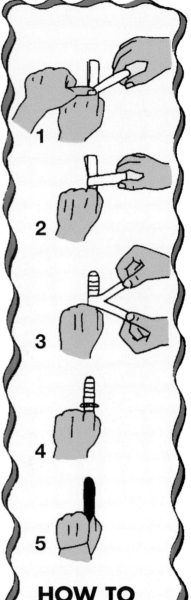

HOW TO BANDAGE A FINGER

Cover the wound with sterile gauze and then a strip of narrow bandage (**1**). Wind the bandage around the finger toward the tip and down again (**2**), split the end (**3**), and tie around the base (**4**). A finger stock (**5**) helps keep the bandage clean and secure.

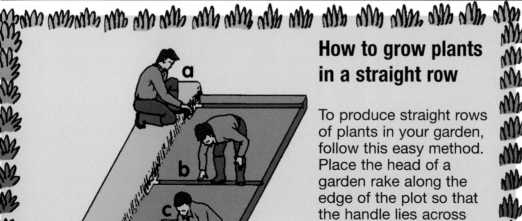

How to grow plants in a straight row

To produce straight rows of plants in your garden, follow this easy method. Place the head of a garden rake along the edge of the plot so that the handle lies across the soil (**a**). Tread gently on the handle to make an indent (**b**). Remove the rake and sow seeds along the indent (**c**), and the plants will come up in neat parallel rows (**d**).

How to freshen up your paint box

It you open up your paint box, and find the lozenges of watercolor dry, cracked and unresponsive to your water-loaded brush don't let it dampen your artistic enthusiasm, or rush out to buy new colors. A drop or two of glycerin brushed on to each little block of paint will make them usable again.

HOW TO PLEASE A PIRANHA

Feed it meat and keep it in running or constantly circulating water at about 77°F (25°C), for it comes from the warm rivers of South America. It prefers its food live and since it can grow to 9 inches (23cm) long, keep your fingers out of the water or it may bite the end off one of them. Watch these carnivores in action and you won't take any risks.

How to spot the Pole Star

Polaris, the Pole Star or North Star, is relatively easy to find in the night sky if you can first find Ursa Major, a constellation which is known by many local names: the Great Bear, the Big Dipper or the Plow.

This constellation is, thankfully, quite easy to locate and – looks a bit like a saucepan with a bent handle. The two stars on the right are known as the pointers. Imagine a line drawn through them and extend it for about five times the distance between the pointers and there is Polaris.

How to fold a suit for packing

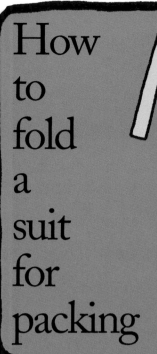

Jacket Lay it flat on its back, bring the two fronts together and fasten one button. Lay the upper part of the sleeves parallel with the sides of the jacket, then fold over at the elbows so that the sleeves cross on the "chest." Fold the bottom of the jacket upward from the waist to lie flat over the sleeves and the upper part

Pants (trousers) Lay flat, with one leg on top of the other so that the front and back creases align. There's no need to do up the fly, but make sure all pockets are flat. Then fold the legs over from the cuffs upward, either in half or in three depending on the size of your luggage, and lay them on top of the jacket.

HOW TO MAKE A GINGER BEER PLANT

You need:
1 loosely-lidded jar
2 oz (60g) baker's yeast
2 tbsp (level) sugar
2 tbsp (level) ground ginger
1 cup (250ml) water

Mix the sugar and yeast together until they form a liquid, to this add the ginger and the water. Stir well and bottle in the jar. That is your ginger beer plant. To produce ginger beer feed the plant with one teaspoon of sugar and one teaspoon of ground ginger each day. After ten days dissolve 2 cups (500ml) of sugar in 3 cups (750ml) of water. Bring this sugar mixture to the boil, then let it cool slightly; add the strained juice of two lemons.

Now strain the contents of the ginger beer plant through muslin and add to the sugar water. Add 6 cups of cold water. Stir well and bottle in strong beer or cider bottles. If you use a corked bottle tie on the cork – otherwise the build-up of gas in the bottle will force it out. Store in a cool place and use at any time after three days.

The sediment from the ginger beer plant is now split in half to form two new ginger beer plants which should be fed as before. If you begin to produce more ginger beer than you need you can give a plant away – if you don't, you'll find they multiply like rabbits!

How to mix the perfect martini

A martini – the cocktail, not the proprietary vermouth – consists of gin and vermouth in varying proportions according to taste, with a few other ingredients. It should be well stirred or, better still, shaken with cracked or crushed ice. If you do not have a shaker a screwtop jar will serve the purpose. Recipes:

Extra dry $1/7$ dry vermouth, $6/7$ dry gin, twist of lemon peel.

Dry $1/5$ dry vermouth, $4/5$ dry gin, twist of lemon peel.

Standard $1/3$ dry vermouth, $2/3$ dry gin, dash of orange bitters, twist of lemon peel, optional green olive.

Medium $1/4$ dry vermouth, $1/4$ sweet vermouth, $1/2$ dry gin, twist of lemon peel, optional green olive.

Sweet $1/3$ sweet vermouth, $2/3$ dry gin, dash of orange bitters, maraschino cherry.

Note: The olive or cherry should be impaled on a cocktail stick so that it can be removed while drinking.

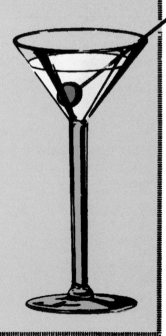

80

HOW TO TELL A NUTMEG FROM A MACE

It's not easy for they have a similar taste but nutmeg is a hard nut kernel which is usually grated and mace is usually obtained as a powdered spice. Both grow in Grenada in the West Indies and once, during colonial times, the local governor received instructions from London recommending that the island concentrate on growing mace, since its sales were increasing whilst the nutmeg market was in decline. This gave the governor an insurmountable problem: for the nutmeg is the kernel (**a**) of the nut of the nutmeg tree and mace is the layer between the nutmeg and the outer casing of the fruit (**b**).

a   b

How to stand for the British Parliament

In Britain, and countries following British practice, it's a pretty simple matter to stand (run) for Parliament. When an election or a by-election is called, you must be nominated as a candidate by at least ten people who are registered electors in the constituency where you are standing. This nomination is handed to the returning officer, an official appointed for the purpose in each constituency. With the nomination you must deposit a certain amount of money – but this sum is returned if you poll at least one-eighth of the votes. You must also appoint an agent, and there is a limit on the amount of money you can spend on your election campaign. There's no limit on the number of unpaid helpers you can have. But you mustn't bribe people to vote for you.

Certain people are disqualified from standing for Parliament. They are: peers (unless they have renounced their peerage); priests and ministers of the Churches of England and Scotland, the Episcopalian Church of Scotland, and the Roman Catholic Church; people who hold public offices, such as judges, civil servants, members of the armed forces, and the police; people under 21 years old; aliens; people with severe mental drsorder; bankrupts; and people convicted of certain crimes.

All you have to do then is to persuade people to vote for you!

HOW TO DO THE COBRA

THE COBRA IS A YOGA POSITION DESIGNED TO EXERCISE THE CHEST, ARMS, BUTTOCKS AND BACK.

1 LIE DOWN ON YOUR FRONT, FOREHEAD ON THE FLOOR, HANDS PALM-DOWNWARD BENEATH THE SHOULDERS.
2 VERY SLOWLY RAISE THE HEAD AND PUSH DOWN WITH THE HANDS.
3 STILL MOVING SLOWLY, ARCH THE SPINE AS FAR AS POSSIBLE WITHOUT STRAINING, AND HOLD THIS POSITION FOR A FEW MOMENTS.
4 LOWER YOURSELF TO POSITION 1, THEN RELAX, HANDS BY THE SIDES, AND HEAD TURNED TO ONE SIDE. REPEAT THE WHOLE SEQUENCE.

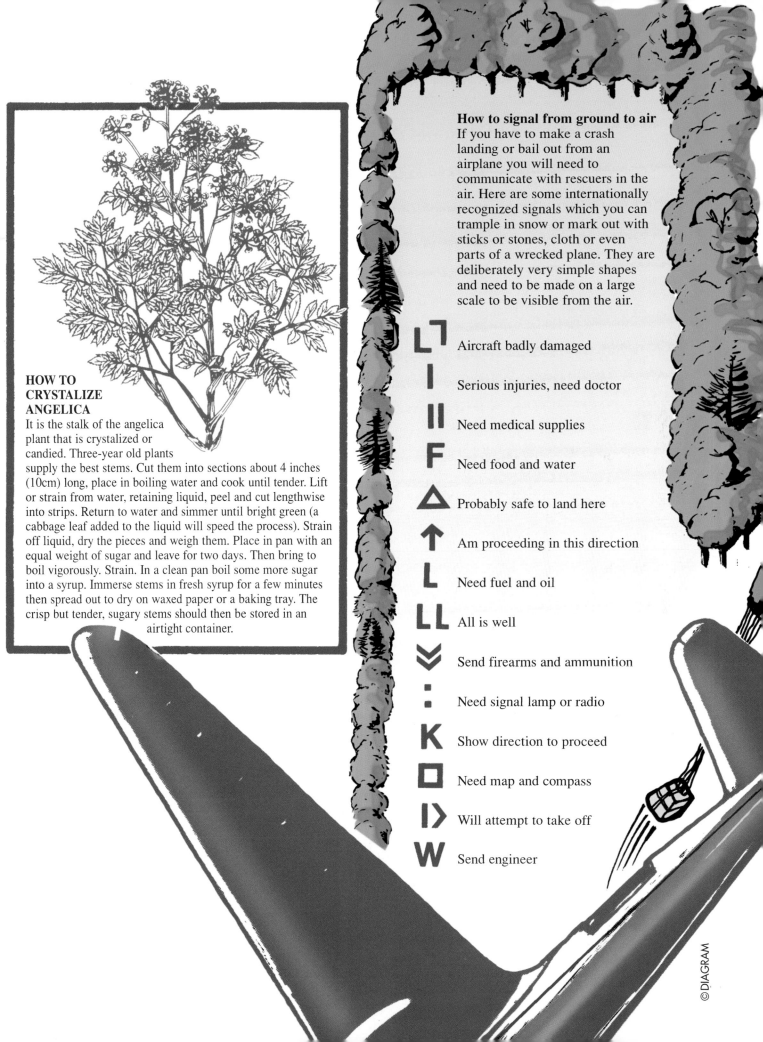

HOW TO CRYSTALIZE ANGELICA

It is the stalk of the angelica plant that is crystalized or candied. Three-year old plants supply the best stems. Cut them into sections about 4 inches (10cm) long, place in boiling water and cook until tender. Lift or strain from water, retaining liquid, peel and cut lengthwise into strips. Return to water and simmer until bright green (a cabbage leaf added to the liquid will speed the process). Strain off liquid, dry the pieces and weigh them. Place in pan with an equal weight of sugar and leave for two days. Then bring to boil vigorously. Strain. In a clean pan boil some more sugar into a syrup. Immerse stems in fresh syrup for a few minutes then spread out to dry on waxed paper or a baking tray. The crisp but tender, sugary stems should then be stored in an airtight container.

How to signal from ground to air

If you have to make a crash landing or bail out from an airplane you will need to communicate with rescuers in the air. Here are some internationally recognized signals which you can trample in snow or mark out with sticks or stones, cloth or even parts of a wrecked plane. They are deliberately very simple shapes and need to be made on a large scale to be visible from the air.

⌐ Aircraft badly damaged

‖ Serious injuries, need doctor

‖ Need medical supplies

F Need food and water

△ Probably safe to land here

↑ Am proceeding in this direction

L Need fuel and oil

LL All is well

⋙ Send firearms and ammunition

⁝ Need signal lamp or radio

K Show direction to proceed

□ Need map and compass

I⟩ Will attempt to take off

W Send engineer

HOW TO REMOVE CIGARETTE STAINS

If nicotine stained fingers reveal that you have not kicked the habit, rub them with a piece of lemon or with cotton dipped in hydrogen peroxide. Rinse in water immediately afterward.

How to convert Centigrade to Fahrenheit (and back again)

Gabriel Daniel Fahrenheit, born in Danzig (now Gdansk), developed his thermometer scale in 1714. Centigrade was devised in 1742 by Anders Celsius, a Swede. Although Centigrade remains a popularly accepted name for the 100-based scale it was officially renamed Celsius, in honor of its originator, by an international conference in 1948.

There are exactly 100 (0°–100°) degrees on a Celsius thermometer between the temperature points at which water will freeze and boil, and 180 degrees (32°–212°) on the Fahrenheit scale. To convert one to the other apply the following formulae:

Centigrade to Fahrenheit:
$(F=\frac{9C}{5}+32)$. Multiply the Centigrade temperature by 9 then divide by 5 and add 32. Thus boiling point of 100°C becomes 9×100=900 divided by 5=180 plus 32=212°F.

From Fahrenheit to Centigrade
$(C=\frac{F-32}{9}\times5)$. Deduct 32 from the Fahrenheit temperature divide by 9 and multiply the result by 5. Thus boiling point 212°–32=180 which divided by 9 is 20 which multiplied by 5 equals 100°C.

Normal blood heat (for humans) is 98.6°F or 37°C.
1 Boiling point of water
2 Blood temperature
3 Freezing point.

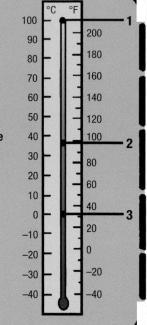

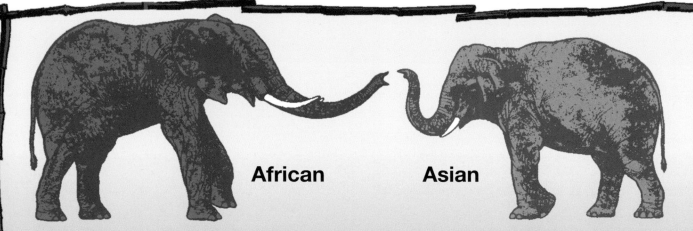

African   Asian

HOW TO SPOT AFRICAN AND ASIAN ELEPHANTS

You may think that an elephant is an elephant is an elephant. But observe the specimens at the zoo carefully, and you will be able to see many differences. If the elephant has a slightly hollowed back, two knobs at the tip of its trunk, large tusks and ears, and is dark gray in color, it is African. If it is smaller, lighter, with a slightly arched back and one knob at the tip of its trunk, it is Asian.

HOW TO ESTIMATE TEA AND COFFEE FOR A PARTY

If you are offering tea or coffee in large quantities you can calculate on getting about 90 cupfuls from 15 pounds of coffee (200 from 1kg) and about 100 cupfuls from 1pound of tea (220 from 1kg).

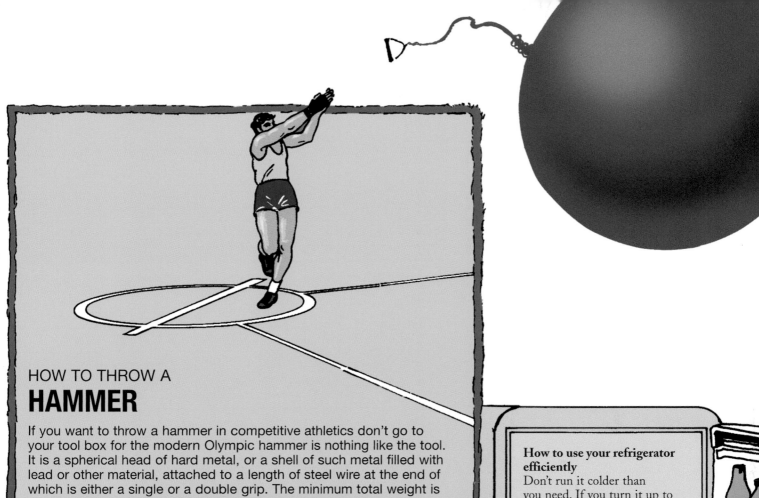

HOW TO THROW A
HAMMER

If you want to throw a hammer in competitive athletics don't go to your tool box for the modern Olympic hammer is nothing like the tool. It is a spherical head of hard metal, or a shell of such metal filled with lead or other material, attached to a length of steel wire at the end of which is either a single or a double grip. The minimum total weight is 16 pounds (7.260kg). It is usual for competitors to wear a glove on the hand which comes in contact with the wire grip.

Keeping within a circle 7 feet (2.135m) in diameter, you begin with the sphere on the ground and turn to swing it up into the air, releasing your grip when the momentum developed will carry it farthest. Its release must be within a 40° arc and it must land within that arc. It is usual to cage the rest of the circle so that the release point may be placed close to spectators away from the direction of the cast. The distance thrown is measured from the nearest mark made by the sphere when it lands to the inner edge of the ring bounding the throwing circle. In competition the winner is the best after six trials.

How to use your refrigerator efficiently

Don't run it colder than you need. If you turn it up to make ice rapidly, turn it down again.

Allow cooked food to cool before putting it inside. Cover liquids to prevent evaporation; this will keep down the amount of ice formed.

Open the door gently and for as short a time as possible. Never allow more than 1/4 inch (1/2cm) of ice to accumulate on the freezing compartment.

Defrost regularly, but not unnecessarily. You can speed defrosting by filling the ice trays with very hot water, and refilling when they cool.

HOW TO CHAIN STITCH

Bring the thread up to the surface of the fabric. Insert the needle close to where the thread emerges, and bring it up again a little further on, over a loop of thread. Pull this stitch, and form subsequent stitches in the same way.

©DIAGRAM

How to stop raisins from sinking

Coating raisins with flour before using them will stop them from sinking to the bottom of cake batters.

How to worship at a Shinto shrine

Stand erect and throw a coin into the offering box of the shrine. Call upon the god within by clapping your hands two or three times at chest level. Align your palms and fingers when you clap; don't clap as if you were applauding at a theater. Keep your hands together, fingers upward, and bend slightly at the waist with your eyes closed. Wish now for a safe journey, a good marriage, a healthy life.

How to check the engine of a used car

Remove the cap from where you add oil to the engine and place your palm over the opening. Rev the engine. If the seals and gaskets are in good condition you will feel suction on your palm. Then scoop out some oil from just inside the rim and rub it between your fingers. If the oil feels gritty, the engine, sooner or later, is going to give you trouble. Take great care not to put your hands near any moving parts.

How to calculate the distance of a thunderstorm

Sound and light travel at different speeds which is convenient in measuring roughly how far away a thunderstorm is. A lightning flash may be seen at almost the moment it occurs since its light travels at approximately 186,000 miles (300,000 km) per second. Sound travels much more slowly, at about 760 mph (1,223 kmph), so that by timing the difference between seeing the flash and hearing the peal of thunder, we can estimate how far away the storm is. One second difference is about a fifth of a mile or 340 meters away.

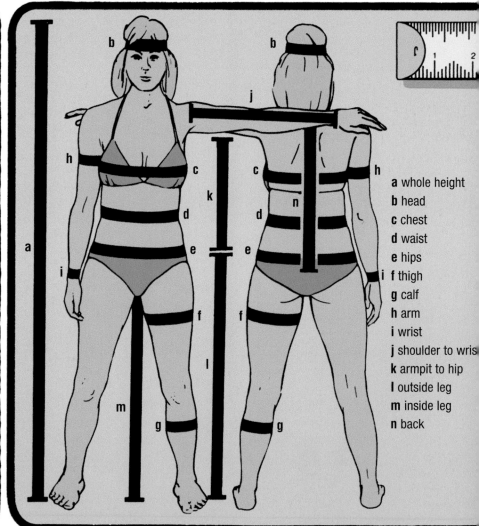

a whole height
b head
c chest
d waist
e hips
f thigh
g calf
h arm
i wrist
j shoulder to wrist
k armpit to hip
l outside leg
m inside leg
n back

HOW TO PLAY THE CASTANETS

A pair of castanets consists of two pieces of hollowed-out hardwood, linked by a cord threaded through two holes in each piece. You wind the cord around the thumb and click the two plates together with your fingers. Take a pair of castanets in each hand. The left hand pair plays a simple rhythm, while with the right hand you perform the full complicated rhythm of the dance. Don't be too dismayed if you aren't as good as a Spanish dancer – the great percussionist James Blades said, "The superb artistry of the Spanish player defies imitation."

HOW TO MEASURE YOUR OWN BODY

Equip yourself with a measuring tape – a real measuring tape, not a metal one that won't be flexible enough to go closely around your body – and paper and pencil to record your findings. One method is to stand against a wall and mark positions against it which you can then measure flat. It is not easy to do this accurately, but it is the only practical way of measuring your own height. If you stand opposite a mirror you will be able to see if your hand is level with the top of your head. Hold a book or other flat surface on top of your head. Keep it in position while you turn and make your mark on the wall. Stay in front of the mirror to take horizontal measures too, then you will be able to make sure the tape is level and that it is not twisted. To measure your head, chest, waist, or hips, settle the tape around you and then draw it against you with the end of the tape (which is frequently reinforced with a small piece of metal) overlapping the free end. Grip the point of overlap on the free end with your thumb exactly on that point. Keep hold as you release the tape and read off the measure at that point. Measure your chest both relaxed and expanded, and if you measure with your stomach pulled in be honest and measure it relaxed as well! Thighs and calves are easy; just wrap the tape around them. Wrists and arms are more difficult because you have to manipulate the tape with one hand. Shoulder to wrist: you'll need to hold the tape end at the shoulder and the other end between the fingers while contriving to keep the tape running along your elbow. Grip the tape between your fingers and pull it tight toward the shoulder until the top end is in place. Then with a little contortion you should be able to read off the measure at your wrist for both the bent and straight arm. From armpit to waist or thigh hold the end in your armpit and use the other hand to grip the lower point. For outside leg length stand on the tape and draw it up under your foot until the end is at your waist. Keeping your foot firmly on the tape, bend your knees and read the measure. Do the inside leg in the same way. Measurements down the back: hold the end at your neck, let the tape hang against your body, and then use the other hand to grip the point at which you need the measurement.

How to play
RINGO

Players Ringo is a game of strategy for two players that originated in Germany.

The board comprises a large circle divided into six concentric rings. From the inner ring outward the circle is further divided into eight segments of equal size. The central circle (**a**) is shaded and is known as the "fortress." One of the segments is marked off as a "neutral zone" (**b**). The six sections in each of the other segments are alternatively shaded in or left blank so that each segment has three shaded and three unshaded sections.

Pieces Each player has counters (four for the defender, seven for the attacker) distinguishable from his opponent's. At the start of the game the defender's pieces are arranged around the fortress in the center of the board (**c**) and the attacker's pieces are arranged on the outermost ring (**d**). Neither player may station his pieces in the neutral zone.

Objective The attacker must capture the fortress by getting two of his pieces into it; the defender must prevent him from doing so. Both must try to capture or immobilize as many enemy pieces as possible in order to achieve their objective.

Play The players decide which of them is to attack and which to defend. The attacker is the first to move, and thereafter players take alternate turns. The attacker may only move his pieces forward – toward the center or sideways (**e**). To compensate for having fewer pieces the defender is able to move his in any direction except diagonally (**f**). Although he may not actually enter the fortress, he is allowed to jump over it when capturing. When moving sideways into another segment pieces must remain on the same ring as the one on which they were standing. Both players may move their pieces into the neutral zone although the attacker may have only as many pieces in the neutral zone as the defender has on the board (i.e. if the defender has only two pieces left on the board, the attacker may have only two pieces within the neutral zone).

Capturing Both players may capture enemy pieces, though there is no compulsion to do so. A piece is captured by jumping over it from a touching section onto a vacant section beyond it (**g**). The captured piece is then removed from the board. As in ordinary moves, the attacker is restricted to capturing in a forward or sideways direction, while the defender may also capture in a backward direction. When making a sideways capture, the taking piece and the piece being captured must both be on the same ring. A player may capture only one piece in a move. All pieces are safe from capture when within the neutral zone. It is permissible for a piece to use the neutral zone as its "take off" or "landing" area in a capturing move. Although the defender may not actually enter the fortress, he may jump over it in order to capture an enemy piece within it, provided the section directly opposite is vacant (**h**).

End play The attacker may enter the fortress from any segment (including the neutral zone). Should a defending piece be positioned on the innermost ring, an attacking piece may jump over it into the fortress (thereby capturing the defending piece). If the attacker gets one of his pieces into the fortress, it is still prone to capture by a defending piece. Should the attacker succeed in getting two of his pieces into the fortress, however, he wins the game. The defender wins the game if he either captures all but one of the attacker's pieces, or immobilizes the attacker's pieces so that he is unable to get two pieces into the fortress.

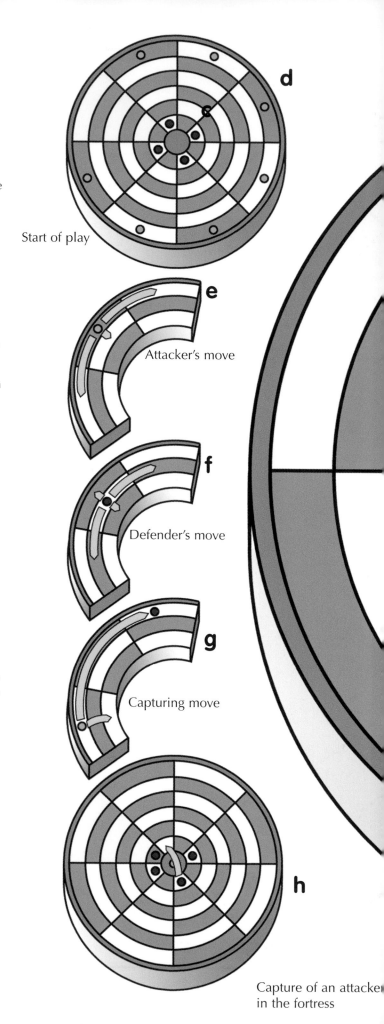

Start of play

Attacker's move

Defender's move

Capturing move

Capture of an attacker in the fortress

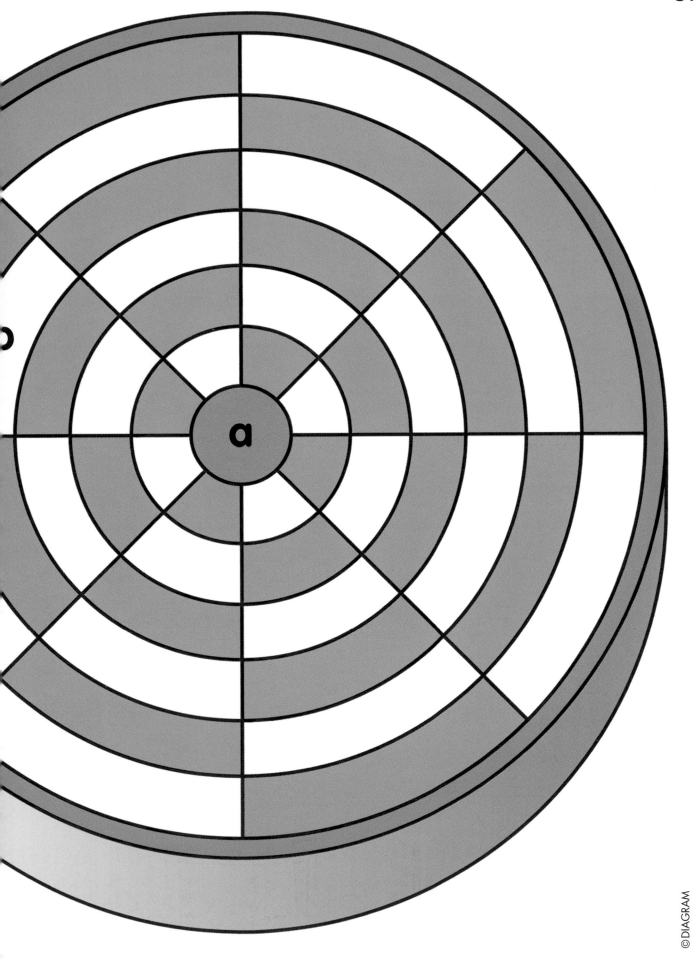

How to hold a goldfish

Holding a fish may remove the mucus that coats its body and protects its skin from organisms in the water, but sometimes it may be necessary when inspecting or treating it for disease. First put your hand in the water with the fish until it cools down to the fish's temperature. Fish do not easily tolerate sudden changes to hot or cold. Whether taking a fish from the water or lifting it from a net allow the fish to swim or slide into the lightly cupped hand between thumb and index finger and then close them upon it. The fish must be gripped firmly so it cannot wriggle and damage itself, and its fins must lie naturally against the body. Whenever possible transfer fish in a net or even a spoon or ladle.

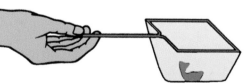

HOW TO PLAY POLO

Polo is an expensive game to play. To begin with you need eight horses or ponies – four for each side – a few more in reserve, and two extra for the mounted umpires. Then you have to find a field 300 yards (274.3m) long and 160 yards (146.3m) wide with a generous margin round it. At each end set a goal mouth 8 yards (7.32m) wide.

The players are mounted and each carries a long-handled mallet with which to strike a wooden ball weighing 4^1/$_2$oz (127.6g). The object of the game is to drive the ball into the goal defended by the opposing team. The side scoring the most goals wins. Playing time is usually 56 minutes, divided into 8 "chukkas," (7-minute periods) separated by 3-minute intervals. A timekeeper signals these divisions on a bell and keeps the score. A judge stationed behind each goal decides whether a goal has been scored. There are strict rules based on the right of a player to follow the ball on its exact line. Ponies may be of any height but must have good sight in both eyes and have bandages or leggings on all four legs.

How to play a jew's harp

The name of this instrument probably has nothing to do with the Hebrew race but comes from "jaws harp". Play it by holding the instrument in your mouth while you pluck the free end of the metal tongue, using the shape of your mouth and lips to alter the pitch.

How to identify a member of the US Government

You would probably recognize the seal of the President of the United States, for the design is often displayed when the President is making public speeches or giving interviews, but did you know the President also has a flag? It does not fly on the White House but it is flown by cars, ships and even airplanes in which the President travels.

The Vice President also has a personal flag, as do the members of the Presidential Cabinet and other leading government figures – although not the Secretaries for Labor or the Interior who only have departmental flags.

President

Vice President

Secretary of State

Secretary of Agriculture

Secretary of Commerce

HOW TO CALCULATE THE SURFACE AREA OF CONES, CYCLINDERS AND SPHERES

Cones First measure the **slant height** of the cone: the distance from the perimeter of the base to the **vertex**, the point of the cone. The area of the lateral surface equals half of the slant height multiplied by the circumference of the base ($2\pi r$) or, more simply, $\pi r \times$ the slant height. Add on the area of the base (πr^2).

Cylinders If you could roll out a cylinder flat the lateral surface would measure the same as a rectangle formed by the length of the cylinder and the length of the circumference. The lateral area, therefore, equals the length multiplied by the circumference: length $\times 2\pi r^2$. Add the area of the cylinder ends ($2 \times \pi r^2$).

Spheres Multiply the area of the Great Circle (where the radius is longest) by four: $4\pi r^2$.

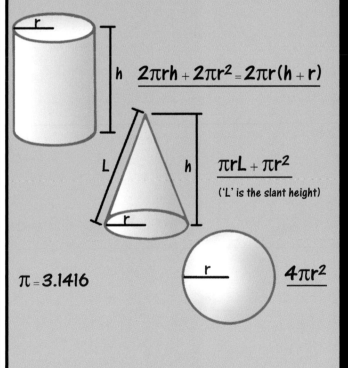

$$2\pi rh + 2\pi r^2 = 2\pi r(h + r)$$

$$\pi rL + \pi r^2$$
('L' is the slant height)

$$\pi = 3.1416$$

$$4\pi r^2$$

©DIAGRAM

How to describe the strength of the wind

The international scale used to describe the strength of winds was devised by Sir Francis Beaufort, a British admiral of the time of Nelson. It rates winds from calm to hurricane "that which no canvas could withstand" as Beaufort originally put it. For official readings measurements are taken at 32.8 feet (10m) above the ground, where speed will be considerably more than at ground level. When a meteorological report says that a wind is of Force 4, or Gale Force 9, it is the Beaufort Scale to which it refers.

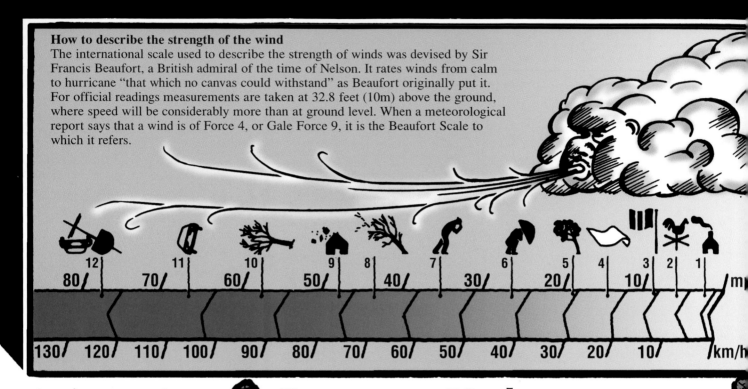

12	11	10	9	8	7	6	5	4	3	2	1	
80/	70/	60/	50/	40/	30/	20/	10/					m
130/	120/	110/	100/	90/	80/	70/	60/	50/	40/	30/	20/	10/	km/h

HOW TO COAT A PAINTBRUSH

Too much paint on your brush will lead to uneven application, run back into the roots of the bristles and even spread onto the handle. Make sure that you charge it evenly and well. Stretch a thin wire across the top of the open paint can. If the can has a handle you can attach it to its ends, or to a circle of wire below the edge, or tape it on. Every time you load your brush with paint wipe it against this wire and excess paint will drip back into the can. That saves paint, mess and trouble.

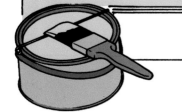

ħow to make Anglo-Saxon mead

Mead is a British alcholic beverage known since the earliest times, drunk by the Saxons and right through the middle ages. This is a modern version of the recipe. You need:

4–5lb (about 2kg) honey
2oz (60g) hops
the rind from 3–4 lemons
a small cloth bag

Sew the hops and the lemon rind into the bag. Add the honey to a gallon of water and boil it for an hour and a half; carefully remove the scum from the top. Add the bag and its contents. Allow to cool. When cold place in a flask (preferably stoneware) and closely stopper it. Allow to stand for 8–9 months before drinking.

Beaufort Scale #	character of wind	effects of wind inland	wind speed mph	km/h
0	calm	calm, smoke rises vertically	<1	<1
1	light air	wind direction shown by smoke but not by flags	1–3	1–5
2	slight breeze	wind felt on face, leaves whisper, flags move	4–7	6–12
3	gentle breeze	leaves and thin twigs move, pennants extended fully	8–12	13–20
4	moderate breeze	paper and dust lifted, twigs and thin branches move	13–18	21–29
5	fresh breeze	small trees in leaf begin to sway, white caps on lakes	19–24	30–39
6	strong breeze	thicker branches move, whistling in telephone lines, umbrellas difficult to use	25–31	40–50
7	moderate gale	whole trees moving, resistance to movement against wind perceptible	32–38	51–61
8	fresh gale	twigs broken from trees, movement in open difficult	39–46	62–74
9	strong gale	minor damage to houses (awnings and T.V. aerials)	47–54	75–87
10	whole gale	trees uprooted, major damage to houses	55–63	88–102
11	storm	widespread damage	64–75	103–120
12	hurricane	severe destruction	>75	>120

How to stop smoking, Chinese-style

A Chinese peasant's method: Take a betel nut, and make a hole in it. Fill the hole with tobacco tar. Place the nut in boiling water for two hours, remove it. Whenever you feel the urge to smoke, sniff the nut instead. After three days you should no longer feel the need to smoke.

How to name an animal family

Just as human beings are known as man, woman or child, according to sex and age, animals have special terms to distinguish them. An adult male swan, for example, is a cob, the female a pen, and young swans are known as cygnets. Here are some others:

Animal	Male	Female	Juvenile
Kangaroo	buck	doe	joey
Elephant	bull	cow	calf
Lion	lion	lioness	cub
Deer	buck	doe	fawn
Hare	buck	doe	leveret
Tiger	tiger	tigress	cub
Bear	bear	she-bear	cub
Fox	fox	vixen	cub
Pig	boar	sow	piglet
Goat	billy	nanny	kid
Donkey	donkey	jennet	foal
Dog	dog	bitch	puppy
Sheep	ram	ewe	lamb
Horse	stallion	mare or dam	foal
Cattle	bull	cow	calf
Seal	bull	cow	pup
Whale	bull	cow	calf
Goose	gander	goose	gosling
Duck	drake	duck	duckling
Most birds	cock	hen	chick

How To Enter A Religious Order

Most Christian religious orders and religious congregations are part of the Roman Catholic Church, though the Eastern Orthodox Church and some Protestant Churches, including the Anglican Church, also have religious communities. The difference between an order and a congregation lies largely in the kind of vows taken.

To enter a Roman Catholic order you must first convince your own priest that you have a vocation. You are then accepted into a novitiate house of a religious congregation, which exists for the preliminary training of would-be monks or nuns. At first you are a postulant, a probationary state lasting at least six months. You must be over the age of 16.

If you have satisfied the superiors of the house of your genuine vocation, you are then accepted as a novice. The novitiate lasts between one and two years. You wear the dress and follow the Rule of the community. At the end of your novitiate you make temporary vows, and leave the novitiate house to take your place in an ordinary community. Your temporary vows last for three years, at the end of which time you take your final vows of poverty, chastity and obedience, and are accepted as a full member of the community.

Anglican religious orders, which first came into existence in the mid-1800s, are organized on much the same lines as those of the Roman Catholic Church. Most monasteries of the Eastern Orthodox Church are controlled by local bishops.

HOW TO TALK TO A DEAF PERSON

Most deaf people learn to lip-read, so always face a deaf person when you're talking to them. Make sure you enunciate your words clearly and don't mumble – then your lips and tongue make easily visible movements which a deaf person can interpret.
If you use the sign language of the deaf-and-dumb alphabet, make sure you're using the same version as the deaf person – there is an international system covering many objects and ideas and two alphabetical systems, one using both hands, and one

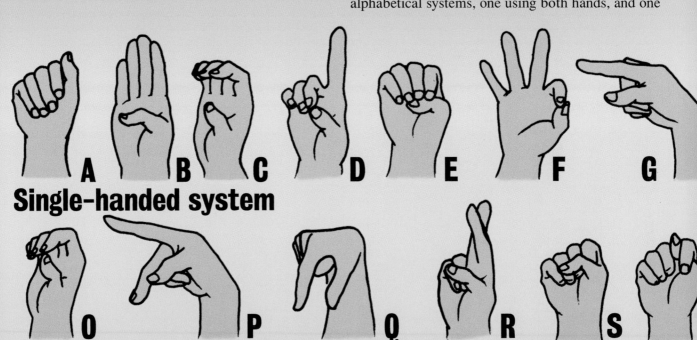

Single-handed system

A   B   C   D   E   F   G

O   P   Q   R   S

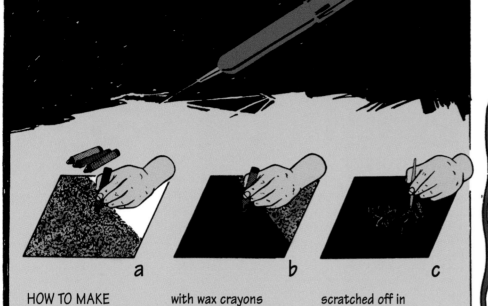

HOW TO MAKE YOUR OWN SCRATCHBOARD

Color the entire surface of a piece of strong cardboard

with wax crayons (a), then cover this layer with a coating of black wax crayon (b). The black surface can then be

scratched off in designs to reveal the colors underneath (c). Use a stylus or blunt needle for scratching.

How to coil a garden hose
Attach it to the hot water faucet – this will warm the hose. Both plastic and rubber are easier to coil when warm.

a single-handed method. Make your movements clear and precise, and keep your hands where the deaf person can see them clearly. With the alphabetical systems you'll have to spell almost everything out except numbers, but in time you can use a number of abbreviations – for example, the familiar thumbs-up sign is usually used for "good". Mark breaks between words by snapping the fingers or separating the hands and jerking them downward.

READ THESE SIGNS TO FIND A CITY

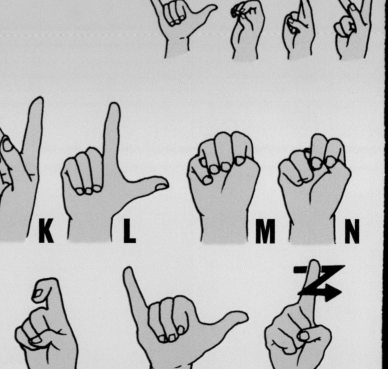

H   I   J   K   L   M   N

U   V   W   X   Y   Z

HOW TO BRANDISH A BATON

In beating time the point of the baton marks the beat. Remember that a white baton does not show up against a white shirt, so keep the baton clear of your body as far as possible. The three basic beats are for 2, 3 and 4 beats in a bar, and are as follows (as seen from the conductor's point of view).

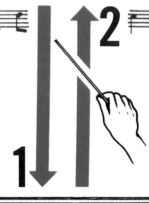

How to grow beansprouts

The easiest beans to sprout are the green mung beans; soak 1/4 cup (50ml) of beans in 1 cup (250ml) of water overnight. Drain the soaked beans, and place them in a thin layer on the bottom of a shallow dish, covered with a damp paper towel. Twice a day rinse them, shake off excess water and replace in the dish; in about 4 days your sprouts, with or without the beans attached, will be ready for use.

How to fire a cannon

The simplest cannon to practice on is an old-fashioned muzzle-loader. You need half-a-dozen brawny men to form the gun's crew. First put a charge of powder, sewn up in a linen cartridge, into the muzzle and ram it tightly down with a long-handled rammer (**a**). Next put in a thick wad of linen and cotton, to form a pad, and ram that home. Now roll a cannonball (**b**) down the barrel to rest on the wad. The gun barrel is mounted on a wheeled carriage, and you can pivot it up and down to get the range, by means of wooden wedges under the breech. For side to side changes you must lever the whole gun-carriage around by hand. On the upper surface at the rear of the cannon is a touchhole (**c**), which you prime with gunpowder. To fire the cannon you take a piece of smoldering slowmatch – slowly burning rope held in a staff called a linstock (**d**) – and apply it to the touchhole. Stand clear for the recoil, as the cannon jumps back on firing. Note: Before reloading, swab the cannon out with a wet sponge on a long handle (**e**) to cool it and remove glowing traces of gunpowder and wadding.

a Rammer
b Cannon ball
c Touch hole
d Linstock
e Sponge & bucket

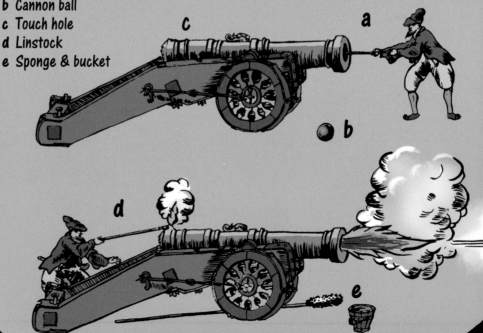

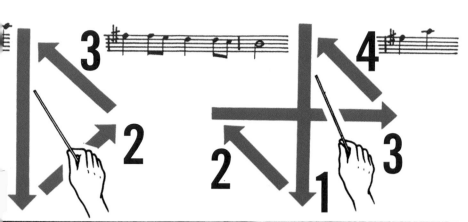

How to date the year

The Christian calendar used in most of the Western world today reckons the years from the birth of Jesus Christ – subsequent years counting forward as Annus Domini (the year of Our Lord), or A.D., and years before counting backward as Before Christ (B.C.). Unfortunately Dionysius Exiguas, a monk who calculated the date of Christ's birth in about A.D. 525, made a mistake as Jesus was actually born at least four years earlier.

The Islamic calendar, used in all Muslim countries, reckons time from the flight of Muhammad from Mecca in the Christian year A.D. 622. The Christian year 2003 is the Islamic year 1424, because the year in that calendar contains only 354 or 355 days, against the 365 of the Christian calendar.

The Jewish calendar is reckoned from a traditional date for the Creation, according to Scripture. The Jewish year A.M. (Anno Mundi) 5764 covers the period September 2003 to September 2004. There are six different lengths of year, containing 353, 354, 355, 383, 384 or 385 days respectively.

The Roman calendar counted its years from the foundation of the city of Rome in 753 B.C.; by this calendar A.D. 2003 equals MMDCCLVI (2756) A.U.C. (*Ab Urbe Condita* "from the foundation of the city").

The Greek calendar counted the years in various ways, none of them satisfactory, reckoned mostly from the date of foundation of the various cities. Some historians used Olympiads, the four-year periods between Olympic Games, each Olympiad bearing the name of the victor of that particular games.

The Mayan calendar, and the calendars of other Central American civilizations, were based on a complicated cycle of days and months lasting 18,980 days (52 years). Chronology was accurate within these 52 year cycles, but confusion can arise between one cycle and another.

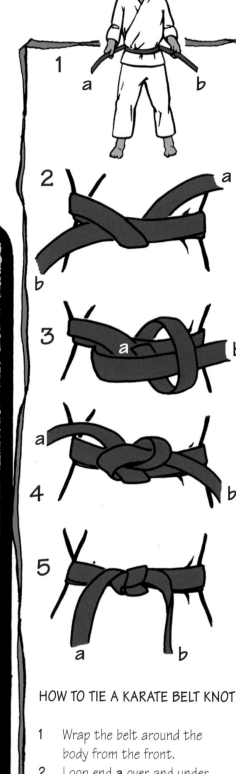

HOW TO TIE A KARATE BELT KNOT

1 Wrap the belt around the body from the front.
2 Loop end **a** over and under end **b** as shown.
3 Loop end **b** back and thread end **a** up through it as shown.
4,5 Pull ends **a** and **b** tight to complete the knot.

HOW TO READ CHINESE NUMERALS

THE FOLLOWING SYMBOLS ARE THE CHINESE CHARACTERS USED FOR NUMBERS 1 TO 10.

1 一
2 二
3 三
4 四
5 五
6 六
7 七
8 八
9 九
10 十

HOW TO COOK IN HAY

Take a solid-sided wooden box, fill it with hay, and scoop a hole just big enough to take a casserole or firmly-lidded pot. Having brought your soup or stew to the boil in an oven, put it inside the hay box, cover the top with hay and reseal the box with a close-fitting lid. Your food will go on slowly cooking, for it will be well insulated and retain the heat for hours.

These days you can do the same thing even more efficiently with a block of expanded polystyrene. Hollow out a hole for your pot in the center, leaving at least 4 inches (10cm) thickness all round, including the lid. Or use a polystyrene cool chest and fill it up with polystyrene granules for a hot picnic box!

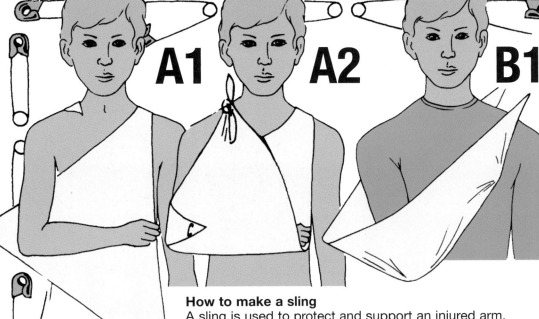

A1 **A2** **B1**

How to make a sling

A sling is used to protect and support an injured arm. The professional way of making one is to use a triangular bandage, though a square of cloth folded along the diagonal will do. You also need a safety pin.

Basic Method

A1 Place the arm across the body with the hand a little higher than the elbow. Put the open triangle of cloth between the body and the arm with one corner stretching beyond the elbow. Another corner goes around the neck.

A2 Bring the third corner up and tie in front of the hollow above the collar bone. Fold the elbow corner forward and secure it with the safety pin.

How to give the wind direction

You can tell the direction of the wind by wetting a finger and holding it up – the windward side feels cold. A swiveling vane or weathercock will point to windward and a tube of fabric, narrowing in a cone shape but open at both ends (a windsock) will trail from a pole in the direction the wind is blowing and away from windward. Wind direction is indicated by the direction from which it blows. The West wind blows **from** the west. The wind used always to be called after the compass points and their divisions, but in meteorology the direction is now given in degrees of a circle.

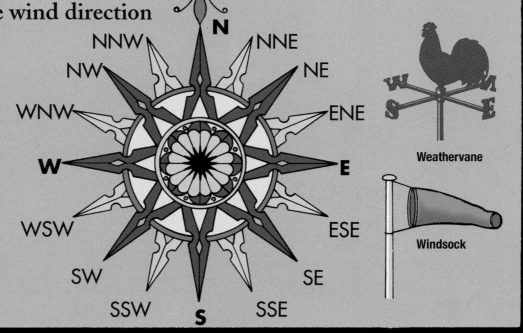

Weathervane

Windsock

©DIAGRAM

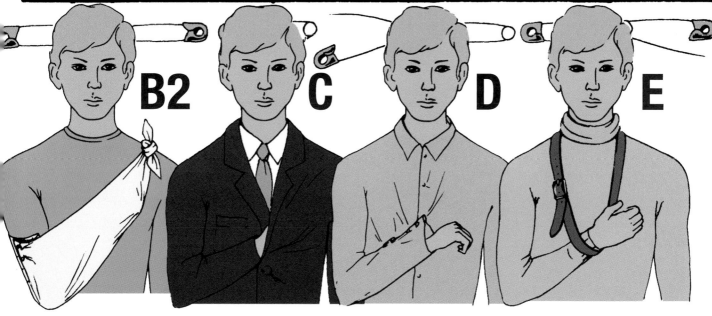

For a more raised position
If a more raised position is required, as in the case of an injured hand, fractured ribs, or if the patient needs extra support for a rough journey:
B1 Place the triangle over the arm, one corner well beyond the elbow. Ease the edge of the bandage between the arm and the body, cupping hand and arm, and carry the free end behind the body.
B2 Adjust to the required position and tie at the shoulder. Tuck the loose corner between the arm and the front part of the bandage and secure with the safety pin

Improvised slings
Here are three ways to improvise a sling if no bandage or cloth is available:
C Place the hand and arm inside the buttoned jacket.
D Pin the sleeve containing the injured arm to the clothing.
E Make a supporting loop with a scarf, belt or tie and suspend around the neck.

HOW TO PLAY AN ALPHORN

An alphorn is a wind instrument up to 13 feet (4 meters) long, with a wooden cup-shaped mouthpiece. It produces a series of harmonic sounds (not a true musical scale) and only a limited range of tunes can be played. To blow it you need to form an embouchure: you press your lips against the mouth piece and, keeping the lips slightly tensed, blow gently into it. The varying tension of the lips and the amount you blow produce different notes. You probably won't be able to do it easily if you have dentures.

how to deal with NAILS

1

2

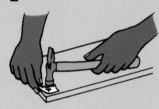

3

4

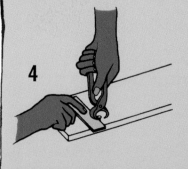

Thin materials may be secured by using a pin punch (1), which leaves no hammer marks and makes location easier.

Small nails may be held by pressing them into paper or thin cardboard (2) which can be torn away when the nails begin to bite.

Bent nails are usually caused by not striking the head in the direction of the nail's course (3).

When removing nails, protect the surface from damage from the pliers with another piece of wood (4).

HOW TO MAKE A BIRCH BARK TORCH

You need a strip of very thick birch bark about 6 inches (15cm) wide and 2 feet (60cm) or so long. It may curl into a natural coil but if it doesn't, coil it and pull it into a tube and then tie with string at the outside end to keep it coiled. Insert a stick into the opening at that end, before you tie the string, as a handle.

Simply light the end and hold the torch upright and

it will give you light for about 15 minutes. If the flame looks like failing, wave it around for a moment or two. This kind of torch is not so reliable as a static illumination, as it needs the movement of being carried. Birch bark torches were used to light the trail by the Chippewa Indians of the Great Lakes area.

HOW TO SEASON BARBECUED MEAT

As the meat is cooking, brush on oil or marinade with a sprig of fresh rosemary; just before the meat is ready, put the sprig on the burning charcoal so that aromatic smoke surrounds the meat.

HOW TO GROW YOUR NAME

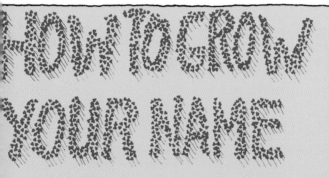

ON A FLAT PIECE OF DAMP COTTON WOOL SPRINKLE SMALL SEEDS – CRESS SEEDS ARE IDEAL – IN THE LETTERS OF YOUR NAME. KEEP THE COTTON WOOL MOIST, AND IN A FEW DAYS YOUR NAME WILL START TO GROW.

HOW TO MAKE A QUILL PEN

Use one of the largest wing feathers of a bird such as a goose, turkey or crow. Heat some sand in a pan until very hot. Remove from the heat and place the end of the quill in the sand for a few minutes. This will dry out the oils and harden the quill. Dissolve a little alum in boiling water. Dip the end of the quill in this. With a knife cut the end of quill at an oblique angle to form a writing point, making a vertical slit to complete the nib.

HOW TO GET A TAN

A suntan is the skin's natural defense against the ultra-violet rays of the sun. People with dark skins already have this defense. This advice is for people with fair skins:

1 Use a good suntan lotion or cream with a sunscreen to cut out harmful rays. Use it freely, paying special attention to chest and shoulders, nose, feet, tops of thighs and backs of knees, which burn most quickly, and any other parts that you expose which rarely see the sun.

2 Sunbathe for between 5 minutes (very fair skin) and 20 minutes at a time, then swim or shower, reapply suntan lotion, and spend half an hour in the shade; then you can sunbathe again. Follow this routine several times a day and you'll build up a tan without burning.

3 Because the Sun's rays dry the skin, apply moisturizing cream every night–this may not be necessary if you have very greasy skin.

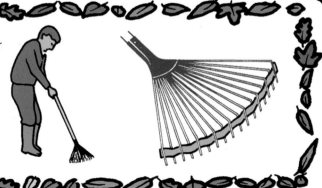

How to rake small leaves
If you use a big semicircular wire rake small leaves often seem to slip through the prongs. You can prevent this by threading a strip of cardboard or plastic between the prongs just wide enough to block all except the last 1/2 inch (13mm) of their length.

HOW TO TIE A BOWLINE

*FIRST MAKE AN OVER-HAND LOOP IN THE MAIN PART OF THE ROPE (**A**), BRING THE FREE END UP THROUGH THE LOOP, BEHIND THE MAIN LINE, THEN DOWN AGAIN THROUGH THE LOOP (**B**); PULL THE KNOT TIGHT. USE A BOWLINE TO TIE A ROPE TO A POLE, OR AROUND YOUR WAIST.*

A

B

HOW TO MAKE A HOUSE MORE HUMID

If the air in your home is dried out by central heating, improve the humidity by placing a saucer of water in each room; the water will evaporate into the air.

How to address an ambassador

Every country has its own forms of ceremonial address for people in high office. An American citizen would address a letter to one of his country's ambassadors as follows:

The Honorable John Smith
Ambassador of the United States of America
followed by the address, and would begin a letter "Sir," or, less formally "Dear Mr. Ambassador." A woman ambassador would be addressed as "Madam" or "Dear Madam Ambassador." A letter to another country's ambassador in the United States would be addressed to His (Her) Excellency, The Ambassador of ———. A letter would begin as for an American ambassador.

A British citizen writing to his own ambassador would address the letter as follows:

His (Her) Excellency H.B.M.'s Ambassador and Plenipotentiary
H.B.M. standing for "Her Britannic Majesty." The ambassador's name would follow according to rank and title, and in the same way the letter would begin "Sir," "Madam" or according to whatever title the ambassador held. The ambassador would be addressed in speech as "Your Excellency."

1   2   3   4

DOLPHIN

How to swim the butterfly

The butterfly stroke was first developed in the 1930s but not recognized for competitive swimming until 1953, when it was known as the butterfly breast stroke. It was a development of the breast stroke with bent elbows flapping out of the water like fluttering wings. It is a difficult and exhausting stroke to execute but is second only to the crawl in speed. For the leg kick, both legs move together to give an up and down motion like a dolphin's tail. There are two leg beats to one arm stroke. Breathing, which can be either with the head turned to one side as in the crawl or with the head kept forward and lifted out of the water, always takes place at the end of the arm pull and the second downbeat of the legs.

How to split bamboo
Long, split pieces of bamboo make attractive fence sidings. Drive a wedge into the top of a bamboo pole. Grasp the two separate halves in your left and right hands and pull them apart with a strong, steady motion (wearing gloves to avoid slivers). Use the wedge again at the joints if necessary.

HOW TO SURRENDER

If you are close to your enemy, hold your hands above your head. At a distance, wave or fly a white flag. If you are flying your own colors, in a ship or on a fortress, for example – you should haul them down.

HOW TO TRACK A RACOON

THE TRACKS SHOWN HERE INDICATE THAT A RACOON HAS RECENTLY USED THE PATH.

1 arms enter water in line with shoulder; legs kick downward
2 feet straightened level with body; hips rise to surface
3 hands pressed out and down, elbows bent and kept high
4 hands nearly meet under chest
5 legs complete downbeat then
6 arms leave water, legs brought upward without bending
7 arms recovered over the water, head lowered, feet almost break surface at start of second kick
8 swimmer exhales at start of arm pull
9 arms finish pull, second kick made, breath taken
10 arms recovered over water, head lowered face down

HOW TO BREAK IN A PAINTBRUSH

Use a new brush for painting undercoats before painting topcoats.

HOW TO MAKE FOOD LESS SALTY

Cook a whole, peeled potato in with over-salted food; the potato will attract a great deal of the salt and can be removed before serving. Alternatively, a little sugar will disguise a salty taste.

How to calculate compound interest

In compound interest the principal (the amount of money invested) is increased by the amount of interest earned, as happens in a bank savings account. There is a formula for calculating this. You need to know:

P the principal

T the time invested

R the amount for one unit invested plus the interest earned over one unit of time: ($1 at 5% per annum = 1.05)

The amount accruing over a period will then be $P \times R^T$

For example: to find the compound interest on $460 invested over 4 years at 9% per annum (R= 1.09)

$P \times R^T = $460 (1.09 \times 1.09 \times 1.09 \times 1.09) = 460 \times 1.4115816 = 649.32753

Take away the original sum ($460) and the total interest earned = $189.32753

How to recognize a pharaoh

1 Cheops (or Khufu, who built the Great Pyramid at Giza).
2 Akhenaten (who introduced the worship of a single god). After his death priests tried to eradicate his memory and defaced any carvings bearing his name and portrait.
3 Tutankhamun (whose mummy and tomb treasure were discovered by Howard Carter).
4 Ramesses II (whose statues front the great rock temple of Abu Simbel).
5 Alexander the Great (the Macedonian who created an empire from Greece to India).
6 Cleopatra VII (the mistress of Julius Caesar and Mark Antony).

Horus

Seth

King of Upper and lower Egypt

Son of Re

The good God

Assuming that you are not already familiar with an Egyptian king's appearance, and when unwrapping his mummy or confronted with a carving you would not have an instant flash of recognition, you will have to look for some identification. There will almost certainly be a label close by telling you exactly who he is. The actual names are usually enclosed in an oblong cartouche (or frame), or later an oval one with the symbols clearly showing the king's titles set above or beside them. The earliest kings of the First Dynasty have a cartouche surmounted by a falcon, the symbol of the god Horus, the sky god identified with kingship. In one instance a king used the symbol of Seth, god of

1　　　　**2**　　　　**3**

How to attract birds

In summer, birds feed themselves, but they like somewhere to drink and bathe. So make a shallow stone or cement birdbath, no more than 2 inches (50mm) deep, with a rough edge and bottom so the birds can get a footing. Put it on top of a pillar or post that cats can't climb.

In winter, birds appreciate help with finding food. Make a bird feeder, also on a cat-proof post. Ideally, make one with two platforms, one open, the other enclosed with 1½ inch (40mm) mesh wire netting to let in small birds and keep the bigger bullies out. For food put out grain such as rice (boiled or raw), bread, seeds, scraps of meat and bacon, and a lump of suet which they can peck at and which won't freeze. Chickadees and other titmice will appreciate nuts, hung in a wire cage to which they can cling and other birds can't.

storms and violence, a quadruped, and once, both were used. More obvious is a symbol meaning King of Upper and Lower Egypt, used by almost all except the very earliest kings. An ibis and a cobra form another royal symbol, and from the Old Kingdom on, the symbol meaning Son of Re, the sun god, is usual. In later centuries when the throne of all Egypt was disputed, a symbol meaning the good god was used.

If you find these symbols separately or together in conjunction with a personal name cartouche you know the man was a pharoah. Reading personal names is much more difficult, but here are those of some famous Egyptian rulers.

4

5

6

How to throw a boomerang

A boomerang is a form of throwing stick, used as a hunting weapon. Its airfoil shape carries it much further than a plain throwing stick of the same size and weight because its contour gives it lift. The wings rotate, giving the boomerang stability, and they present only a small angle to the airflow, thus reducing air resistance. Throw an ordinary boomerang in the plane of rotation, almost horizontally, so that it spins through the air. The lifting force then acts in a direction opposite to that of gravity. You'll need a lot of practice before you can hit what you are aiming at.

A return boomerang is much less often used, although that is the kind that comes to mind when most people hear the word. They are sometimes used for hunting but are more frequently used for frightening birds so that they will fly into the hunters' nets. A return boomerang is thrown vertically and its trajectory turns to the left. Boomerangs are not restricted to the Australian aborigines. They were used for hunting in southern and northwestern India, and among the Hopi people of North America, and were used by the ancient Egyptians and in prehistoric Europe.

HOW TO IDENTIFY THE SIGNS OF THE ZODIAC

1 Aries	March 21–April 20
2 Taurus	April 21–May 20
3 Gemini	May 21–June 20
4 Cancer	June 21–July 21

1 ♈ **2** ♉ **3** ♊ **4** ♋ **5** ♌ **6** ♍ **7** ♎

how to eat WINKLES

Winkles (or periwinkles) are a type of snail. They used to be a very popular food among the poorer classes in Britain, France and the Netherlands and many people still consider them a delicacy. In 1858, a bumper year for winkles, London markets sold about 76,000 bushels, and you can still buy them, ready cooked, from street stalls in many British cities.

To cook them, simply boil them in a small amount of heavily salted water. This loosens the animal from the shell. Then you can pick them out with a pin – you "winkle" out the meat, that's the derivation of the expression. You can eat them with a dressing of vinegar, serve them with butter or a variety of sauces, as with oysters or snails, or make them into periwinkle soup.

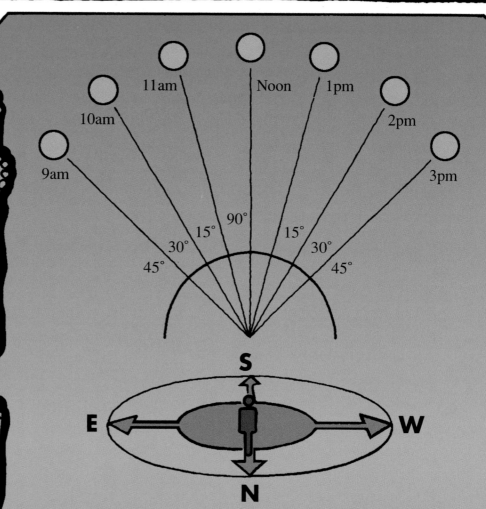

How to tell the time by the sun

At noon the sun is due south of an observer in the northern hemisphere (due north of an observer in the southern hemisphere). So if you know the direction of due south you can also tell when it is noon. The change from night to day is caused by the Earth turning upon its own axis, and so is the apparent movement of the sun across the sky from east to west. The spinning movement of the Earth is regular and the sun appears to move through 15⅓ every hour. So, knowing that the sun is due south at noon, and that the sun is moving through 15⅓ every hour, enables us to be able to locate roughly where the sun will be at any given time – that is, when it's daylight!

<table>
<tr><td>5 Leo</td><td>July 22–August 21</td><td>9 Sagittarius</td><td>November 22–December 20</td></tr>
<tr><td>6 Virgo</td><td>August 22–September 21</td><td>10 Capricorn</td><td>December 21–January 19</td></tr>
<tr><td>7 Libra</td><td>September 22–October 22</td><td>11 Aquarius</td><td>January 20–February 18</td></tr>
<tr><td>8 Scorpio</td><td>October 23–November 21</td><td>12 Pisces</td><td>February 19–March 20</td></tr>
</table>

For ease in making notes when calculating someone's birth chart, astrologers use the traditional symbols for the signs of the zodiac. For the layman it is useful to be able to recognize at least one's own birth sign, as the symbols still appear in some newspaper horoscopes.

How to drain a swamp

A swamp is land saturated with water. To make it usable for farming, you must lower the water table – the saturation level – to at least 4 feet (1.2 meters) below the surface. You need a channel to take the water away to a nearby river or lake, or to the sea. The simplest channel is a large open ditch, which you can dig with a power shovel. But it is better to install underground drainage channels, and in any case you will need such channels to carry water into your open channel. You dig ditches varying between 2½ feet and 5 feet (0.75–1.50 meters) below the surface of the ground, sloping downward with the natural slope of the ground. Put hollow tiles or lengths of clay pipe in the ditches, but leave the joints open so that water can get in and soil cannot. Then fill in the ditches. A word of warning: drainage can cause the level of the land to sink, and may threaten natural plant and animal life – including crocodiles, if you happen to have any!

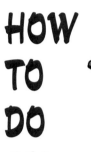

HOW TO DO AN ARABESQUE

Raise the body onto the toes of one foot, keeping the leg straight and fully extended. If wearing point shoes the weight should be carried on the blocked tip. Extend the other leg backward until just above the horizontal, the foot following the line of the leg with the toes pointed. Extend the arm on the same side as the supporting leg in a fluid motion to a half raised position slightly open from the body, the hand following the line but relaxed. Extend the other arm backward. The head should be kept upright and facing forward. The overall effect should be of arrested flight or of poise for flight.

An alternative form is an arabesquc with the supporting leg half bent: Russian dancers often bend the rear leg upward from the knee. There are a number of variations in position which are used by choreographers.

HOW TO TRACK A DEER

DEER TRACKS CAN BE RECOGNIZED BY THEIR COMMA-LIKE SHAPES. THE SIZE OF THE PRINTS INDICATES THE TYPE OF DEER THAT MADE THEM.

HOW TO POLISH ACRYLIC

Remove the tiny scratches that dull the surface by rubbing on a little metal polish on a soft rag. Finish polishing with a clean rag.

 ©DIAGRAM

HOW TO PLAY
CHINESE REBELS

Players One player operates the "general," the other operates the rebelling "soldiers" in this game which is thought to have originated in China.

The board is label-shaped enclosing 39 small circles – it can easily be drawn on a sheet of paper. One of the circles is distinctly marked and represents the "camp," as shown in the illustration.

Pieces Counters or other small objects may be used. One piece representing the general must be different in appearance from the 20 pieces representing soldiers.

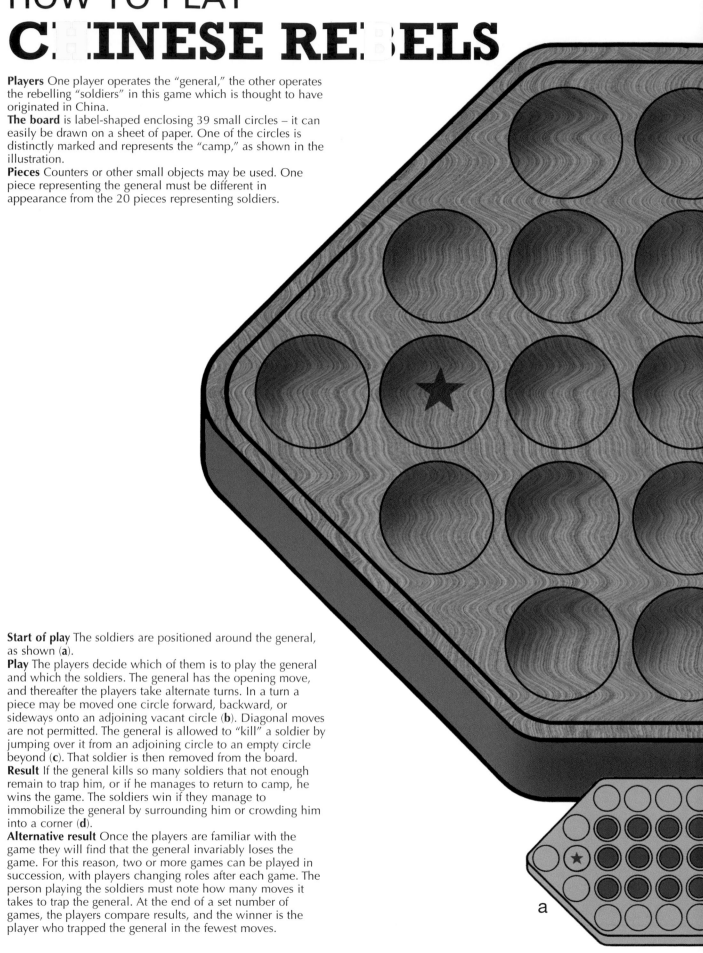

a

Start of play The soldiers are positioned around the general, as shown (**a**).

Play The players decide which of them is to play the general and which the soldiers. The general has the opening move, and thereafter the players take alternate turns. In a turn a piece may be moved one circle forward, backward, or sideways onto an adjoining vacant circle (**b**). Diagonal moves are not permitted. The general is allowed to "kill" a soldier by jumping over it from an adjoining circle to an empty circle beyond (**c**). That soldier is then removed from the board.

Result If the general kills so many soldiers that not enough remain to trap him, or if he manages to return to camp, he wins the game. The soldiers win if they manage to immobilize the general by surrounding him or crowding him into a corner (**d**).

Alternative result Once the players are familiar with the game they will find that the general invariably loses the game. For this reason, two or more games can be played in succession, with players changing roles after each game. The person playing the soldiers must note how many moves it takes to trap the general. At the end of a set number of games, the players compare results, and the winner is the player who trapped the general in the fewest moves.

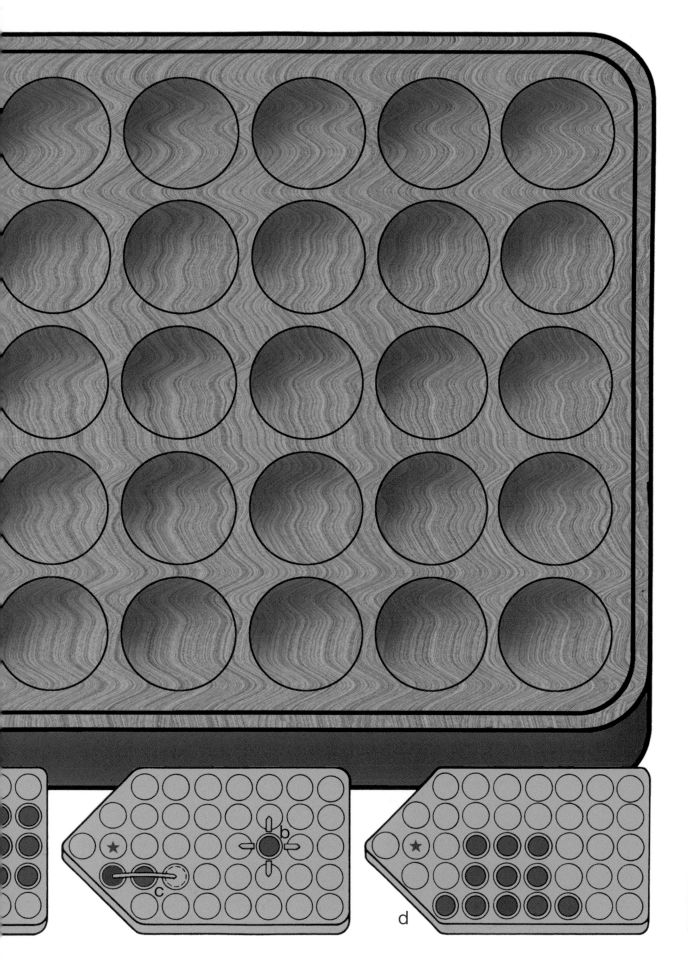

HOW TO ATTRACT BUTTERFLIES

YOU CAN DO THIS BY GROWING AUBRETIA, HONESTY (SILVER DOLLARS), PETUNIAS, LAVENDER, BUDDLEIA, ASTERS AND CABBAGES IN YOUR GARDEN.

HOW TO PIPE A MAN ABROAD

In the British Navy the arrival on board a Royal Naval vessel of a captain or other senior officer is greeted ceremonially by a long whistle on the calls, or pipes, of the ship's boatswain's mates. A similar ceremony marks such an officer's departure. Customs in other navies vary.

How to drink sake

Drinking of sake is a delicate ceremony in Japan. Serve it hot in tiny porcelain bowls holding about an ounce. Sip it. You can buy a sake jug and cups at a local Asian store. Sake is the national brew of Japan. It is a beer made from rice. It is mistakenly believed to be a wine because its alcoholic content is high (17–18%).

How to play the teacups

Take a number of teacups of different sizes and thicknesses, and tie each individually to a line stretched between two uprights. Strike them with a spoon or stick. Retain any cups which produce a good note and replace the others with new cups until you have the scale or range of notes that you require. The British composer Benjamin Britten, when visiting schools in East Anglia to choose singers and instrumentalists to appear in his *Noyes Fludde*, found a schoolboy who had made himself just such an instrument, so he wrote a special part for it and the young musician, in his lively setting of this medieval version of the Old Testament story. It matches perfectly the falling of raindrops at the beginning of the rains and the flurries of rain in the storm.

HOW TO MAKE AN INTRODUCTION

The basic rule is to present the visitor to the host, the younger to the elder, the male to the female and the person of lower rank to the person of higher. In the most formal of circumstances you might say: "May I present Mr. James Smith," but more colloquial forms are quite acceptable except in the case of royalty. In the case of titled people, address the person informally yourself but use their title in the introduction so that it is clear to the other party. This ensures that should they wish to write to each other they will not make an error of etiquette. You might say: "John, I'd like you to meet Dr. Mary Butler; Mary, this is Lord John Smith," or "Elizabeth, may I introduce Captain Robert Brown; Robert, this is Mrs James Green." Ladies do not rise from their seats on being introduced, gentlemen always do. Titles such as Honorable are not used in introductions. Remember to introduce:

> younger to older
> commoner to peer
> gentleman to lady
> unmarried lady to married lady

If you are writing a letter of introduction you should both write to say that a visitor known to you will call and explain who they are, and give the visitor a formal letter of identification which he will deliver in an unsealed envelope on arrival. It should simply say, "Dear William, I am sending this letter to introduce you to Mr. Joseph Gilliflower..." Of course in less formal circumstances you can just write a letter ahead and the visitor can call on the telephone on his or her arrival.

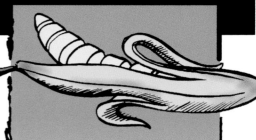

HOW TO SLICE A BANANA BEFORE PEELING IT!

Insert a long needle into the flesh of the banana through the skin, and move it as far as possible from side to side. Do this at regular intervals along the banana, and when it is peeled, the flesh will be in neat slices.

HOW TO MAKE YOGURT

You need milk and a little store-bought live yogurt, one teaspoonful to two cups of milk. Bring the milk to the boil. For a creamier end-product let it simmer for a half hour or longer to reduce. Pour it into a bowl to cool to blood temperature. Mix the bought yogurt with a little of the warm milk and stir the mixture into the bowl. Cover the bowl and leave it in a warm place for five to eight hours. Standing it in a pan of hot water set over the pilot light on a gas stove is ideal. You can use some of your newly-made yogurt to start off your next batch, and so on indefinitely.

How to make perfumes

To make most perfumes you need a still, so that you can extract the essential oils from flowers and other scented raw materials. To make up perfume, dissolve 10 parts of essential oils in 90 parts of pure alcohol; colognes consist of essential oils 3–5 percent, alcohol 80–90 percent, water to 100 percent; toilet waters contain 2 percent essential oils, 60–80 percent alcohol, the rest water. For those of you who haven't got a still, here's a simple recipe for lavender water:

Essence of musk	*¹/₂ fl oz or 15 ml*
Essence of ambergris	*¹/₂ fl oz or 15 ml*
Oil of cinnamon	*10 drops*
English lavender	*³/₄ fl oz or 7.5 ml*
Oil of geranium	*¹/₄ fl oz or 4 ml*
Spirit of wine	*20 fl oz or 600 ml*

Use either the US or metric measurements. Mix together well, and keep in a well-stoppered bottle. If you have a still, steep flower heads or other perfume ingredients, such as sandalwood, in spirits of wine for several weeks, then distill the infusion.

HOW TO OFFER FOOD TO A HORSE, DONKEY OR CAMEL

All may be fed by fitting a nose bag over the animal's head or by placing the food in a manger at a convenient height. If you offer tidbits from your hand, hold your hand absolutely flat with the food lying on top or you may find it is your fingers that get eaten.

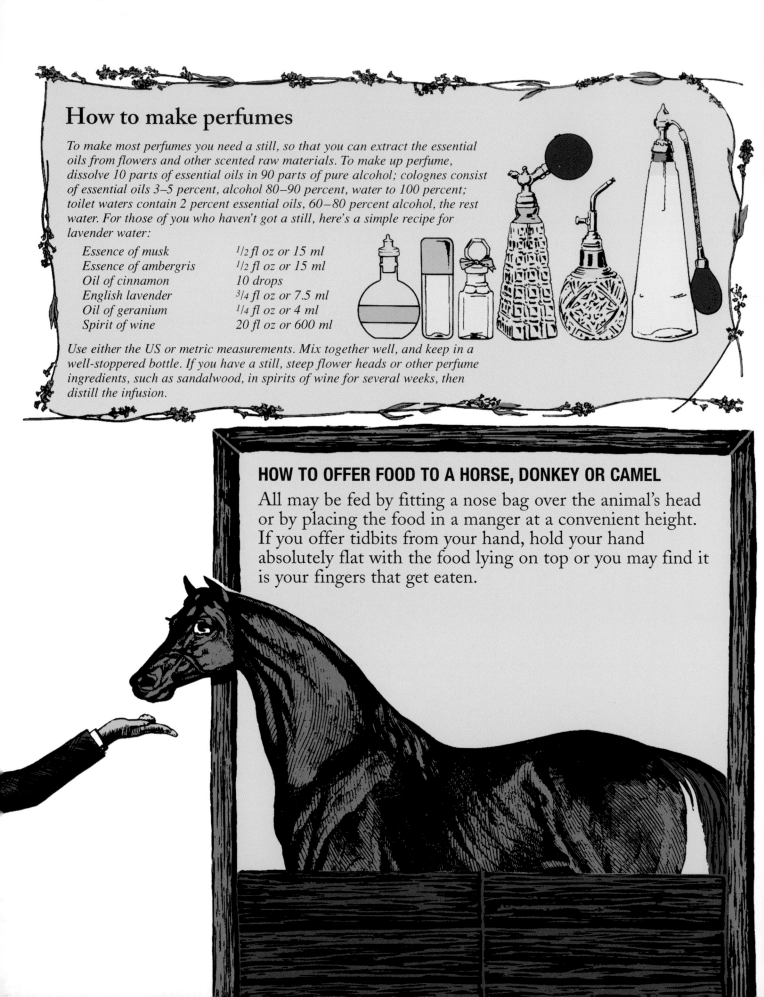

How to become Pope

To become Pope you would first have to be a Roman Catholic and begin as a priest, rising through the ranks of bishops and archbishops to become a cardinal and member of the Sacred College. Between the 15th and 18th days after the death of a Pope, the members of the college go into conclave, shut off from the outside world to choose a new one, and you have your chance. If a conclusive vote is reached in your favor, it will be signaled to the waiting world by white smoke. You would be asked if you accepted; if so, you would become Pope from that moment, receiving the homage of the other cardinals. You would be dressed in the white robes of office and appear on the balcony of St. Peter's in Rome to bless the assembled multitude and the world, and your formal coronation would take place a few weeks later.

HOW TO MAKE AN EGG SWIM

With a good supply of salt you can make an egg float halfway up a jar of water as if by magic. Fill one jar with plain water; the egg will sink (1). Fill another with a very strong solution of salt dissolved in water; the egg will float (2) because it is less dense than the solution. Fill a third jar with roughly equal quantities of the two liquids, and the egg will be suspended when the density of the solution matches the density of the egg (3).

How to blow a cork into a bottle
*Lay a bottle on its side and in its mouth place a cork of slightly smaller diameter than the neck. Can you blow the cork into the bottle? Get your friends to try. If they blow into the bottle they will increase the pressure of air within and force the cork out rather than in. The method is simple enough if you know the trick: the secret is to **suck** air **out**, so that the pressure is reduced and the cork drawn in. You can produce the same effects by heating the bottle, so that some of the expanded air is expelled; as it cools again the air will contract, sucking in the cork.*

©DIAGRAM

HOW TO MAKE A MOCCASIN

The moccasin was probably the first type of footwear invented by man. The earliest form of moccasin was a simple piece of leather wrapped around the foot and held with rawhide lacings.

You can make that kind of moccasin from a piece of strong, prepared and softened leather. Shaping it around your foot, mark out where to cut so it will fit the heel, around the ankle and up from the sides to meet along the top of the front of the foot, either by overlapping or butting edge to edge. Allow an extra flap to punch holes for lacing. Cut out the pattern (a) and sew the moccasin together with rawhide lacing (b). An extra piece of leather can be glued or stitched to the sole for extra cushioning and strength. Moccasins later became more elaborate but kept the same principle. You can cut out one piece of leather for the sole, and two for the sides (leaving extra pieces at the back to fold double), as well as a separate piece for the top. These should all be held together by tight lacing with rawhide.

a

b

HOW TO WIN AT PACHiNKO

Pachinko is Japan's national pastime. It is a vertical bagatelle-like game: small steel balls shot upward emerge at the top of the playing surface and then descend through a pegged obstacle course. Most balls end up in oblivion at the bottom. But a lucky few make it through the pegs into the "tulip" holes for a payoff. The payoff, of course, is in more pachinko balls. But these can be run through the machine again, traded in for candies, cigarettes, or fountain pens, or surreptitiously (and illegally) carried to the shop next door to exchange for cash.

Like television, pachinko is a mesmerizing recreation. Yet it is not entirely artless. You increase your chances of winning by choosing a good machine. Look for machines whose metal pegs above the payoff holes are a bit flared out of line. This means that they have not been tampered with recently to make the payoffs less frequently. Also look for machines whose ashtrays are full of cigarette butts – a sure sign that someone has just had a big winning streak.

HOW TO FORM A RIGHT ANGLE

You can form a perfect right angle on the ground (say, for marking out a tennis court) with any piece of string, just by marking out a triangle with sides of 3, 4 and 5 units long. Any unit that suits the length will do – try using the length of your shoe. A similar method was used by Ancient Egyptians (right), but not for tennis courts!

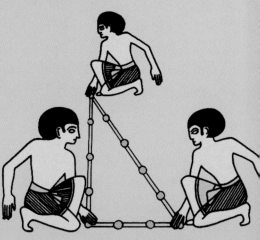

HOW TO CONVERT INCHES TO CENTIMETERS

Multiply the inches by 2.54 to find the equivalent number of centimeters.

Multiply centimeters by 0.394 to find the equivalent in inches.

in x 2.54 = cm
cm x 0.394 = in

How to succeed with rice

There are as many ways of cooking rice as there are cooks. Some cooks toss it into plenty of boiling water, others bring it to the boil from cold, still others steam it in a measured amount of water, with or without salt – it doesn't really matter. The main point to remember is that rice swells to up to three times its bulk in cooking and goes mushy when boiled too long and prodded too much. Brown rice takes longer than white rice.

Use the right kind of rice for your recipe: long-grain rice, such as patna, is best for jambalaya, pilau and curries, as it is not very absorbent; a dish of boiled rice should be fairly dry, with the grains well separated.

Round, more absorbent Italian rice is needed for risotto and paella, which should be moist but not sloppy.

Use round-grain Carolina rice for sweet puddings. It'll take up more liquid than you think, so sprinkle just a little into your pie with plenty of milk, or you'll have to dig it out of the oven.

Save the water from boiled rice as a basis for soup. And dry out the sludge slowly in the oven to make rice-paper for macaroons.

How to paint a room

Work in this order:

1. Edges of ceiling
2. Rest of ceiling
3. Woodwork
4. Edges of walls, beginning at the nearest window
5. Rest of walls

It is quicker, and easier, to use a roller for ceilings and walls.

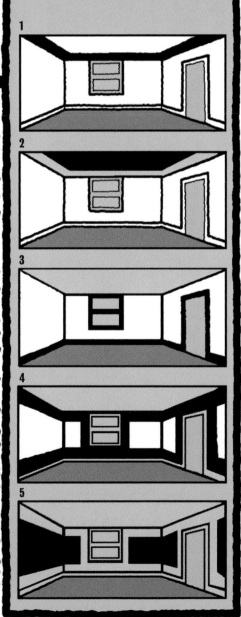

HOW TO DRAW A HEXAGON

Use a compass to draw a circle (A). Keeping the compass at the same radius, place the point anywhere on the circle and mark off a point where the pencil touches the circumference (B). Place the point on that mark, and do the same all the way around the circle (C); you will be able to do this exactly six times. Connect the six marks on the circumference and you will have formed a hexagon (D).

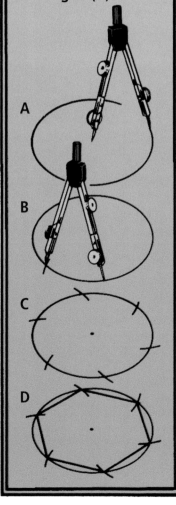

BIRD

DOG

DUCK

SHEEP

HOW TO MAKE HAND SHADOWS

You need a bright light and a clear wall or similar surface. The number of shapes you can make depends on your own skill and ingenuity. Watch the shadow, not your hands, to see the effect you are producing. When you like a shape, keep your hands still and check their position so that you can reproduce it. Here are four simple shapes to start you off. You can make the mouths and wings move too.

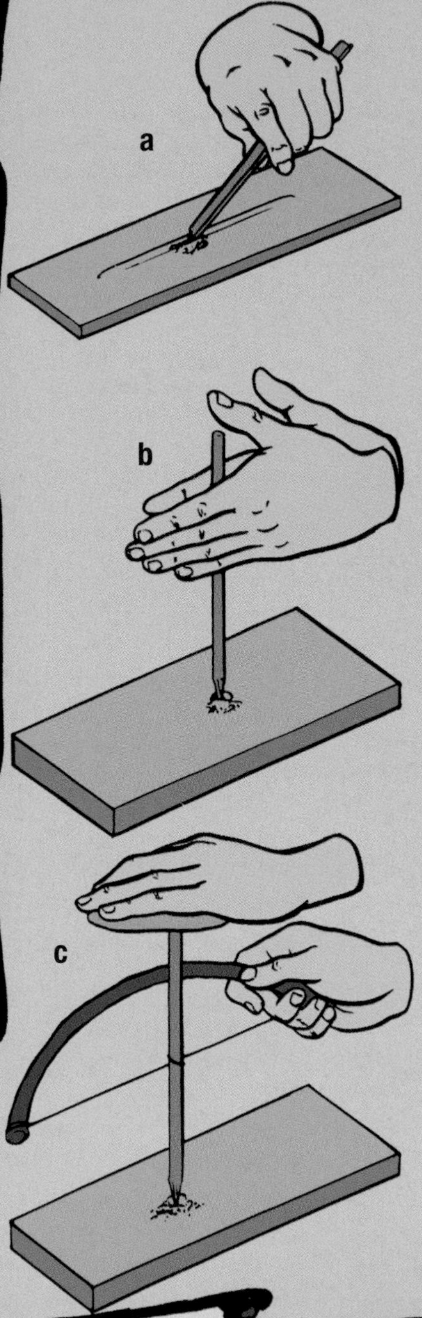

a

b

c

HOW TO USE FIRE STICKS

Friction produces heat, and if the heat becomes sufficiently intense and the materials are sufficiently dry, combustion will follow. Simply rubbing two very dry pieces of wood briskly against each other can generate enough heat to ignite dry moss or grass but there are several ways to make the task easier. Cut a slot in a piece of bamboo. Sharpen another piece to a point. Rub the point up and down briskly in the slot (**a**). This will work off fragments of bamboo which will be set alight with the friction. Make a hole in a piece of dry softwood. Sharpen a hardwood stick to a point. Hold the stick between the palms of your hands and rub it between them so that the point twirls in the hole in the softwood until it powders and catches fire (**b**). Make a bow with a bent stick and a piece of string (or use an archer's bow); use hardwood and softwood as above. Loop the bowstring around the stick. Use another stick, a stone with a hollow in it or a cup to keep the top of the stick steady and saw the bow briskly to and from to twirl the hardwood stick (**c**). In all cases have dry tinder close to the point of friction so that it will ignite.

How to make cut roses last longer

Place the stems of the roses up to their necks in very warm water for several hours. Before arranging, split or crush the ends of the stems.

HOW TO MAKE FRIENDS WITH A FERRET

Ferrets, the domesticated form of the polecat, are bred for their aggressive hunting instincts. The problem is to handle them safely. A ferret should be handled when it is a four-or five-week-old kitten and still too small to sink its teeth in. Given a lot of attention and affection at this age, it will be as friendly and as safe to handle as a domestic cat and will only bite in self-defense or because of pain, though it will attack the small furred and feathered creatures which form its natural prey. Young ferrets can be fed on milk and raw meat, but from about three months old should transfer to a meat and water diet. Canned cat and dog food is satisfactory, especially if supplemented with chicken, eggs, mink feed and extra vitamins. Ferrets should be inoculated against distemper and, where appropriate, against rabies. Continual handling is necessary to keep them tame.

To test for tameness offer the back of your closed fist for the ferret to sniff the tight skin will offer no purchase for its teeth (**a**). If no attempt is made to bite, run your hand gently over the ferret's back (**b**), grasp the back of its neck (**c**) and lift it to be carried with both hands (**d**). Its front feet should protrude between your first and second fingers. Never offer a finger for a ferret to smell, especially a strange one. In parts of the United States a permit is needed to keep ferrets because of the damage to poultry if they escape.

HOW TO STAND AN EGG ON ITS END

SHAKE THE EGG VIGOROUSLY TO MIX UP THE YOLK AND THE WHITE. HOLD THE EGG UPRIGHT FOR SEVERAL MINUTES SO THAT THE HEAVIER YOLK SINKS TO THE BOTTOM, THEN, WITH A LITTLE PERSEVERANCE, YOU WILL BE ABLE TO STAND THE EGG ON ITS BROAD END.

HOW TO RELAX

The illustrations show some resting postures from various parts of the world; many of these positions feel strange to Westerners.

1 American Indian
2 Japan
3 Asia
4 Australian Aborigine

© DIAGRAM

How to hunt for truffles

Find a pig with a sensitive sense of smell and make sure that it has a ring in the end of its nose — otherwise it will snuffle up the truffle itself. Lead the pig around the trunks of trees growing in loamy soil, and when it starts showing interest in a patch, dig down carefully; if you are lucky you will unearth one or more of the highly prized delicacies.

HOW TO KEEP A CAMPFIRE ALIGHT

THE PAPERY BARK OF THE SILVER BIRCH WILL BURN EASILY AND KEEP YOUR FIRE ALIGHT UNTIL LARGER BRANCHES BECOME HOT ENOUGH TO CATCH FIRE.

HOW TO MAKE A FLOWER CHANGE COLOR

PLACE THE STEM OF A PALE-COLORED FLOWER INTO A STRONG SOLUTION OF COLORED INK (**A**); THE FLOWER WILL "DRINK" THE INK AND CHANGE COLOR (**B**). A VARIEGATED FLOWER CAN BE OBTAINED BY SPLITTING THE STEM AND PUTTING HALF INTO A DIFFERENT COLORED INK (**C**).

How to duck a scold

In the days long before women's liberation, a scold (a woman who nagged her husband, or gave other people too much of a tongue-lashing) could be punished by ducking in the village pond or local river. This was a punishment that was also used for traders of both sexes who cheated — although there's no record of its use for a nagging man. The last time it was used in England was at Leominster, in Herefordshire, in 1809, when a woman named Jenny Pipes was ducked in the river.

Ducking was done with a special piece of equipment — a ducking stool — and the Leominster one still survives, along with one or two others up and down the country. It is kept in the Priory Church and makes a good model for your own ducking stool.

You must mount your stool on a stout trolley with four wheels so that you can take it to the water. On this you pivot a long beam about 20 feet (6m) long with a crude chair fixed at one end into which the victim can be strapped with legs astride the beam. At the other end you need a counterweight, heavy enough to balance the other end of the beam, the chair and the victim (or you may not be able to fish him or her out again!). Oak is the best wood to use. It will stand up to a lot of wear and tear if you have a town full of scolding women and crooked storekeepers. Remember that the punishment is a ducking, not a drowning. It is the public shame rather than the physical discomfort that makes this punishment effective.

How to serve beer

Lager beers, popular in the United States, Germany and Scandinavia, are best served very cold. Most British and so-called "heavy" beers, of which there are hundreds of varieties, are served at room temperature – chilling kills the flavor.

To pour bottled or canned beer into a glass, tilt the glass and pour the beer against the side – that way you won't get too big a head on it. Don't shake the can or bottle beforehand. If you want a slight head, use a dry glass: a glass that's been drunk out of tends to inhibit the froth.

Generally, British drinkers like their beer "on draft" – drawn from the barrel. From containers pressurized with carbon dioxide gas you turn a tap to get the beer, but serious British drinkers like "real ale", which is drawn from the barrel by suction with a hand-operated pump.

HOW TO STORE MUSHROOMS

Mushrooms will keep fresh for longer if they are stored in a paper bag rather than a plastic one; the paper helps to absorb the moisture given out by the mushrooms.

HOW TO MAKE A PAPER CUP

1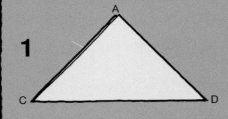

2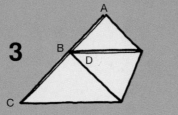

3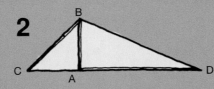

4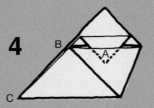

5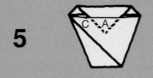

6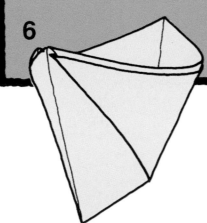

You can make this container quickly and easily from ordinary paper but waxed paper will hold liquids longer.

Take a sheet of paper about 6 inches (15cm) square.

1. Fold it diagonally.

2. Find point B by bringing point A down to the fold line C-D. Fold the edge at B to indicate the position.

3. Open the paper back to the single diagonal fold and bring point D to point B, crease firmly.

4. Tuck the front flap with point A into the pocket you have just formed and crease edge.

5. Turn over and fold point C to the diagonally opposite corner. Tuck the remaining flap into this pocket.

6. Press gently against the outer sides and insert a finger into the center space to open out your cup.

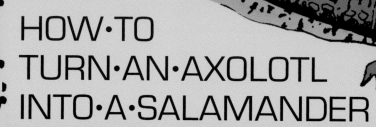

HOW·TO TURN·AN·AXOLOTL INTO·A·SALAMANDER

How to use a Ouija board

The Ouija board has the letters of the alphabet and the numbers one to nine on it. Free to move about the board is the message indicator or pointer, a small board with three legs. It may have an arrow to point to the letters, or a window through which they can be read. Some people use an up-ended glass as a message indicator. Two people are needed to use it. Sitting opposite each other both press their fingers lightly on the message indicator. One asks questions, and the indicator glides about, indicating various letters in turn to spell out a message. If you take it seriously, you may think that spirits guide the message indicator. If you don't, you may attribute any message to one of the two participants. The Ouija board was invented in about 1890 by a Baltimore man, William Fuld.

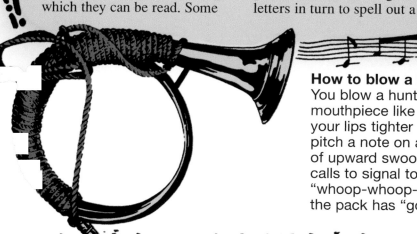

How to blow a hunting horn
You blow a hunting horn through a cup-shaped mouthpiece like an alphorn, but you have to keep your lips tighter and blow harder. You can't really pitch a note on a hunting horn, so you get a series of upward swoops. Each huntsman has his own calls to signal to hounds. A series of repeated "whoop-whoop-whoops" generally indicates that the pack has "gone away" in pursuit of the fox.

An axolotl is a newt-like reptile which breathes through gills and lives in water. Keep it in an aquarium, feed it on worms, raw meat, or slugs. Keep the water clean (and chlorine-free) and below 70°F (21°C). An axolotl starts life as a tadpole, changes into this form and grows to about 9 inches (22cm) long. It may live like this for up to 20 years but if a mechanism is triggered within it by giving it a thyroid extract or, when it is in tip-top condition, removing it to a shallow tank in a vivarium and gradually reducing the water level so that it has difficulty in submerging and eventually cannot submerge at all, it will stop using its gills to breathe and start using the lungs with which it is also equipped. Over a period of weeks it will turn into a salamander. During this time keep the atmosphere in the vivarium very moist and/or spray it with a fine mist of pure water.

HOW TO MILK A COW

Don't take a bucket out into a field. Bring the cow to where you want to milk her, preferably in a stall eating her food. Speak to her to let her know you're there. Get as close to her back leg as you can when milking, in case you accidentally hurt her and she kicks. That way she won't hurt you.

Clean her udder with a cloth dipped in hot water containing a cleansing agent, which you can get from an agricultural merchant. Then place your hand like a slightly open fist around one of her teats. Squeeze the teat gently with the top fingers, then the lower ones, and repeat in a series of smooth, rippling movements. The milk will spurt out of the teat. Do it slowly until you get used to the movements of the fingers. If the milk is not white but has yellow curds in it, that teat is affected by mastitis, and should not be milked. Test all the teats, letting the milk run away. Mastitis is not a serious complaint and it can easily be cured, but the yellow curd would spoil any milk it was mixed with. Now put a clean bucket under the udder and milk in the way described, one teat at a time until the flow ceases.

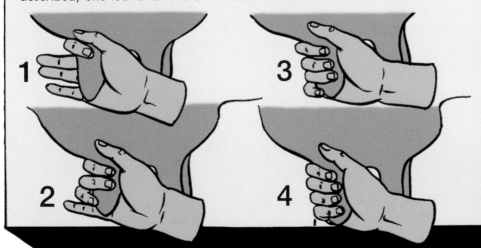

How to store brooms

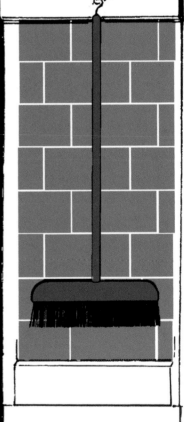

Screw a hook or eye into the end of the broom handle so that you can hang the broom from another hook in the broom closet and therefore keep the brush end off the floor.

How to culture a pearl

Take a healthy, live oyster, preferably one of the species belonging to the genus *Pinctada*, the small oysters used by the commercial pearl industry in Japan, and a tiny bead made from the shell of a freshwater bivalve. Enclose the bead in a small bag of tissue from the mantle of another oyster. Wedge open the living oyster and insert the bag into its reproductive area. Return the oyster to sheltered water in which phytoplanktonic food is abundant. If you wish, remove it after a few weeks to see whether the graft has survived (many do not). If it does a pearl of nacre will be formed around the shell fragment, a process which may take several years. To keep the oysters readily accessible, commercial pearl farms keep them in baskets or cages slung beneath rafts. The pearl will be almost identical to the naturally produced article, the nature of the particle within it being the only difference.

HOW TO TEACH A DOG TO BEG

SIT YOUR DOG IN THE CORNER OF A ROOM WHERE THE ANGLE OF THE WALLS WILL HELP IT TO BALANCE. GIVING THE COMMAND "BEG," LIFT THE DOG'S FORELEGS UP TO ITS CHEST WITH ONE HAND WHILE HOLDING A TREAT ABOVE ITS HEAD WITH THE OTHER. PRACTICE UNTIL YOU CAN TAKE YOUR SUPPORTING HAND AWAY. ALMOST ALL ADULT DOGS CAN BE TAUGHT TO BEG, BUT GREEDY ONES LEARN FASTEST. DO NOT TRY TO TEACH A PUPPY, AS ITS BACK MUSCLES WILL NOT BE STRONG ENOUGH TO HOLD THE POSE. WAIT UNTIL IT IS 9 MONTHS TO 1 YEAR OLD.

HOW TO MAKE GRANITA

To make one quart (one liter) you need:

2 cups (500ml) sugar
1 cup (250ml) water
1 cup (250ml) lemon juice (or other fruit juice)
1 cup (250ml) ice and water
1 tbsp finely grated lemon rind (or other rind if appropriate)

Method

Dissolve the sugar in the water, heating it in a pan to make sure it dissolves completely and easily. Cool. Add lemon juice, rind, and ice and water. Stir until the ice is melted. Pour into freezer trays and freeze. When almost completely solid take from the freezer and break up the mixture. You can use an electric beater to mix it up if you switch it on to very slow, or mix by hand. Return to the freezer for an hour. Take it out and beat or mix again. Freeze again for one hour or until firm. Serve immediately as a dessert or even to accompany meat or salad.

An instant granita

Put some crushed ice in a glass, pour milkshake syrup over it and a dash of cream. The syrup Davors the ice as it trickles through it.

How to tie a knot while holding both ends of a piece of string

Take a piece of string at least 20 inches (50cm) long. Challenge your friends to hold one end in each hand and to tie a knot without letting go of either end. It's easy: fold your arms before you take hold of the string. As you unfold them the knot will tie itself. You can use a scarf or a large handkerchief, held corner to corner, if you don't have any string.

How to make Neapolitan sign language

The people of Naples seem to talk more with their hands than they do with their tongue. This is not just to add emphasis to what they are saying: for centuries Neapolitans have used gestures with very exact meanings. Here are some of them from a book published a century and a half ago but still in use today.

1 Be silent **2** No **3** Beauty **4** Hunger **5** Derision **6** Tiredness **7** Stupidity **8** Beware **9** Dishonest **10** Crafty

Some, such as **1** and **5**, will be understood in many places, but **2** and **8**, although used elsewhere, may have very different meanings. In France, for instance, **8**, instead of meaning "watch out, danger," means "I'm watching you, don't go too far." Farther north in Italy and in France **2** becomes very impolite and means "get lost" – or something stronger.

HOW TO HARVEST WALNUTS

Reach up to the branches of the walnut tree with a long forked stick and shake down the ripe nuts.

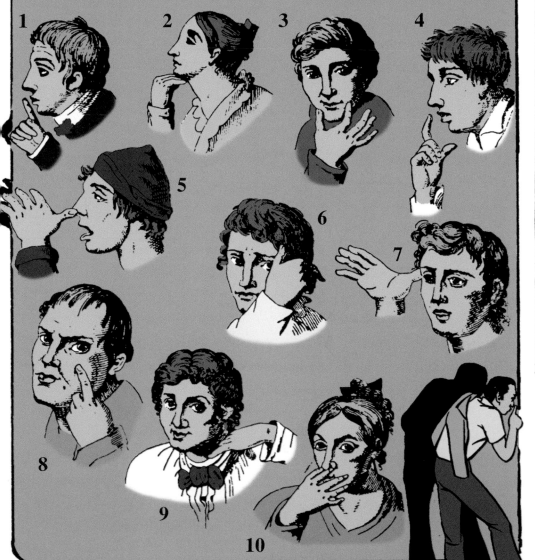

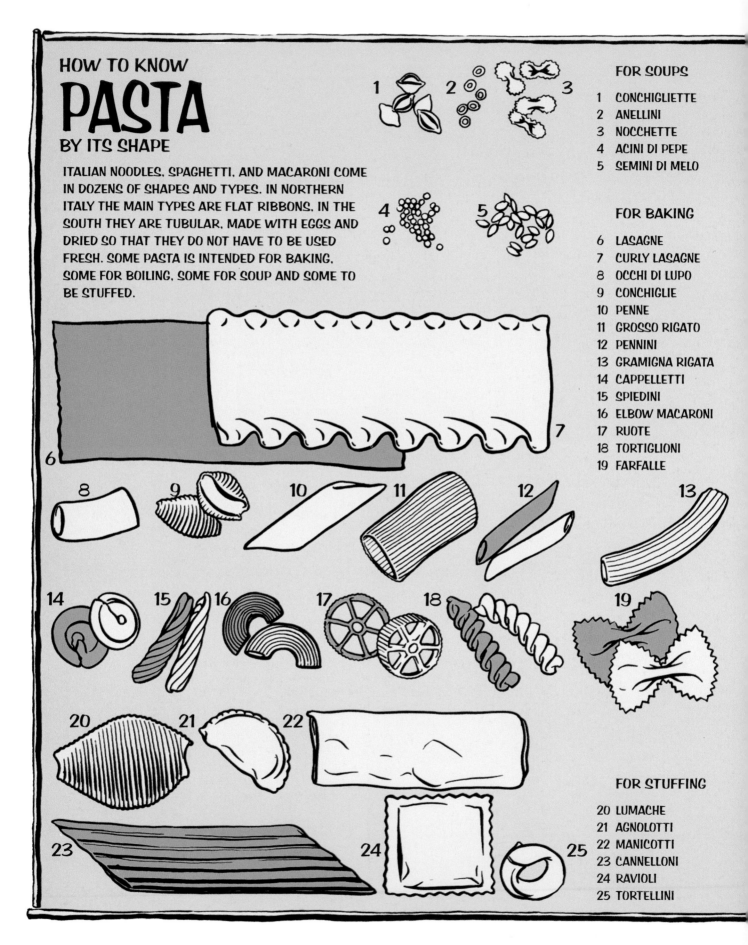

HOW TO KNOW
PASTA
BY ITS SHAPE

ITALIAN NOODLES, SPAGHETTI, AND MACARONI COME IN DOZENS OF SHAPES AND TYPES. IN NORTHERN ITALY THE MAIN TYPES ARE FLAT RIBBONS, IN THE SOUTH THEY ARE TUBULAR, MADE WITH EGGS AND DRIED SO THAT THEY DO NOT HAVE TO BE USED FRESH. SOME PASTA IS INTENDED FOR BAKING, SOME FOR BOILING, SOME FOR SOUP AND SOME TO BE STUFFED.

FOR SOUPS

1 CONCHIGLIETTE
2 ANELLINI
3 NOCCHETTE
4 ACINI DI PEPE
5 SEMINI DI MELO

FOR BAKING

6 LASAGNE
7 CURLY LASAGNE
8 OCCHI DI LUPO
9 CONCHIGLIE
10 PENNE
11 GROSSO RIGATO
12 PENNINI
13 GRAMIGNA RIGATA
14 CAPPELLETTI
15 SPIEDINI
16 ELBOW MACARONI
17 RUOTE
18 TORTIGLIONI
19 FARFALLE

FOR STUFFING

20 LUMACHE
21 AGNOLOTTI
22 MANICOTTI
23 CANNELLONI
24 RAVIOLI
25 TORTELLINI

FOR BOILING

26	FETTUCCINE	36	LASAGNETTE
27	FUSELLI	37	LINGE DI PASSESO
28	CAPELLINI	38	MAFALDINE
29	FEDELINI	39	MAFALDE
30	SPAGHETTI	40	ZITONI
31	SPAGHETTICI		
32	ZITE		
33	MEZZANI		
34	PERCIATELLI		
35	PERCIATELLONI		

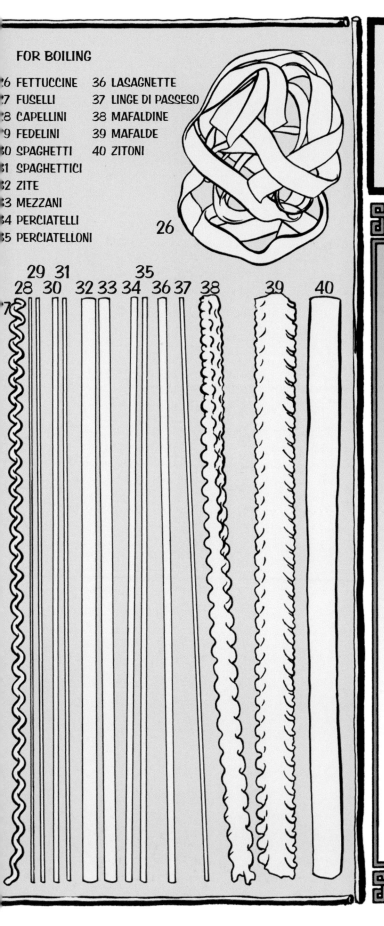

HOW TO LIGHT DAMP MATCHES

Dip them in nail polish and strike them (well away from the nail polish bottle).

How to recover from fainting

If you feel your consciousness becoming hazy and find yourself breaking out in beads of sweat on face, neck and hands, breathe deeply, flex the muscles of your legs, thighs and buttocks, loosen clothing at neck, chest and waist, sit with your head between your legs or lie down where there is a current of fresh air. Fainting is the result of a temporary fall in the supply of blood to the brain and may be caused by a fright, bad news, pain or seeing something upsetting, or it may be due to fatigue or a long subjection to a hot and stuffy atmosphere.

If a person has already fainted you must attempt to increase the supply of blood to his or her brain. Make sure he has plenty of fresh air, lay him down and raise his legs higher than his head and loosen clothing. If he seems to be having difficulty breathing place him gently to lie on one side, bring the upper arm to make a right angle with the body and bend the elbow. Draw the upper leg until the thigh is at right angle to the body and bend the knee, bring the under arm gently backward to extend slightly behind the back and bend the under knee slightly, move the head to one side. The patient's skin will feel cold and clammy and the face may be pale and greenish. As these symptoms disappear, raise the patient to a sitting position, offer reassurance and give sips of water if requested.

How to taste wine

If you're just tasting wine before it's served to you in a restaurant, check the label and make sure the wine is what you ordered before the waiter draws the cork. A small quantity will be poured for you and you may be handed the cork. Some wine buffs believe they can tell everything about a wine by sniffing the cork. Then sniff the wine in the glass to get the aroma, and take a little on your tongue. If you like the flavor of this sip, then you'll enjoy the wine. There are no hard and fast rules, except that red wines should be at room temperature, while white and rosé (pink) wines should be cool. The sweeter the white wine, the cooler it can be. If the wine tastes of cork or is sour, don't accept it.

Professional wine tasters, who have a lot of different wines to try, don't actually swallow their mouthfuls, but spit them out. If they didn't, they'd soon be rolling drunk. They also like to eat a piece of cheese between tastes to cleanse the palate.

How to handle a ladder

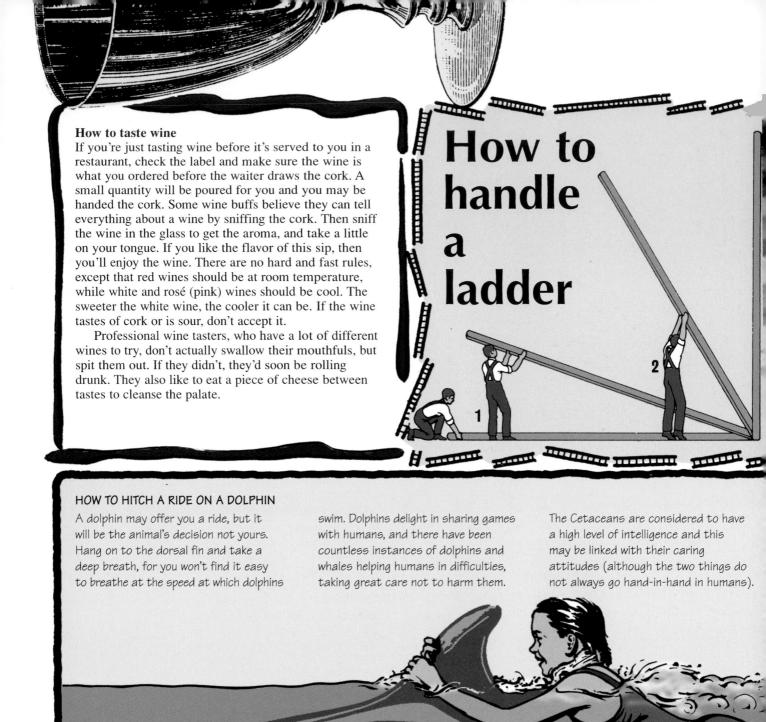

HOW TO HITCH A RIDE ON A DOLPHIN

A dolphin may offer you a ride, but it will be the animal's decision not yours. Hang on to the dorsal fin and take a deep breath, for you won't find it easy to breathe at the speed at which dolphins swim. Dolphins delight in sharing games with humans, and there have been countless instances of dolphins and whales helping humans in difficulties, taking great care not to harm them.

The Cetaceans are considered to have a high level of intelligence and this may be linked with their caring attitudes (although the two things do not always go hand-in-hand in humans).

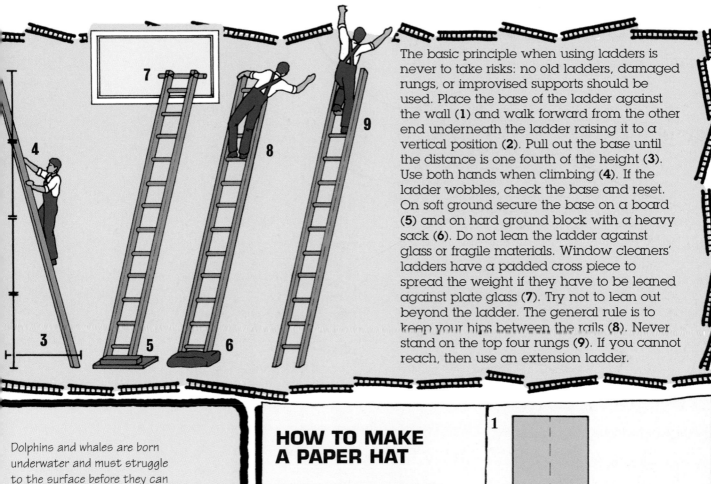

The basic principle when using ladders is never to take risks: no old ladders, damaged rungs, or improvised supports should be used. Place the base of the ladder against the wall (**1**) and walk forward from the other end underneath the ladder raising it to a vertical position (**2**). Pull out the base until the distance is one fourth of the height (**3**). Use both hands when climbing (**4**). If the ladder wobbles, check the base and reset. On soft ground secure the base on a board (**5**) and on hard ground block with a heavy sack (**6**). Do not lean the ladder against glass or fragile materials. Window cleaners' ladders have a padded cross piece to spread the weight if they have to be leaned against plate glass (**7**). Try not to lean out beyond the ladder. The general rule is to keep your hips between the rails (**8**). Never stand on the top four rungs (**9**). If you cannot reach, then use an extension ladder.

Dolphins and whales are born underwater and must struggle to the surface before they can take their first breaths. Adults will help to lift the newborn mammal upward, and may have a similar, instinctive reaction when they find a human in trouble in the water.

HOW TO MAKE A PAPER HAT

Take a sheet of paper with a length of 1$\frac{1}{2}$ times its width; the size will vary according to who is to wear it.

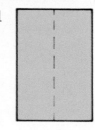
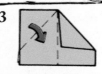
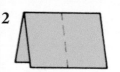
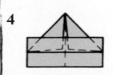

1. **Fold down center, unfold**
2. **Fold in other direction**
3. **Fold top corners into center**
4. **Fold bottom edge. Turn over and fold up other side**
5. **Open out and hat is ready to wear.**

HOW TO PLAY
NINE MEN'S MORRIS

Players Nine Men's Morris is a very old European game for two players in which each player attempts to capture or block his opponent's pieces.

The board The game is played on a board specially marked with three squares one inside the other and with lines radiating from the outer border of the innermost square to the center border of the outer square (as in the illustrations).

Pieces At the start of the game each player has nine "men" (counters, checkers, etc) distinguishable from those of his opponent.

Objective Through the placing and maneuvering of men on the board, each player attempts to capture all but two of his opponent's pieces, or to make it impossible to move any piece in his turn.

Play There are usually three stages of play: 1) placing the pieces on the board; 2) moving the pieces around; 3) "hopping" them. (This third stage is sometimes disallowed, as it gives one player a distinct advantage over his opponent).

Placing the pieces The players decide which of them is to start, then each in turn places one of his own men on the board at any point of intersection not already occupied (**a**). Players aim to get three of their own men into a straight line along one of the lines of the board, so forming a "mill" (**b**).

Pounding Once a player has formed a mill he is entitled to "pound" his opponent by removing one enemy piece from the board (**c**). He may not, however, remove an enemy piece that is part of a mill unless there is no other man available. Once removed from the board, a piece is dead for the rest of the game. Players continue their turns (nine turns each) until each of their men has been placed on the board.

Moving the pieces Still taking alternate turns, players now move their men to try to form new mills and so pound their opponents. A move consists of moving a man from his existing position to any adjoining intersection (**d**). (According to some rules players may take pieces by passing over an enemy piece to a vacant spot beyond it, as in checkers.) Players may form new mills by breaking existing mills. This is achieved by moving a man one place from his position in a mill, and then returning him at the next move to his original position. Mills may be broken and re-made any number of times, and each new mill formation entitles the player to pound his opponent. Play continues until one of the players is reduced by successive poundings to having only two men on the board; or until one player's pieces have been so blocked by his opponent's men that he is unable to make any move. Should a player's only remaining pieces form a mill and it is his turn to move, then he must move even if this results in his losing a piece and the game at his opponent's next move.

Hopping is an optional stage in the game and begins when either player has only three men remaining. The player is now no longer restricted to moving his men along a line to an adjacent point of intersection, but may "hop" to any vacant spot on the board (**e**). This freedom of movement gives him a certain advantage over his opponent, and so restores his chance of winning.

Result A player is defeated when either: he is reduced to having only two pieces; or his pieces are blocked by enemy men in such a way as to prevent further moves. If hopping has been allowed then the game ends when one player has only two pieces remaining.

a

b

c

d

e

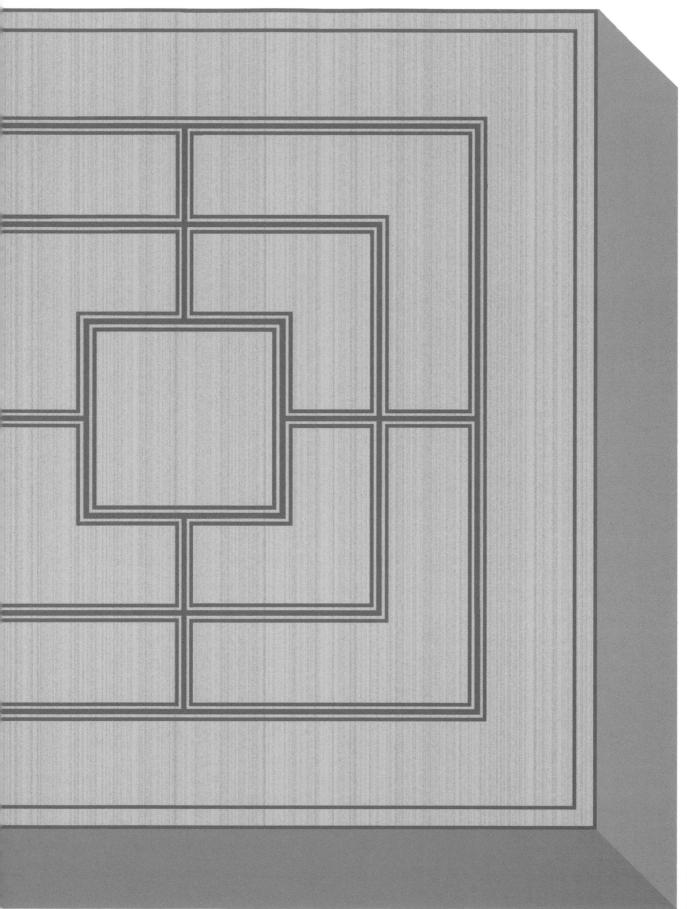

HOW TO READ THE LANGUAGE OF FLOWERS

The language of flowers originated in the harems of Turkey and other Muslim countries. Nineteenth-century flower dictionaries listed hundreds of flowers and their meanings, so that by exchanging bouquets lovers could "write" long messages. Here is a selection:

Acacia friendship
Almond (flowering) hope
Ambrosia love returned
Asphodel my regrets follow you to the grave
Bachelor's Buttons celibacy
Balsam, Red touch me not
Birch meekness
Bluebell constancy
Candytuft indifference
Canterbury Bell acknowledgment
Carnation, striped refusal
Cedar Leaf I live for thee
Clover, Four-leaved be mine
Clover, White think of me
Currant your frown will kill me
Daisy, Garden I share your sentiments

Dock patience
Eglantine I wound to heal
Ficoides (Ice Plant) your looks freeze me
Fleur-de-Lis I burn
French Marigold jealousy
Geranium, Lemon unexpected meeting
Geranium, Nutmeg expected meeting
Hawthorn hope
Honeysuckle devoted affection
Hortensia you are cold
Iris message
Ivy faithfulness
Jasmine, Cape I am too happy
Jasmine, Carolina separation
Jonquil please return my affection
Lady's Slipper win me and wear me

Lavender distrust
Lettuce coldheartedness
Lily of the Valley return of happiness
Marigold grief
Marigold, French jealousy
Michaelmas Daisy farewell
Mountain Ash prudence
Nightshade truth
Oleander beware
Ox Eye patience
Pansy thoughts
Peach Blossom I am your captive
Primrose, Evening inconstancy
Quince temptation
Rose love
Rosemary remembrance

How to flour fish or meat
The quickest and tidiest way is to put the flour into a plastic bag, season it as you would normally, put in the fish or meat, shake the bag, remove the fish or meat nicely covered in flour and throw the bag away. No flour all over the kitchen and no extra dish to wash.

HOW TO SPLICE THE MAINBRACE
Get out the liquor, or to be more precise get the ship's bosun to pipe "up spirits" and call the crew of a vessel of the British Royal Navy on deck, then issue every man with a tot of grog (rum). Perhaps the expression arose because the mainbrace, the rope supporting the main yard or crosspiece of a sailing vessel, was difficult to splice and earned those doing it a reward. Sadly, the free rum issue in the Royal Navy ended in the 1970s.

Rue disdain
Snakesfoot horror
Spearmint warmth of sentiment
Syringa memory
Thorn Apple deceitful charms
Tulip, Red declaration of love
Tulip, Yellow hopeless love
Venus's Car fly with me
Veronica fidelity
Water Lily purity of heart
Willow, Creeping love foresaken
Wormwood absence
Yew sorrow
Zephyr Flower expectation

HOW TO DIVINE FOR WATER

You need a divining rod. The traditional material is a forked stick of hazel, but other twigs have been used. Some dowsers (water diviners) prefer to use Y-shaped rods made of metal or whalebone. Hold the rod between the thumb and first finger of each hand, with the hands palm upward and the elbows into the sides – but not stiffly held. If you have the gift of "finding," the rod will either dip or rise when you are over a source of water. People also use divining rods for locating minerals. Some dowsers use a pendulum, a weight on a short length of string held between finger and thumb. When water is located the pendulum starts to rotate or swing. Some dowsers claim to be able to locate water by holding a pendulum over a map. Scientists say there is no scientific explanation of water divining.

HOW TO KISS AN ESKIMO

It's not a myth. Eskimos kiss by rubbing noses together. It can be a real turn-on. It's a sign of affection, farewell and greeting, like a peck on the cheek or a handshake in some cultures. It can be a nice bit of romance too; but when an Eskimo is in a comfortable hut or igloo and really concentrating, he or she will kiss in the Western fashion too – though in Eskimo culture this is an intimacy kept in more exclusive reserve than in the rest of North America.

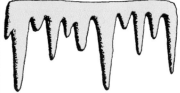

©DIAGRAM

HOW TO MEND STONE

Stone can be joined with an epoxy resin. The edges should be rubbed down with coarse glass-paper and cleaned with a detergent and water. Dry them, and then apply the adhesive. Chips in marble can be masked by building up with a mixture of epoxy resin and whiting, colored appropriately.

HOW TO TELL HOW LONG TILL THE SUN SETS

Face the setting Sun. Hold both arms at full length in front of you. Bend the fingers inward, parallel to the horizon, and fill the space between the horizon and the Sun with your fingers. For each finger count 15 minutes, add that up and you'll know approximately how long it is to sunset. Of course, if you are in hilly country you will have to make allowance for the horizon not being the edge of the Earth as it would be on a wide plain, but even making a guess with an imaginary horizon in woods and hills you'll still be fairly accurate – and it doesn't matter how tall you are or how big your hands are either!

HOW TO GET POWER FROM POTATOES

YOU NEED:
12 STRIPS ZINC
12 STRIPS BRASS
24 PAPER CLIPS
12 POTATOES
COPPER WIRE
1.5 VOLT FLASHLIGHT
BULB AND HOLDER

HOW TO MAKE A FLOW CHART

FLOW CHARTS ARE USED TO SET OUT A SEQUENCE OF ACTIONS AND DECISIONS AS CLEARLY AND LOGICALLY AS POSSIBLE. THEY ARE FREQUENTLY USED IN SCIENCE, INDUSTRY, COMMERCE AND ESPECIALLY IN COMPUTER PROGRAMMING. MAKING YOUR OWN FLOW CHART CAN BE FUN, AND HELPS IMPROVE YOUR POWERS OF LOGICAL THINKING.

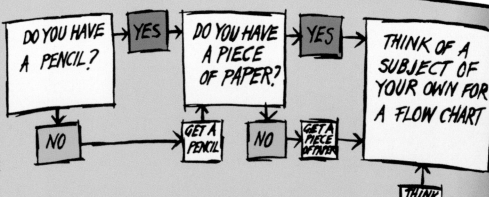

HOW TO TELL LINEAR A FROM LINEAR B

Linear A and Linear B are two very similar scripts found on clay tablets in the ruins of the ancient Cretan civilization at Knossos. Scholars found that Linear B inscriptions are in an early form of Greek. Linear A, the older script, is in a different language which hasn't yet been identified. To the casual eye the two scripts look alike, but the lines of writing on Linear B tablets are separated by rules or guidelines, while there are no such rules on Linear A tablets. Nearly two-thirds of the Linear B symbols are almost identical to those of Linear A, while the rest have no equivalent. Note: The scripts are called linear because they're written in lines.

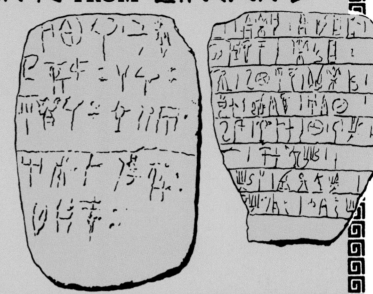

Cut your strips from sheets of scrap metal. Push one strip of each metal into each potato. Link between potatoes, brass strip to zinc, with copper wire. A few twists of wire around each strip can be held firmly by a paper clip. Complete the circuit by connecting the terminals of the bulb holder. Insert the bulb and it will light up.

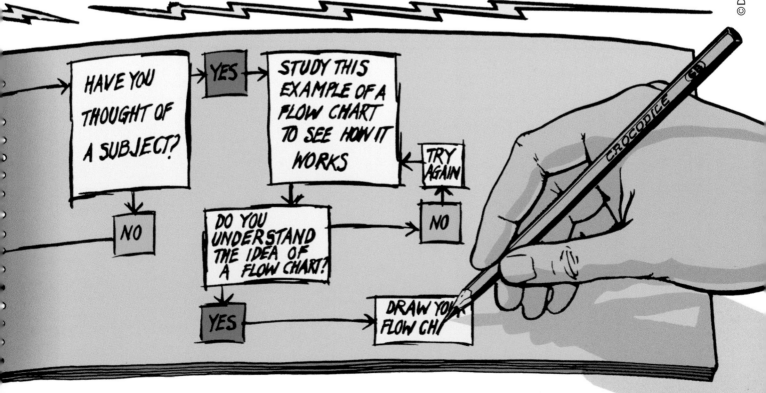

HOW TO WEIGH LESS WITHOUT LOSING WEIGHT

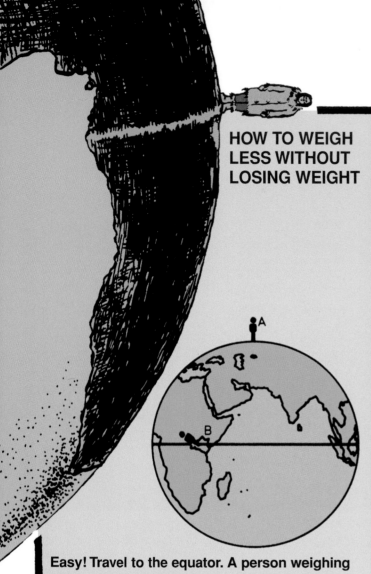

Easy! Travel to the equator. A person weighing 100 pounds (45.3kg) at the North pole (A) will weigh only 99.5 pounds (45.1kg) in, say, Kenya (B). The reason for this is that the pull of gravity on your body – your weight – decreases the farther you are from the Earth's core, and the Earth bulges slightly at the equator. The same person would weigh another 1/4 pound (0.1kg) lighter at the summit of Mt. Kenya, a further 17,058 feet (5199m) from the Earth's core. Of course, if you already live up a mountain at the equator, then this method of reducing is not much use!

HOW TO DISCOVER A TREE'S AGE

EVERY YEAR A TREE GROWS AN EXTRA LAYER ON ITS TRUNK WHICH IN CROSS SECTION SHOWS A SERIES OF CONCENTRIC RINGS. WHEN A TREE IS FELLED YOU CAN COUNT THE RINGS TO DISCOVER THE AGE. WITH A LIVING TREE A HOLLOW BORING INSTRUMENT CAN EXTRACT A SMALL SEGMENT FROM BARK TO CORE. CLIMATIC CONDITIONS AND NUTRIENT AVAILABILITY AFFECT THE SIZE OF EACH ANNUAL RING AND WITH SUITABLE SPECIES CAN TELL US ABOUT PAST CLIMATES.

years |10 |20 |30

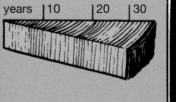

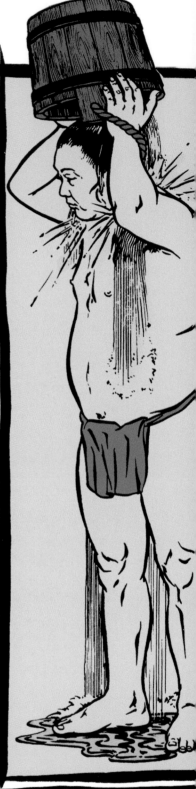

HOW TO MAKE AN ICOSAHEDRON

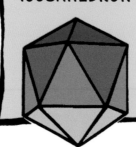

Copy the shape drawn here; it is made up from 20 equilateral triangles (see p. 137). Score along the straight lines with a compass point, fold into shape, and glue the edges into place to form a perfect regular icosahedron.

HOW TO TAKE A JAPANESE BATH

A Japanese bath, ofuro, is for soaking. It is kept hot, at about 105°F (40°C). Before entering the tub, rinse your body thoroughly. There is usually a shower, or water and buckets provided for this purpose; you can also scoop out water from the tub itself. After you've rinsed, climb into the tub (slowly – the water is very hot) and soak for a while. Then get out of the tub and wash with a washcloth, soap, and water. Rinse off any soap then hop back into the tub for a final long, leisurely soak. Try not to dip your used washcloth into the tub. Remember, the same water is used by everyone and is not changed each time. For that reason, too, it's best to take your bath in the late afternoon. By evening, most Japanese baths have lost their limpid clarity. Japanese people always dry themselves with a wrung-out washcloth. Westerners usually use a towel, but try drying yourself the Japanese way. You'll be surprised at how well it works. If you're at a public bathhouse, don't strut around the washing area like a peacock. Even though they are not unisex be modest and keep your washcloth in front of your lower body as you walk to and from the tub, as Japanese men and women do.

How to open a champagne bottle

First make sure that the wine is well chilled, so it won't froth all over everything, and agitate it as little as possible. Champagne is a sparkling wine that builds up pressure within the bottle, which is why champagne bottles are extra thick and have their corks wired on. Twist the wire off the neck of the bottle, remove it and any foil or metal covering the cork. Keeping the bottle steady, gently ease the cork by pressure from the thumbs. Now grip the cork and twist it out very slowly. It should just pop out into the palm of your hand while a plume like a small puff of smoke rises from the bottle. Pour the champagne slowly into tall glasses to retain its effervescence. Of course, if you want to waste good wine you can serve it insufficiently chilled, shake the bottle and push the cork out with your thumbs so that it makes an explosive noise, shoots across the room and drenches everyone around in a fountain of champagne. Then pour it into glasses shaped like sundae dishes, mistakenly thought to be designed for champagne, which will allow it to go flat in no time!

How to name the "points" of a dog

As with the horse, the "points" or anatomical features of the dog have special names, as indicated on the diagram.

1 Stop
2 Muzzle
3 Jaws
4 Shoulder
5 Prosternum
6 Forechest
7 Elbow
8 Pastern
9 Dewclaw
10 Ribs
11 Flank
12 Feet
13 Metatarsus
14 Pastern
15 Hock
16 Lower thigh
17 Stifle
18 Upper thigh
19 Tail
20 Croup
21 Loin
22 Withers
23 Occiput

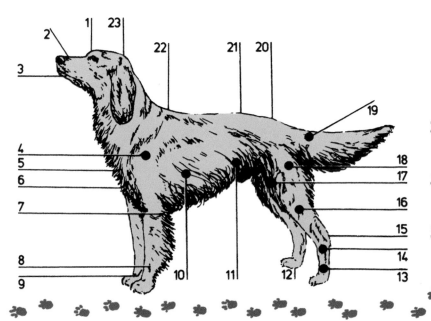

©DIAGRAM

134

How to travel with pets

There are certain points to be remembered when traveling with any pet animal. First and foremost is whether you can take it with you at all. Some countries forbid the import or export of certain kinds of animals. Others impose quarantine or health checks on the pet. You should also check that any airline, rail, boat or bus transport you may be using will accept an animal, whether you need a ticket for it, and what kind of container they advise. For example, boxes for animals traveling on aircraft must conform to certain design requirements. It is also wise to make sure that your pet will be welcome at the end of your journey, since not all hotels tolerate animal guests. Whichever way you travel and whatever animal you want to take, try and make sure you have a suitable box, cage or container for it. This should be large enough for the animal to stand up comfortably and turn around. It should provide protection against drafts and extremes of temperature, yet be well enough ventilated so that under no circumstances can suffocation occur. It is better to feed and water your pets at intervals rather than leave food bowls in the crate to be upset. Make sure the box is labeled clearly with your name and address and the fact that it contains a live animal, just in case the two of you get separated, and, if you can, attach a name tag to the animal as well.

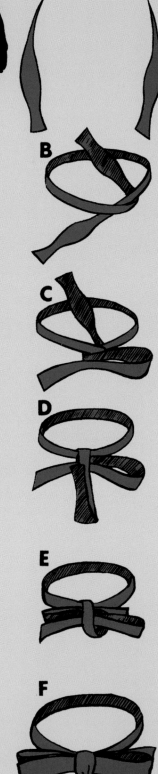

HOW TO TIE A BOW TIE

THE TIE MAY HAVE SHAPED (**A**) OR STRAIGHT ENDS, THE METHOD IS THE SAME FOR BOTH. LEFT AND RIGHT REFER TO YOUR OWN LEFT AND RIGHT IF YOU ARE TYING A TIE ON YOURSELF.

PUT THE TIE AROUND YOUR NECK AND CROSS THE RIGHT END OVER AND UNDER THE LEFT END (**B**). LEAVING A FULL BOW WIDTH ON THE LEFT END FACING FRONT, FOLD THE FABRIC BEHIND IT TO HALFWAY ALONG THE BOW (**C**) BRING THE RIGHT END OVER AND IN FRONT OF THE BOW (**D**) FOLD BACK THE RIGHT END AS YOU DID THE LEFT IN (**B**) AND TUCK THE FOLDED PART INTO THE SPACE BETWEEN THE FOLDED LEFT END AND THE FABRIC AROUND YOUR NECK, PUSHING FROM LEFT TO RIGHT AND LEAVING THE ACTUAL END TO THE RIGHT (**E**). THIS FORMS THE BASIC BOW WHICH YOU CAN NOW ADJUST UNTIL IT IS SMOOTH AND NEAT (**F**). AT FIRST YOU MAY FIND THAT THE LENGTHS AT THE SIDES OF THE BOW ARE UNEVEN OR THAT THE WHOLE TIE IS TOO LOOSE. WITH PRACTICE YOU WILL GET THE BALANCE OF THE BOW CORRECT AND IF THE OVERALL TIE IS LOOSE, YOU SHOULD SHORTEN THE TIE; OBVIOUSLY THIS MUST BE DONE IN THE CENTER TO AVOID HAVING TO RESHAPE THE ENDS. MANY TIES HAVE AN ADJUSTABLE CENTER SECTION TO FACILITATE THIS.

How to ride an OSTRICH

Climb on to the middle of the bird's back and seat yourself as far to the rear as possible while still able to keep your seat and grip the roots of its wings. Then hang on. The ostrich will probably run in the hope of shaking you off. They are large and tough birds. In South Africa, where ostriches are farmed, an ostrich race is often part of rural festivities. If they go in for it in a big way ostrich jockeys tend to wear jockey outfits like those worn for horse racing, but ostrich racing is a rather undisciplined, ad hoc event. Ostriches are curious and friendly but they are independent spirits and not really trainable for organized events.

How to pan for gold

You need pay dirt – that is, soil, rock, gravel or other substance that you think contains gold – and a good supply of water. The pan can be a large frying pan or a shallow bowl. You swirl the gravel around in the pan with the water, allowing it to spill over the edge. The gold, being about seven times as heavy, stays in the bottom of the pan. If you can get yourself a **batea**, a pan with a corrugated bottom, you'll find it works even better than an ordinary pan.

©DIAGRAM

How to make Greek or Turkish coffee

The people of the eastern Mediterranean like their coffee very strong and drink small quantities at a time from small cups. Choose a fairly strong coffee, medium roast, and finely grind or pulverize it. Place it in a copper coffee pot (you can make do with an ordinary small saucepan if the proper equipment is not available); about two tablespoons will do. Add four tablespoons of sugar. Mix, then add two cups of water. Heat until it rises in a froth. Remove from heat. Repeat twice. Add a *little* cold water and pour out gently. Some of the muddy lees will go into the cup but don't worry, that's expected; one never drinks it to the bottom! What you have made is what the Greeks call *glykí vrastos*, sweet and well boiled. If you want very sweet coffee, *poli glybós*, add more sugar. Medium-sweet is known as *métrios*, a little sugar, *me olighi*, no sugar, *skétos*. Because you can boil up small quantities very quickly you can make each cup separately to please the tastes of each of your guests. Sip it slowly and, to increase your enjoyment, serve it with *loukoumi* (Turkish delight).

136

HOW TO HIVE A SWARM OF BEES

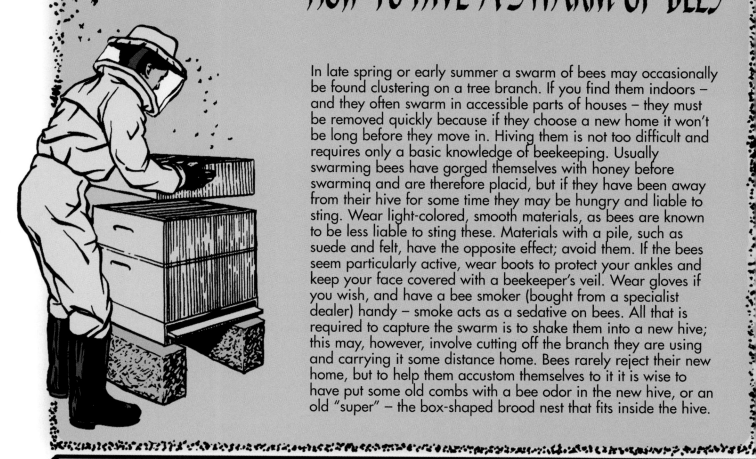

In late spring or early summer a swarm of bees may occasionally be found clustering on a tree branch. If you find them indoors – and they often swarm in accessible parts of houses – they must be removed quickly because if they choose a new home it won't be long before they move in. Hiving them is not too difficult and requires only a basic knowledge of beekeeping. Usually swarming bees have gorged themselves with honey before swarming and are therefore placid, but if they have been away from their hive for some time they may be hungry and liable to sting. Wear light-colored, smooth materials, as bees are known to be less liable to sting these. Materials with a pile, such as suede and felt, have the opposite effect; avoid them. If the bees seem particularly active, wear boots to protect your ankles and keep your face covered with a beekeeper's veil. Wear gloves if you wish, and have a bee smoker (bought from a specialist dealer) handy – smoke acts as a sedative on bees. All that is required to capture the swarm is to shake them into a new hive; this may, however, involve cutting off the branch they are using and carrying it some distance home. Bees rarely reject their new home, but to help them accustom themselves to it it is wise to have put some old combs with a bee odor in the new hive, or an old "super" – the box-shaped brood nest that fits inside the hive.

HOW TO REPAIR A FLAT BICYCLE TIRE

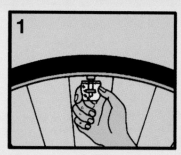  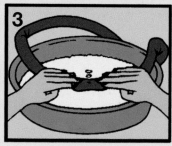

First check the outside of the tire for any sharp objects stuck in it that may have caused the puncture, or any gashes in the tire. Note or mark any such position. If no indication of a puncture is apparent, reinflate the tire and check the valve. You may be able to feel air escaping, but if not, place the valve at the top of the wheel, and immerse it in water (**1**). If it is leaking, renew the rubber or replace. If the valve is satisfactory, remove the wheel and

unscrew the valve. Starting opposite the valve, insert tire levers between the tire and the rim and lever one side of the tire off (**2**). Then pull the inner tube out.

Replace the valve and inflate the tube, and check for leaks by squeezing the tube and passing it slowly through a bowl of water (**3**) and watch for air escaping. Check the whole tube for punctures – there may be more than one – and mark them; a wax crayon is best for this.

HOW TO DRAW AN EQUILATERAL TRIANGLE

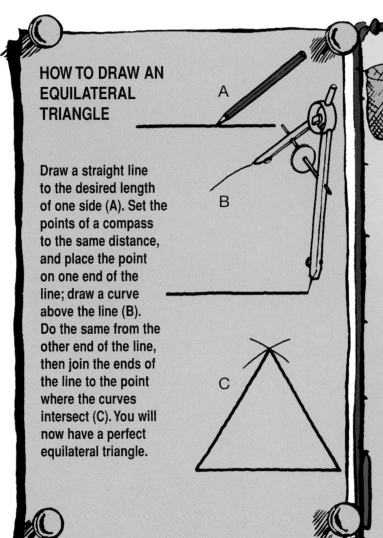

Draw a straight line to the desired length of one side (A). Set the points of a compass to the same distance, and place the point on one end of the line; draw a curve above the line (B). Do the same from the other end of the line, then join the ends of the line to the point where the curves intersect (C). You will now have a perfect equilateral triangle.

How to pick the apple from the top of the tree

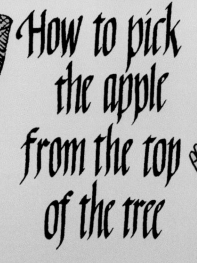

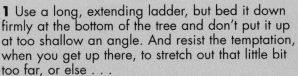

1 Use a long, extending ladder, but bed it down firmly at the bottom of the tree and don't put it up at too shallow an angle. And resist the temptation, when you get up there, to stretch out that little bit too far, or else . . .

2 Obtain, or make, a simple but effective device consisting basically of an extremely long-handled pair of pruning shears, operated remotely from the ground end, which will cut the apple stalk or a convenient twig and let the apple drop into a soft net alongside the blades of the pruning shears. Commercial fruit growers avoid the problem by pruning their trees to a shape that enables a fork-lift truck to be operated between the rows.

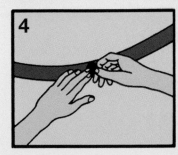
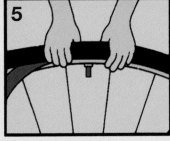

Deflate the tube and clean up the puncture area with glass paper. Spread adhesive over the area, and when tacky apply the patch (**4**). Dust with chalk.

Replace the tube and insert the valve. Slightly inflate the tube and tuck it into the tire. Press the tire over the rim (**5**), starting opposite the valve, making sure that the tube is not pinched. Then inflate the tire fully.

HOW TO MAKE MUESLI

TO MAKE THIS HEALTHY BREAKFAST CEREAL, MIX TOGETHER VARYING AMOUNTS OF THE FOLLOWING INGREDIENTS UNTIL YOU FIND A MIXTURE THAT PLEASES YOU: DRIED OATMEAL, BRAN, FLAKED WHEAT OR CORN, WHEATGERM, BROWN SUGAR, RAISINS, DATES, DRIED BANANAS, DRIED APPLE, CHOPPED NUTS, DRIED APRICOTS.

HOW TO FIND YOUR BLIND SPOT

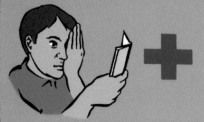

Hold this page at arm's length. Close or cover your left eye. Now look at the cross with your right eye. Slowly move the book toward you. At one point the dot will disappear. Now look at the dot with your left eye in the same way. You will find that the cross will now disappear.

How to tell the speed of the wind at sea

Take a look at the surface of the water and you can readily judge the force of the wind. It is possible that even when the air is still there may be waves originating from some distant wind center, but normally waves are a useful indicator.

Effect of wind on sea	Wind speed on Beaufort Scale (See p. 90)
Sea absolutely calm (mirror-like)	0
Scale-like ripples but no foaming crests	1
Small wavelets, short but more pronounced crests that still do not break	2
Crests beginning to break with foam of glassy appearance, some scattered "white caps"	3
Small waves, becoming longer, quite frequent "white caps"	4
Moderate waves, more noticeably long in form, many "white caps," perhaps some spray	5
Large waves forming, crests break with patches of white foam, some spray	6
Sea begins to tower, foam from the breaking waves blows in streaks in direction of wind	
Moderately high waves of considerable length, crests begin to break in spindrift, foam blown in noticeable streaks	8
Mountainous waves, dense streaks of foam, rollers beginning to appear, spray probably affecting visibility	9
Very mountainous waves, long overturning crests, sea white with foam, heavy rollers, visibility reduced by spray	10
Exceptionally mountainous waves, visibility much reduced by spray	11
Air filled with foam and spray, sea completely white, visibility severely reduced – no distant objects can be seen	12

How to extract a broken cork

Use a crochet hook. It's worth keeping one in the house as a tool for removing broken corks from bottles even though you may never want to do any crocheting!

How to find a CORYPHEE

A coryphee is a ballerina who is halfway between the *corps de ballet* and prima ballerina; coryphees lead the *corps de ballet* or dance in small groups.

How to take the temperature of a cat or dog
Do *not* use a normal clinical thermometer intended for humans which could snap and cause serious harm. More robust kinds are made for animals. Prepare the thermometer as for taking a human temperature. Get someone whom the animal trusts to hold it firmly and confidently. Smear the thermometer with a lubricant jelly. Insert the bulb end of the thermometer very gently into the animal's rectum. Rotate it gently, do not push. Leave for two minutes. Remove it and read the temperature. The animal must be restrained and reassured the whole time. The average normal temperature for a cat is 101.5°F (38.6°C) but may fluctuate between 100.5°F (38.05°C) and 102°F (38.88°C) without significance. For a dog it is between 101.5°F (38.61°C) and 101.6°F (38.66°C). A puppy's healthy temperature may be higher, up to 101.8°F (38.77°C).

How to tell a cockatrice from a basilisk
You can't for they are one and the same thing. Fortunately you are not likely to meet one, for it is a legendary and heraldic monster said to have been hatched from a cock's egg by a serpent. It had the combed head of a cock, the tail of a dragon or serpent, and the wings of a fowl, and its very look, even its breath, were said to be fatal. Only the weasel, which was said to secrete a venom deadly to the cockatrice, was believed to be safe from the creature.

How to ride an ELEPHANT

Ask (politely) the elephant to kneel down on its forelegs. Step up onto its left knee, hold onto the top of its ear, and climb aboard after gaining a foothold on one of the numerous lumps and bumps along its neck. Straddle the elephant just behind its neck. Grip tightly with your knees, and instead of letting your legs dangle, bend them slightly backward so that each leg grips the elephant's body along the inside of the calf all the way to the ankle. As the elephant walks, roll your body from side to side with its lumbering motion; this will prevent your backside from getting sore. Do not attempt to ride an elephant in the mating season, at which time it becomes intractable. Treat the elephant firmly but with kindness. Elephants do have long memories, and should you abuse one, it will remember you and get its own back later.

HOW TO DO THE LOTUS

This is an advanced yoga position, and many people will find it impossible at first. Go easy!

1. Sit on the floor and place the left foot as high up the right thigh as possible.
2. Bring the right foot into a similar position, crossing it over the lower left leg.
3. Form an "o" with the forefinger and thumb of each hand, and rest the fingers on each knee. Hold the posture as long as is comfortable.

1

HOW TO CONFUSE YOUR ENGLISH

Though it's the same basic language, American (and much of Canadian) English is quite different from English as she is spoke in England in certain details. For instance, if you go into Woolworth's in London, England and ask for **thumb tacks** they won't know what to give you; any more than if you go into Woolworth's in London, Ontario or Oxford, Mississippi and ask for **drawing pins**. They are, of course, the same thing. An American hangs his clothes up in the **closet**, but an English person uses a **wardrobe** or **cupboard**. In America, the law **enjoins** you (i.e forbids you) from spitting on the sidewalk; while in England, the law **enjoins** you to drive on the left hand side of the road (i.e. compels or requires you to do so). You can get into a lot of trouble if you don't know some of the different usages. For instance, you can go to the wrong address. If your friend lives on the **first floor** in New York, he or she lives on the **ground floor**, or the floor that is the same as the one with the entrance should there be a half basement. In England, someone living on the first floor lives on what Americans would consider to be the second floor. English people, in common with other Europeans, begin with the ground floor and call the next floor up the first floor and so on. Here are some more examples of words that could lead to embarrassment or misunderstanding:

American English	British English
Purse	Handbag
Coin purse	Purse
Pants	Trousers
Underpants	Pants
Vest	Waistcoat
Undershirt	Vest
Rummage sale	Jumble sale
Zee (Z)	Zed
Monkey wrench	Spanner
Zip code	Post code
Truck	Lorry
Checkers	Draughts
Diapers	Nappies
Elevator	Lift
Kerosene	Paraffin
Gas	Petrol
Drugstore	Chemist (and they don't serve refreshment)

HOW TO TELL THE BOW FROM THE STERN

NOTHING IRRITATES A SEAMAN AS MUCH AS A LAND LUBBER REFERRING TO THE "SHARP END" AND THE "BLUNT END" OF HIS SHIP. THE CORRECT TERMS ARE "BOW" (a) AND "STERN" (b).

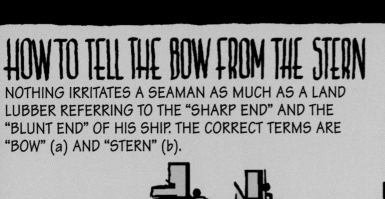

b

2 3

HOW TO MEASURE A FLEA'S LEAP

ACCORDING TO ARISTOTLE, YOU CATCH YOUR FLEA. HOLDING IT DELICATELY IN TWEEZERS, YOU DIP ITS LEGS IN WARM WAX. YOU PLACE THE FLEA ON A TABLE; IT JUMPS; AND YOU THEN MEASURE THE DISTANCE BETWEEN ONE SET OF FOOT-PRINTS OF THE FLEA AND THE NEXT.

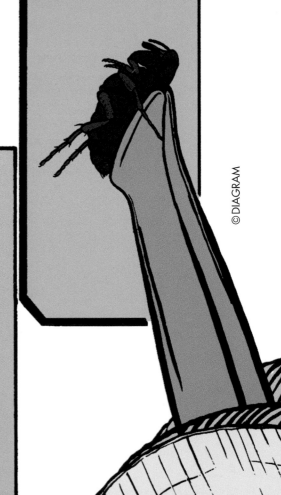

©DIAGRAM

And for some more that mean something different:
Mad American: angry; British: crazy, insane.
Mason American: worker in brick or stone; British: only in stone.
Char American: to burn; British: to burn, but also to clean for someone else, and as a noun, a house cleaner; as slang, in America: coffee; British: tea (from the Mandarin Chinese for tea).
Sack American: bed, as in "hit the sack"; British: to fire from a job (and a coarse cloth bag in both)
Nosh American: a snack between meals; British: a big, slap-up meal as in "nosh-up".

Measures differ too:

	American	British and International
Gallon	231 cubic inches	277 cubic inches
Pint	28.87 cubic inches liquid measure (16oz)	34.68 cubic inches (there is only one
	33.6 cubic inches dry measure	British pint) (20oz)
Quart	57.8 cubic inches liquid measure (32oz)	69.4 cubic inches
	67.2 cubic inches dry measure	
Ton	2,000 pounds = a short ton in Britain	2,240 pounds
Billion	1 thousand million (1,000,000,000)	1 million million (1,000,000,000,000)
Trillion	1 million million (1,000,000,000,000)	1 million billion (1,000,000,000,000,000,000)
Quadrillion	1 million billion (1,000,000,000,000,000)	1 million trillion (1,000,000,000,000,000,000,000,000)

How to build a Great Pyramid

HOW TO CELEBRATE THE CHINESE NEW YEAR

Traditionally Chinese all over the world celebrate New Year on the day of the second new moon after the winter solstice – varying between January 20 and February 20.

Three weeks before, make a sweet pudding of at least eight ingredients – different kinds of rice, beans, dates, chestnuts, red and white sugar, melon seeds, pine nuts and similar items. You serve this to family and friends.

Seven days before New Year, Tsao Wang-yeh, the Kitchen God, ascends to Heaven to report on the family's doings for the year. So you offer him sticky molasses candy so that he can't speak, and burn the paper image in his shrine so that he can't watch your activities until you paste in a new one on New Year's Eve. Meanwhile your children eat the candy.

On New Year's Eve you strew the courtyard of your house with sesame stalks, which crackle when stepped on and so ward off evil spirits. Decorate the household altar, put up the new picture of Tsao Wang-yeh, and hang lighted lanterns everywhere. Then you seal the doors with strips of paper to prevent the entry of evil spirits, and settle down to a banquet. Shortly before dawn the strips of paper are removed, and everyone lets off fire crackers to mark the beginning of the New Year.

On New Year's Day everyone wears at least some brand-new clothes, and people visit relatives and friends to exchange greetings and gifts. Celebrations-visits to theaters, fairs, and bazaars, gambling, and parties – go on for several days. The celebrations end on the 15th day with the Festival of Lanterns: temples and streets are decorated with hundreds of beautiful paper lanterns, and huge lions, with fierce head masks and cloth bodies (operated by men inside), dance in the streets.

HOW TO SPLINT A BIRD'S LEG

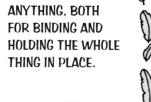

IF YOU ARE THE CLUMSY TYPE, DON'T TRY. IF YOU CAN'T GET EXPERT HELP, SEEK SPLINTS OF AN APPROPRIATE SIZE SUCH AS SPLIT MATCHSTICKS. WITH THE LIMB AS STRAIGHT AS POSSIBLE AND THE SPLINTS LIGHTLY PADDED WITH AN ABSORBANT COTTON BALL, BIND THEM ON, BEING CAREFUL NOT TO GET THEM TOO TIGHT. MASKING TAPE IS AS GOOD AS ANYTHING, BOTH FOR BINDING AND HOLDING THE WHOLE THING IN PLACE.

If you really want to go down in history and leave your mark for all to see, why not follow an old Egyptian tradition by building a pyramid? To construct one on the scale of the Great Pyramid at Giza – and it is hardly worth considering anything less – you will need about 100,000 laborers. Naturally you'll want to use traditional techniques, none of this new-fangled modern technology, so allow ten years for clearing the site, which should cover 571,530 square feet (53,095 sq m), plus working and storage space. Now take 2,300,000 blocks of good stone. It should take only 20 years to stack them properly, large ones at the bottom, to produce a fine pyramid 481 feet (146.6m) high.

How to read an Alchemist's formula

The alchemists of the middle ages tried for centuries to make gold from less valuable substances. Should you find one of their recipes, you would need to understand the symbols used – but don't get excited – none of the concoctions worked.

Lead

Arsenic

Tin

Steel

Iron

Glass

Brimstone

How to dress crab and lobster

Twist the limbs off the boiled shellfish, crack the claws open with a hammer and extract the meat. A lobster needs to be split along its entire length with a knife. Empty out all the meat from the body, keeping the white and brown meat of the crab separate. The only parts you can't eat are the stomach sacs, the gills, the dark intestinal vein which runs down the tail and the "dead men's fingers" found between the legs on the underside. The greenish-looking liver in the lobster's head is delicious and so is the coral – that's the bright red roe of the female lobster.

Scrub out and polish the shells. Mix the brown crab meat with seasoning and breadcrumbs, then pile it back into the center of the shell with the finely-chopped white meat arranged artistically around it. Lobster looks best if the pieces of meat are kept as whole as possible.

The dressed crustacean may be decorated with hard-boiled egg, mayonnaise and lettuce.

©DIAGRAM

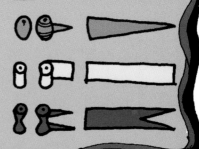

How to make beads from paper

Cut strips of paper, glue them on one side, and roll them around a knitting needle. When they are dry, slip them off, paint them and string them into jewelry.

How to recognize classical columns

The Ancient Greeks devised three main styles of architecture, most easily recognized by the different capitals on their columns, although the fluting of the columns, the arrangement of the base, and the entablature (the bands of moldings above the columns) all differ in their pure form. These are the Doric, the Ionic and the Corinthian. The Romans adopted the Greek forms but also devised another version of the Doric, often known as the Tuscan order, and an elaborate combination of the Ionic and Corinthian shapes in the Composite order. The classical architects and builders also noticed that if a column is built of exactly the same diameter through all its length it does not look right. An optical illusion of an inward curve appears. To correct this appearance they gave a convex curve to columns, whether cylindrical or tapering, a technique known as entasis.

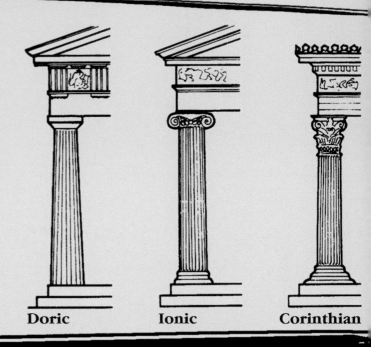

Doric   **Ionic**   **Corinthian**

How to catch a cockroach

Switch off the light at night so that the cockroaches are tempted to emerge, and have a bar of soft soap ready. Switch the light on suddenly, and pounce on the cockroaches as they scurry for safety; trap them by pressing the bar of soap over them.

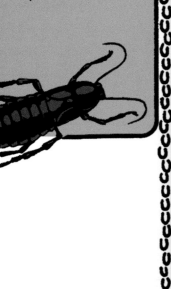

HOW TO MOUNT A HORSE

Always stand on the left-hand side of the horse when you mount. Position yourself sideways on to the horse, facing its tail. Mounting should be done quickly and efficiently so that the horse does not get bored and start moving, or feel that it has to put up with an inexperienced rider, which may unnerve it. Take the reins in your left hand and place your left foot in the stirrup, facing the tail (**1**). Grasp the back of the saddle with your right hand and pull yourself up (**2**). Let go with your right hand and swing your right leg over the horse (**3**). Put your right foot in the right stirrup.

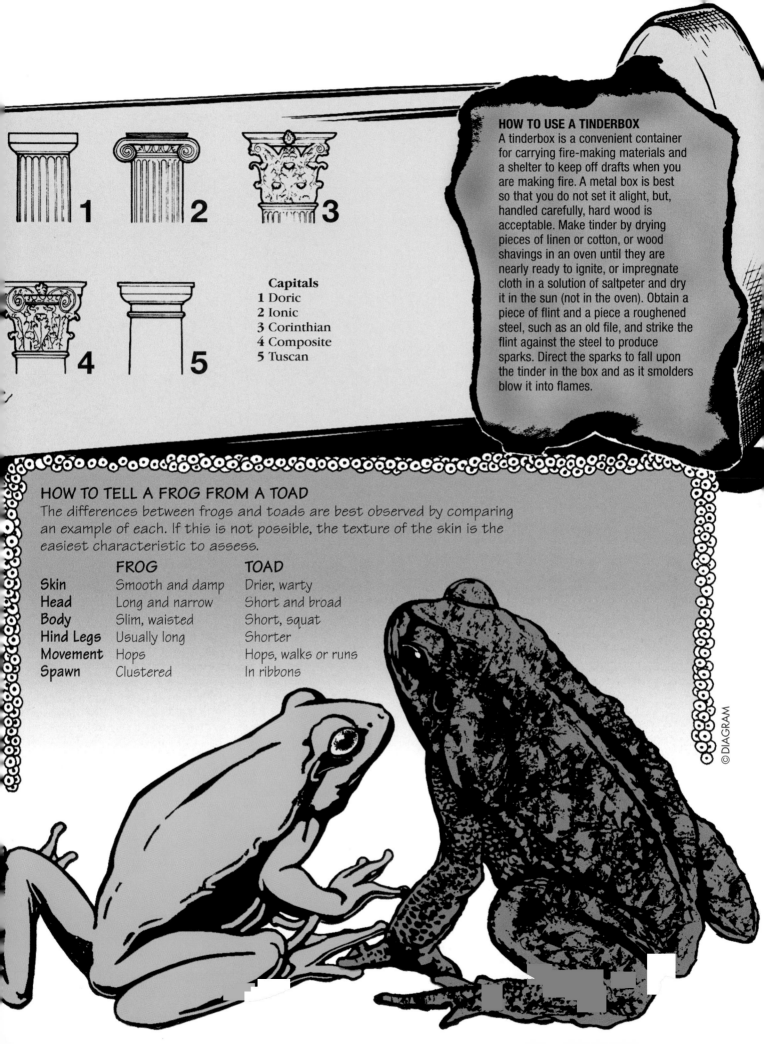

Capitals
1 Doric
2 Ionic
3 Corinthian
4 Composite
5 Tuscan

HOW TO USE A TINDERBOX
A tinderbox is a convenient container for carrying fire-making materials and a shelter to keep off drafts when you are making fire. A metal box is best so that you do not set it alight, but, handled carefully, hard wood is acceptable. Make tinder by drying pieces of linen or cotton, or wood shavings in an oven until they are nearly ready to ignite, or impregnate cloth in a solution of saltpeter and dry it in the sun (not in the oven). Obtain a piece of flint and a piece a roughened steel, such as an old file, and strike the flint against the steel to produce sparks. Direct the sparks to fall upon the tinder in the box and as it smolders blow it into flames.

HOW TO TELL A FROG FROM A TOAD
The differences between frogs and toads are best observed by comparing an example of each. If this is not possible, the texture of the skin is the easiest characteristic to assess.

	FROG	TOAD
Skin	Smooth and damp	Drier, warty
Head	Long and narrow	Short and broad
Body	Slim, waisted	Short, squat
Hind Legs	Usually long	Shorter
Movement	Hops	Hops, walks or runs
Spawn	Clustered	In ribbons

©DIAGRAM

How to play
PACHISI

Players This version of Pachisi comes from the Indian subcontinent and is for two or four players.

Board The playing area is in the form of a cross which is divided into small squares – 24 in each arm. Three squares in each arm (12 in all) are marked off as "resting" squares, where any number of pieces is safe from capture.

Pieces Each player has four shells, stones, counters or other objects that must be easily distinguishable from those of his opponents.

Objective In this race game each player tries to be the first to get all four of his pieces around the board from starting point to finish.

Dice Traditionally cowrie shells were used, and the number of moves calculated by the number of shells that fell with their openings uppermost. In this version a die is used and the following method of scoring adopted: 1=10 moves, 2=2 moves, 3=3 moves, 4=4 moves, 5=5 moves, 6=25 moves; any player throwing 1 or 6 is also entitled to a further throw.

Play Each player in turn throws the die and moves one of his pieces the number of squares scored. Pieces are moved in a clockwise direction around the board (see illustrations **2**, **3**, **4**). At the start of the game each player's first piece may enter the race with any throw, but subsequent pieces (or the first piece if it is made to return to the start) may only enter the game if a 10 or 25 is thrown. A player may have any number of his pieces on the board at any time. After the players have each had one turn, they may if they wish miss a turn or decline to move their pieces after making their throw.

Taking If a piece lands on any square (other than a resting square) occupied by an opponent's piece, the opponent's piece is obliged to return to the start. It may only enter the game again after the correct number has been thrown. The player who took the opponent's piece is allowed another throw. Once a piece has reached the central column of his own arm, leading to the finish, it cannot be taken.

Double pieces If a piece is moved on to a square already occupied by a piece belonging to the same player, both pieces may be moved together as a "double piece" on subsequent moves. A double piece may never be overtaken by other pieces, whether the player's or an opponent's, and can only be taken if an enemy piece of equal strength lands directly on its square.

End of play The finish can only be reached by a direct throw. If, for example, a piece is seven squares away from the finish and the player throws more than a 7, he is obliged to wait his next turn, or move one of his other pieces. As soon as a piece lands on the finish the piece is removed from the board. The winner of the game is the first player to get all four of his pieces to the finish, and the game may be continued to determine the finishing order of the other players.

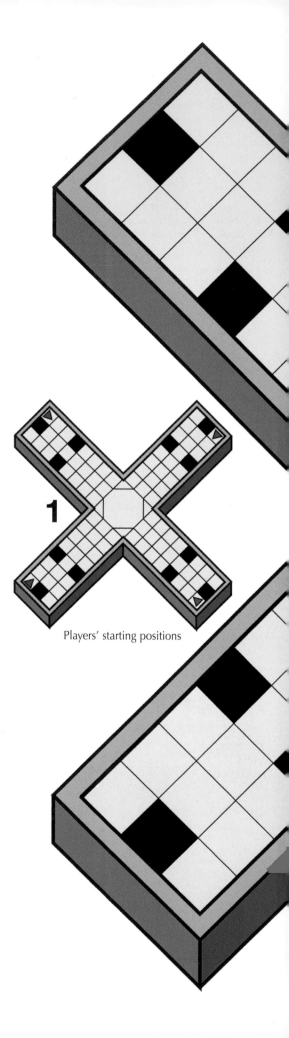

1

Players' starting positions

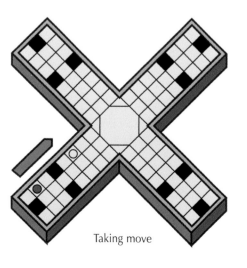

Taking move

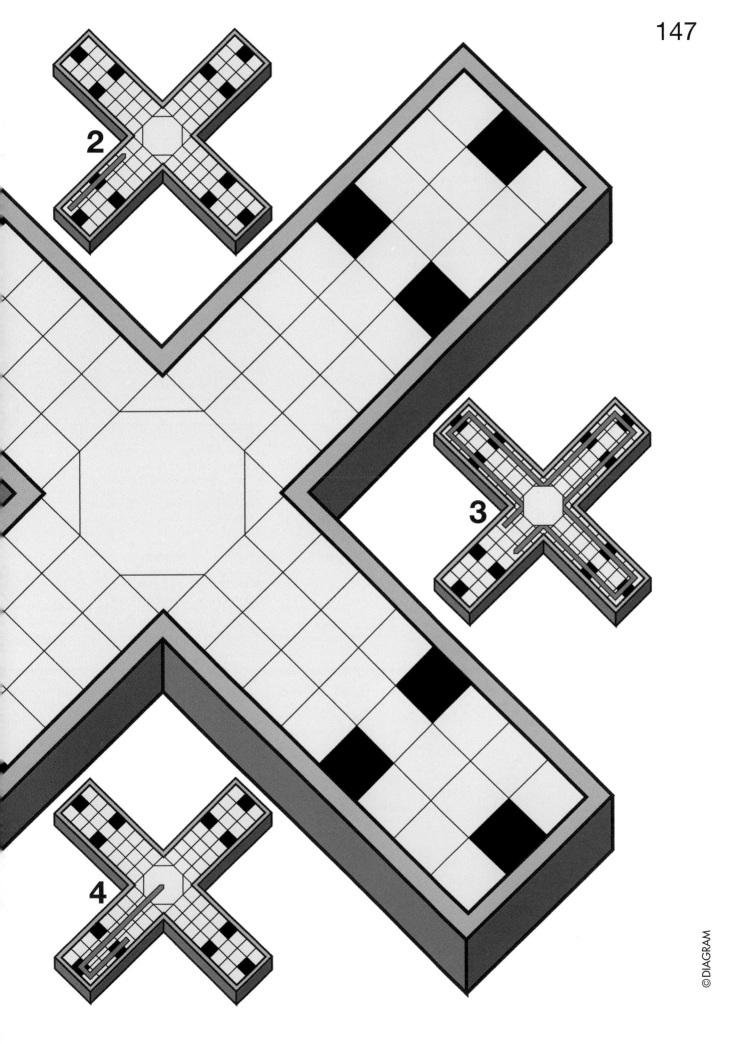

How to have a black dinner

For an all-black feast, make your meal from the following ingredients. Rye bread, caviar, sloes, black olives, poppy seeds, blackcurrants, black bass, truffles, black cherries, black-eyed peas, blackberries, black bun, black pudding, licorice and black pepper.

How to get to sleep without pills
First close your eyes then: The traditional method is to count sheep – but for it to work you should make an effort to visualize each sheep jumping over a fence before you count it.
Or
Breathe regularly and as you breathe out visualize your breath forming a cloud in front of you, as it does on a cold day.
Or
Take deep breaths, hold the breath and then exhale, counting each breath as you breathe out. In many people this produces a mildly hypnotic state.
Or
Read a book – but not one with a gripping story or you will find you stay awake even longer!

Or
Listen to the radio at low level (using a time switch to turn it off after you have gone to sleep).
Or
Do mental arithmetic – if you have a digital clock try to factorize the number on the clock screen – though that kind of mental stimulus may keep some people awake. Presumably it works by crowding other more disturbing thoughts from your surface consciousness. As an aid to sleep avoid heavy meals shortly before bedtime, or drinks containing caffeine (tea, coffee and cola). Ensure that the mattress is firm and supports your body and that you are neither too hot nor too cold. And attend to nature's needs before retiring – a desire to empty the bladder or bowels is a common cause of sleeplessness.

HOW TO NAME THE PARTS OF A GUN

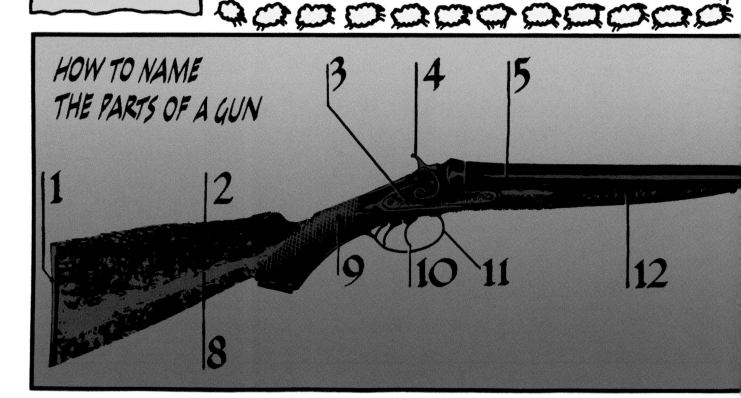

1 2 3 4 5 8 9 10 11 12

HOW TO BE A BUTLER

ACCORDING TO THE 19TH CENTURY ENGLISH WRITER MRS BEETON, THE DUTIES OF THE BUTLER IN A HOUSEHOLD WERE AS FOLLOWS:

1. TO SUPERVISE ALL OTHER MALE SERVANTS, TO PAY BILLS, AND TO RUN THE WINE CELLAR.
2. TO SERVE BREAKFAST, ASSISTED BY THE FOOTMAN.
3. TO ARRANGE AND SERVE LUNCHEON.
4. AT DINNER TO SET OUT THE SILVERWARE, ANNOUNCE THAT THE MEAL IS READY, BRING IN THE FIRST DISH, CARVE THE MEAT, SERVE THE WINES. DURING DESSERT, HE SHOULD STAND BEHIND THE MASTER'S CHAIR.
5. AT BEDTIME, TO BRING CANDLES FOR THE HOUSEHOLD, TO LOCK THE WINDOWS AND DOORS, AND TO SEE THAT THE FIRES ARE IN A SAFE STATE.

CAN YOU IDENTIFY ALL THE PARTS OF A GUN "LOCK, STOCK AND BARREL" AS THE SAYING GOES? HERE ARE THE MAJOR PARTS OF A TYPICAL LONGARM.

6 7

1 BUTT-PLATE	7 MUZZLE
2 COMB	8 BUTT OR STOCK
3 LOCK	9 SMALL OF THE STOCK
4 HAMMER	10 TRIGGER
5 BREECH	11 TRIGGER-GUARD
6 BARREL	12 FORE END

HOW TO WEAR THE KILT

First, are you entitled to wear a particular tartan – the woven, check-like pattern of the fabric? Each highland clan has its own design and colors, though they are not necessarily of great antiquity. If you are not a Scot or of Scottish ancestry there are many to choose from, although you will run the risk of offending purists who consider you should not wear a tartan but some other plaid, and that you probably ought not to wear a kilt at all.

The original highland "belted plaid" was a mantle 6 feet wide by 12–18 feet long (1.8 x 4–5m) which was laid on the ground and folded into pleats until its length was reduced to about 5 feet (1.5m) with one end unpleated to cover the front of the body. The wearer lay upon it, the lower edge level with his knees, folded it around him, fastened it around the waist with a leather belt and threw the remaining plaid over his shoulder.

The modern kilt is just the lower part of the "belted plaid," with two sets of buckles sewn at either end of a length of fabric that wraps around the waist. This must be long enough to cover the bottom of the knees. Place one end of the fabric on the hip, buckles uppermost, and wind it across in front and then behind you. Push the buckle straps through the slots in the fabric that should now cover them, and do them up. The remaining fabric goes across your front and buckles on the other hip.

Over the kilt you should wear a sporran, a sort of purse threaded to a belt that is slung on the hips, purse to the front, protecting the crotch, as it were. It can be either of plain leather with plain tassels, or it can be much more decorative, trimmed with fur and silver. Either way, it is an extremely convenient place to keep your credit cards and whiskey miniatures. Now for your waistcoat and jacket. These are specially designed for wear with the kilt and can be either informal and tweedy-looking or more formal and black. Any old jacket will not do. Shirts should be plain-colored, preferably white. Ties should also be plain or tartan. For formal occasions, try a lace bib.

To finish off: socks must be calf-length and be of plain, heavy wool. An optional extra is the dirk, a small dagger. This is worn inside one of the socks, handle protruding at the top of the calf. Shoes? That is up to you. You can buy the special shoes that are suited to formal occasions. Otherwise, plain shoes or brogues, rather than high-fashion shoes, are best. As for what you wear underneath your kilt. Well, that would be telling, wouldn't it?

HOW TO GET INTO A LIFE PRESERVER

LEARN THIS ONE OFF BY HEART OR PRACTICE IN A SHALLOW POOL – THE TRICK IS HARDER THAN YOU'D THINK, AND YOU WON'T HAVE THE BOOK WITH YOU IN THE WATER!

1. GRIP THE NEAR EDGE OF THE LIFE PRESERVER, WITH YOUR HANDS **ON TOP.**
2. PULL THE RING CLOSE TO YOUR CHIN, THEN PUSH DOWNWARD.
3. AS THE RING REACHES A VERTICAL POSITION, PUSH THE BOTTOM EDGE AWAY.
4. AS THE RING FALLS OVER YOUR HEAD, PUSH YOUR ARMS AND SHOULDERS THROUGH IT.

How to follow the language of the fan

Fan language, much used by fashionable ladies in the 18th century, was of help in carrying out love affairs under the chaperones watchful eye.

Here are some of the more useful signals:

With the fan open
I love you hide the eyes behind the fan
I do not love you give quick brushing away movements, holding the fan pointing downward, the back of the hand on top
You are welcome hold the fan palm uppermost and extend toward the other person
I must avoid you hold the fan over the head

With the fan closed, and holding its tip to the face
Yes touch the right cheek
No touch the left cheek
Hush touch the lips
Do not give us away touch the left ear
I love you point toward the heart
Go away, you're boring me yawn behind the fan

HOW TO DRINK Чай

Pronounced *chai*, Russian tea seems to center on the *samovar*, always steaming and ready to provide a refreshing drink. But the *samovar*, an urn with a coiled heating tube inside, fueled by charcoal, is not really necessary, for its tap does not deliver *chai* but hot water, although the little platform on its top is useful for keeping the teapot hot. Any source of boiling water will serve. You need broad-leaved tea of the Chinese type, which makes a clear, light-colored brew. Warm a ceramic pot (metal pots slightly affect the taste) with some of the hot water, pour it away, put in a spoonful of tea per person, add boiling water and allow it to brew for several minutes. If you've got a samovar leave the pot on top to keep it hot. Pour into glasses, not into cups. The glasses should have metal, preferably silver, holders, because the glass will be very hot to hold. Add a slice of lemon. If you must sweeten it with a little sugar. Don't drink it from cups, it doesn't taste quite the same, and do drink it piping hot.

How to track a fieldmouse

The fieldmouse's tiny tracks will probably only be visible in the snow; they consist of tiny footprints with curved marks of the tail through the center of the tracks.

HOW TO FOLD A NAPKIN INTO A FAN

To fold a napkin into a spectacular fan shape takes time, but the method is quite simple.

1. Lay the napkin on a table, and make a deep pleat at two opposite edges.
2. Fold it in half, with the pleats inside.
3. Next form one inch pleats, back and forth, from end to end.
4. Place the thinner end in a glass, and pinch down the inner fold of each pleat at the top edge, alternately at each side. This will fill out the final impressive shape, and both glass and napkin are ready to place on the dinner table.

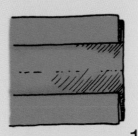

1

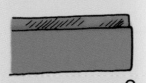

2

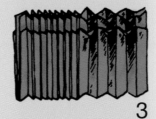

3

4

HOW TO REMOVE BAGS UNDER THE EYES

A TEMPORARY METHOD FOR REMOVING BAGS UNDER THE EYES IS TO SMEAR UNCOOKED EGG-WHITE OVER THE AFFECTED SKIN; AS IT DRYS THE SKIN WILL BECOME TAUT, BUT THE EFFECTS ONLY LAST FOR AN HOUR OR TWO.

© DIAGRAM

How to play the spoons

Choose a pair of stout spoons, and hold them, bowl to back, between the middle finger and the thumb, with the forefinger between them, so that they can pivot and the bowl of one can clap into the bowl of the other. You can use them as a pair of clappers by bouncing them off your knee, or rub them up and down the folds in your coat sleeve to get a trilling effect.

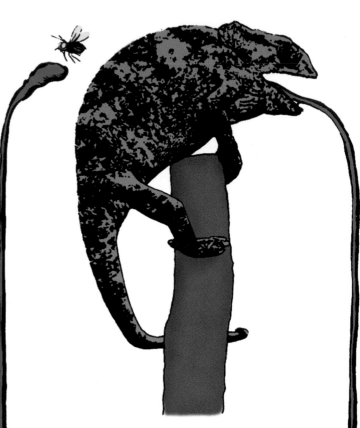

HOW TO KEEP A CHAMELEON

Chameleons need to be kept in a vivarium at a temperature of 75–85°F (24–29°C) with twigs and branches for them to climb on. The foliage should be sprayed daily with water for them to sip and they need a varied diet with plenty of caterpillars and flies which they catch by shooting out their long, sticky tongue. They move slowly and deliberately and can change color to camouflage themselves to match their background. Sadly they do not live for very long.

HOW TO CHEAT FATTENING SQUASH/VEGETABLE MARROWS

Do you want to win at your local vegetable show? Select a young growing squash and thread a strand of yarn through its neck. Bury a large jar by the plant with its rim level with the surface of the earth. Fill the jar with water, stir in some sugar and lower the end of the yarn into it. The yarn will act as a wick, drawing up the sugar solution and feeding the squash. Keep the jar well supplied with sugar-water and your neighbors will be amazed at the size of your entry.

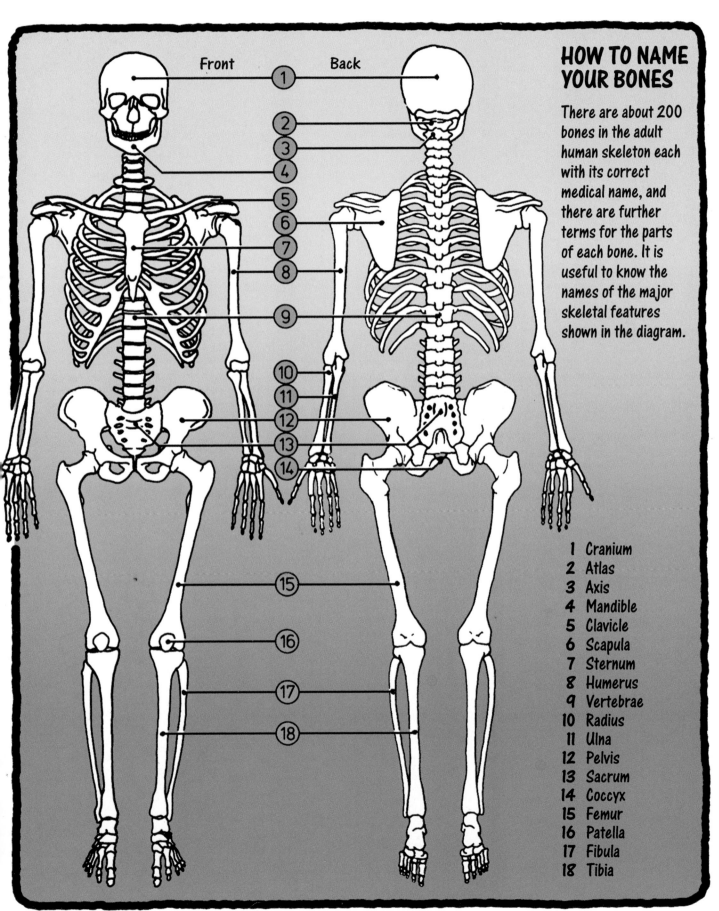

Front   Back

HOW TO NAME YOUR BONES

There are about 200 bones in the adult human skeleton each with its correct medical name, and there are further terms for the parts of each bone. It is useful to know the names of the major skeletal features shown in the diagram.

1 Cranium
2 Atlas
3 Axis
4 Mandible
5 Clavicle
6 Scapula
7 Sternum
8 Humerus
9 Vertebrae
10 Radius
11 Ulna
12 Pelvis
13 Sacrum
14 Coccyx
15 Femur
16 Patella
17 Fibula
18 Tibia

© DIAGRAM

HOW TO MIX CONCRETE

1 2 3 4 5

Concrete is a mixture of four elements. Aggregates (usually small stones, broken up brick or slag), sand, cement and water. An excess of any one of these elements makes the substance weak or unstable. The substances vary in proportion depending on the form of setting required. For foundations or heavy duty work: 1 part cement, 2$\frac{1}{2}$ parts sand, 4 parts coarse aggregate. For paving and thin sections: 1 part cement, 2 parts sand, 3 parts coarse aggregate. For step treads or bedding-in slabs, one part cement and 3 parts sand. When storing materials, care must be taking to keep them dry and clean at all times.
(**1**) Store sacks off the ground and cover them.
(**2**) Store half-used sacks in plastic bags.
(**3**) Keep aggregates and sand apart on a smooth flat surface.

Mixing concrete
Measure the ingredients, using a box or bucket, onto a clean, flat surface (**4**). This is usually a sheet of iron, wooden board, or

How to make a daisy chain

Pick daisies with stalks over 1 inch (25mm) long. Part way down the stalk make a slit along its length with your fingernail or a knife. Thread another slit daisy through the first slit. When your chain is long enough, choose a daisy with a longer stem and make a bigger slit in it. Thread this lasts stem onto your chain. Carefully open up the slit and pass it over the head of the first daisy.

How to know when Easter Day will be

In the Western Church, Easter is celebrated on the first Sunday after the full moon on or after March 21 – but it must not be before March 22 or after April 25.

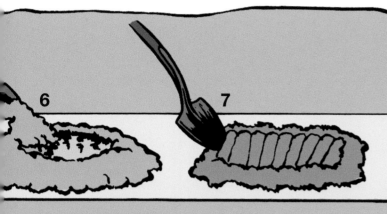

6 7

existing concrete floor. First measure out the sand evenly over the area, then measure out the cement and spread on top. Mix together until they are an even gray, and then add in the aggregate in the same way (**5**). Make a hole in the center of the pile and gradually add water,

mixing from the edge as you go (**6**). Thoroughly turn until the concrete is a smooth thick (paste-like) substance. Avoid adding water too quickly or in excess. You should be able to mark the final mixture with a shovel, so that the mark does not fill in (**7**).

HOW TO UNDERSTAND ANIMAL LANGUAGE

Animals communicate in a number of ways, with coloration, body posture, movement and vocalization. The message from the brightly striped caterpillar reads "Don't eat me. I'm bitter." The skunk's striped tail is a similar warning to leave well enough alone. The sudden flip of the rabbit's scut to show the white presses the panic button for the whole warren, just as the shape of the hawk overhead causes small birds to scatter for shelter. Man has always known some animal languages since, as a primitive hunter, his success depended very much on close observation. Today more and more animal signals are being studied. However, watching closely is not always the answer. The bear is considered the most dangerous of performing circus animals. A trainer, even though his safety depends on it, finds it very difficult to gauge a bear's mood. Lack of facial muscles and markings make the bear pretty inscrutable – except presumably to other bears.

How to empty bottles quickly

If you have to wash out a large number of bottles, the slowest part of the process is emptying out the water. If you give the upturned bottle a couple of shakes with a circular motion, a whirlpool effect lets the air rush in and the water will flow out twice as fast.

HOW TO SPLIT A LOG

INSTEAD OF TRYING TO SAW A LOG IN HALF, MAKE A SLIT IN THE TOP OF THE LOG WITH A SAW AND INSERT A METAL WEDGE (A).

STRIKE THE WEDGE SHARPLY SEVERAL TIMES WITH A MALLET (B), AND THE LOG SHOULD SPLIT ALONG THE GRAIN.

How to avoid your creditors

According to a medieval herbalist, putting poppy seeds in your shoes will enable you to walk unnoticed among people to which you owe money.

HOW TO FEED A PANDA

THE MENU SERVED TWICE DAILY TO PANDAS AT THE NATIONAL ZOO, WASHINGTON D.C., CONSISTS OF 4 OR 5 CARROTS, 4 OR 5 APPLES, 2 SWEET POTATOES, RICE MIXED WITH MILK AND VITAMINS, 20 POUNDS (9KG) OF BAMBOO, AND 2 DOG BISCUITS. AS BETWEEN-MEAL SNACKS THEY ARE SOMETIMES GIVEN HONEY SANDWICHES.

HOW TO KNOW WHAT CLOUDS BRING

1 Cirrus are fine wispy clouds made from tiny spikelets of ice. They are sometimes called "mares' tails," and if more cloud follows them it is likely to rain.

2 Fine Weather Cumulus are small fluffy clouds, a little like those in children's drawings. If they are well spread out in a clear sky you can expect fine weather. But if before noon they form into rows, or "streets" as they are called, then you can expect the weather to deteriorate.

3 Cirrostratus are high-flying clouds frequently giving an almost complete overcast. Halos around the Sun usually mean that rain is on its way.

4 Altocumulus these are long, flattish-looking clouds which frequently herald changeable weather.

5 Cumulonimbus Big "anvil heads" often mean thunder, lightning and sometimes hail. The upcurrents in these clouds are very powerful. Watch and you will see the clouds continually changing shape.

6 Cumulus are big bumpy looking clouds which often mean showery weather.

HOW TO KNOW YOUR PATRON SAINT

The idea of patron saints, that is saints with special power to intercede with God for particular purposes or for people following particular occupations, arose in the Middle Ages. The reasons are sometimes obscure, and often attached to legends for which there is no foundation. Here is a small selection:

Occupation	Patron saint(s)	Reason for choice
Accountants and bookkeepers	Matthew	Taxgatherer
Aviators	Joseph of Copertino	Levitator
Artists	Luke	Said to have been artist
Athletes	Sebastian	Martyred by arrows
Authors	Francis de Sales	Writer
Bakers	Elizabeth of Hungary	Legend says she concealed bread for the poor in her apron
Blacksmiths	Dunstan	Metalworker
Cabdrivers	Fiacre	First Paris cab stand was outside Hotel de Fiacre
Carpenters	Joseph	Carpenter
Cooks	Lawrence	Martyred by roasting
Dentists	Apollonia	Had her teeth knocked out during martyrdom
Editors	John Bosco	Writer and teacher
Farmers	Isidore Farm	Laborer
Gardeners	Dorothea, Fiacre, Phocas	As Dorothea was being led to martyrdom she sent fruit to one who mocked her; the others were gardeners
Lawyers	Ivo, Thomas More	Both lawyers
Librarians	Jerome	Scholar and writer
Miners	Barbara	Her father, who martyred her, was killed by lightning; hence she became patron of protection from lightning, and of miners who blew things up
Musicians	Cecilia, Dunstan, Gregory the Great	Cecilia is said "to have sung to God in her heart"; the others reformed Church music and liturgy
Nurses	Camillus de Lellis	Hospital bursar
Physicians	Cosmas and Damian, Luke, Pantaleon	All physicians
Poets	Cecilia	By association with music
Printers	Augustine of Hippo	Writer
Sailors	Brendan, Christopher, Cuthbert,	Brendan and Cuthbert sailed on missionary journeys; Erasmus – martyred by having his bowels wound out by a windlass, a piece of nautical apparatus. Christopher – see Travelers below
Scientists	Albert the Great	13th-century teacher of all sorts of subjects, including the sciences
Scouts	George	By tradition a soldier; but his existence is doubted
Secretaries	Cassian	Schoolmaster, stabbed to death with pens
Soldiers	Adrian, George, Joan of Arc, Martin, Sebastian	All soldiers at some stage in their careers
Surgeons	Cosmas and Damian	Physicians
Teachers	John Baptist de la Salle,	John was an educationist; a scholar and reformer
Television, radio, tele-communications and postal workers	Archangel Gabriel	By tradition, the angel of the Annunciation
Travelers	Christopher	Legend says he carried the Christ-child across a river; his existence is doubted

How to climb a rope

Begin by gripping the rope with both hands in front of your face and securing it between the sole of one foot and the top of the other (a).

Climb by moving first your hand grip and then your foot grip farther up the rope (b).

158

How to repel cavalry

How to keep an octopus

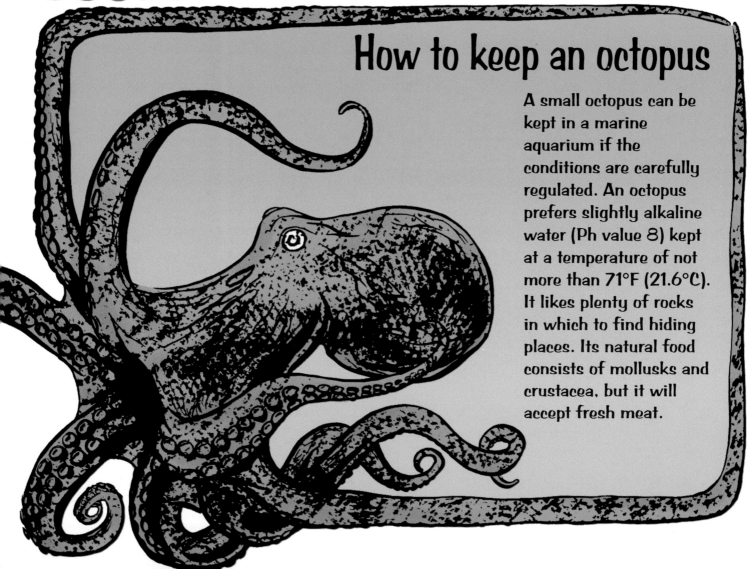

A small octopus can be kept in a marine aquarium if the conditions are carefully regulated. An octopus prefers slightly alkaline water (Ph value 8) kept at a temperature of not more than 71°F (21.6°C). It likes plenty of rocks in which to find hiding places. Its natural food consists of mollusks and crustacea, but it will accept fresh meat.

NEXT TIME YOU DREAM OF BEING STONEWALL JACKSON OR NAPOLEON BUONAPARTE, AND ARE ATTACKED BY CAVALRY, HERE'S WHAT TO DO! CAVALRY ALWAYS TRY TO ATTACK THE ENEMY'S UNPROTECTED FLANKS, TO BREAK UP THEIR FORMATION: SO ADOPT A FORMATION THAT HAS NO FLANKS – A SQUARE. THE THEORY IS BASED ON HORSE SENSE. HORSES WILL NOT CHARGE STRAIGHT AT AN OBSTACLE THEY THINK THEY CAN'T JUMP, ESPECIALLY IF THE OBSTACLE IS A HUMAN "WALL" BRISTLING WITH BAYONETS. THEY WILL SHY TO ONE SIDE OR PULL UP SHORT, LEAVING THEIR RIDERS HELPLESS TARGETS, MILLING AROUND YOUR SQUARE.

How to recognize comedians and tragedians
If you went to a Greek or Roman theater in classical times you only had to look at an actor's feet. If he was wearing light, soft shoes (called *socci* – yes, the word does have a familiar sound) he was a comedian in a comedy; if he was wearing high boots with thick soles (called *colthurni*) he was appearing in a tragedy. The colthurnus later became known as the "buskin" from which the English word "busker" is derived for a traveling or street entertainer.

HOW TO BUILD A LOG CABIN
Choose your cabin site. Stake out the cabin perimeter with the help of pegs and string, making sure that its corners are at 90° angles. Four large cornerstones should be used as foundations; other stones embedded and tamped in along the lines of your walls will help stability. Chop your timber into logs of suitable lengths.

Set down the front and back logs first. Fit the two end logs in between, laying them on top of the front and back logs, use U-shaped notches to marry them together. Notch logs on the lower side only, so that the notch fits snugly over the log beneath. Once each log is in place it should be spiked into the log below with 12-inch (30cm) spikes: One at each end and at intervals of 4–6 feet (1.2–1.8m) in between. Mark the center of each log with a vertical line, then you can check their alignment to make sure that the foundation is still square. If you mark a vertical line through the center of the end of each log you will be able to check that the laying is vertical. Horizontal level can be checked by balancing a board along the top log and placing a spirit level on it.

Trim the logs carefully where you want to insert windows or doors and nail planks or split logs along the ends of the logs to make a frame. Keep openings small to avoid heat loss. At about 6 feet (1.8m) high or a little higher begin to shorten the side logs to create the roof slope. Plan the slope to match the final height you need. On a small cabin you can split the roof timbers along their length to give a level upper surface and then lay half timbers vertically up the finished slope, extending them beyond the walls to give an overhang. Pack the spaces between them with peat or turf to keep the roof watertight.

If you do not want to roof with logs, chop the ends to a slant anyway, securing each log to the one below with spikes. A log serving as ridgepole should be spiked into the last of the side pieces. From this rafters should be attached roughly 18 inches (45cm) apart running from the ridgepole down to the front and back and overlapping the walls by a foot or so. Roof boards can then be laid lengthwise across the rafters and a final covering of asphalt, crushed slate, shingles or tar paper added.

HOW TO MIX CHINESE INK

ORIENTAL INK COMES IN HARD STICKS. TO MIX IT, HOLD THE STICK UPRIGHT AND RUB IT ON A FLAT SURFACE TO WHICH YOU HAVE ADDED A LITTLE WATER; IT WILL TAKE A LONG TIME TO PRODUCE THE DENSE COLOR USED FOR MOST ORIENTAL CALLIGRAPHY.

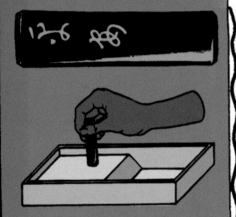

HOW TO IMPROVE YOUR MEMORY

EAT CHERVIL; ACCORDING TO ONE ANCIENT SOURCE, THIS WILL PROD THE MEMORY OF OLD PEOPLE.

HOW TO THROW A LASSO

A   B

1

IT IS POINTLESS TO TRY THROWING A LASSO MADE FROM UNSUITABLE ROPE. YOU NEED GOOD MANILA ROPE, ABOUT 3/8 INCHES (1CM) THICK, TO PROVIDE THE RIGHT DEGREE OF STIFFNESS. THE BEST LENGTH IS ABOUT 35 FEET (10.5M).

PREPARING THE ROPE: FORM A LOOP ABOUT 4 INCHES (10CM) LONG (A,B). PLACE THE OTHER END THROUGH THE LOOP TO FORM A NOOSE ABOUT 4 FEET (1,2M) LONG WHEN IT HANGS, HOLD IT AS SHOWN (C). COIL THE REST OF THE ROPE AND TRANSFER IT TO THE LEFT HAND, WITH THE STRAND THAT LEADS TO THE NOOSE GRIPPED BETWEEN THUMB AND FOREFINGER (D).

HOW TO KEEP A HEDGEHOG HAPPY

IF YOU SEE A HEDGEHOG NEAR YOUR HOUSE, AND WANT TO GIVE IT A TREAT, PUT OUT A SHALLOW SAUCER OF BREAD AND MILK AT NIGHT. HEDGEHOGS ALSO LIKE MEAT SCRAPS, BUT THESE MAY ATTRACT MORE UNDESIRABLE ANIMAL VISITORS!

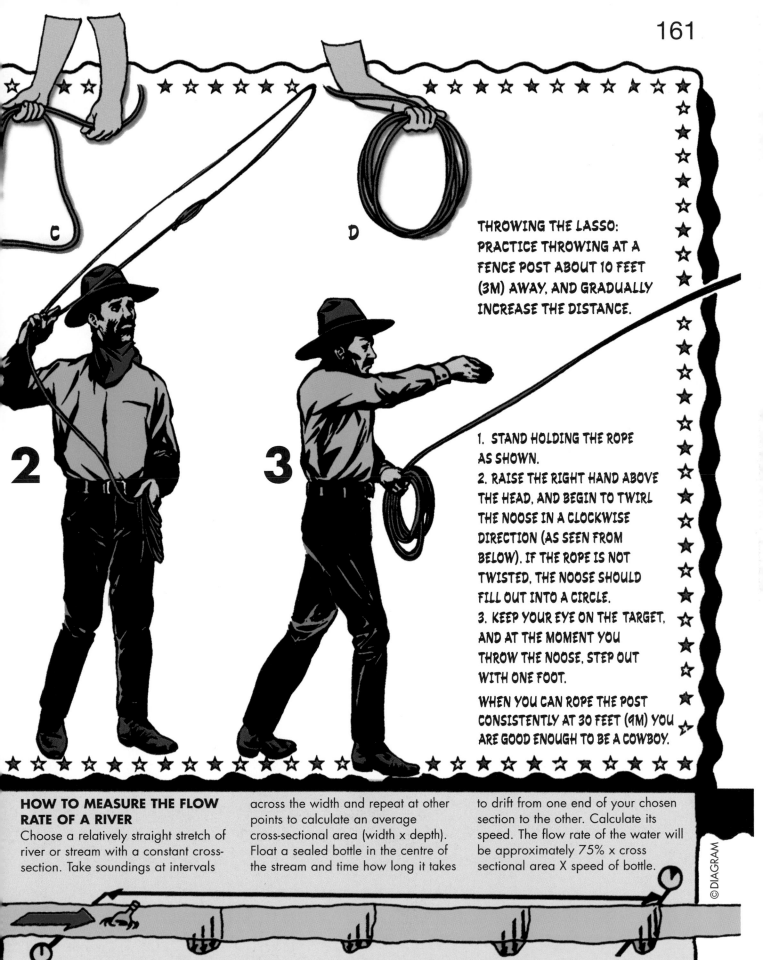

C

D

2

3

THROWING THE LASSO: PRACTICE THROWING AT A FENCE POST ABOUT 10 FEET (3M) AWAY, AND GRADUALLY INCREASE THE DISTANCE.

1. STAND HOLDING THE ROPE AS SHOWN.

2. RAISE THE RIGHT HAND ABOVE THE HEAD, AND BEGIN TO TWIRL THE NOOSE IN A CLOCKWISE DIRECTION (AS SEEN FROM BELOW). IF THE ROPE IS NOT TWISTED, THE NOOSE SHOULD FILL OUT INTO A CIRCLE.

3. KEEP YOUR EYE ON THE TARGET, AND AT THE MOMENT YOU THROW THE NOOSE, STEP OUT WITH ONE FOOT.

WHEN YOU CAN ROPE THE POST CONSISTENTLY AT 30 FEET (9M) YOU ARE GOOD ENOUGH TO BE A COWBOY.

HOW TO MEASURE THE FLOW RATE OF A RIVER

Choose a relatively straight stretch of river or stream with a constant cross-section. Take soundings at intervals across the width and repeat at other points to calculate an average cross-sectional area (width x depth). Float a sealed bottle in the centre of the stream and time how long it takes to drift from one end of your chosen section to the other. Calculate its speed. The flow rate of the water will be approximately 75% x cross sectional area X speed of bottle.

HOW TO SEAT GUESTS AT TABLE

At formal dinner parties in the western world the host and hostess sit at either end of the table, giving it two "heads". The gentleman whom they wish to honor most, or whom they consider most important because of rank, position or interest, sits on the hostess's right; the lady of greatest honor or importance on the host's right. The places on the side of both host and hostess are assigned to the next most important people and so on to adjoining places down the table. The sexes are placed alternately and men face women across the table if it is an equally mixed guest list, which is what most people aim at. Nowadays, if entertaining privately, formal precedence will give way to the host or hostess's opinion as to who would most interest whom as conversational partners across the table or to the side. At official banquets the rules of rank and diplomatic precedence should be followed. This places the guests of "least importance" in the center of the table, farthest from the host and hostess. In private it is usual for members of the family or close friends of the hosts to be placed among other guests in the center to look after guests who are too far away to be given the host and hostess' attention. In medieval times, in the household of a king or great lord, the host and his most important guests would be seated at one table, and lesser ranks sat separately. The ceremonial salt, a symbolic rather than a purely functional salt holder which was usually a fine example of the goldsmith or silversmith's art, was placed at the nobleman's left. The most important guests sat on his right, although sometimes with quite a wide gap between him and the first guests, especially if there was a big difference in rank. Guests of lesser rank sat on the host's left, below the salt. They were served by a lower grade of servant who did not carry napkins and the gap before their places was greater. Thus "below the salt" came to indicate those not considered important or worthy of a great man's attention.

HOW TO RAISE SILKWORMS

Obtain eggs of the moth **Bombyx mori**. These will hatch into caterpillars which must be fed on the leaves of the mulberry tree. Eggs may be kept refrigerated until leaves are available – May in northern temperate climates. Hatching takes eight to ten days in a warm room. When the caterpillars first hatch and are very small keep them in a cage with fine mesh sides. As they grow larger keep them on an open tray; they will not crawl away. Lay mulberry leaves flat on the bottom of the cage or tray. Feed the silkworms twice a day. As the caterpillars grow, place straw or woodwool around the edges of the tray to provide a place where they can spin their cocoons of silk. The moths will emerge from the cocoons in about five weeks. They cannot fly. Line the tray with paper on which they will then lay their eggs. Store the paper with the eggs in a box and keep it in a cool place ready for hatching next spring.

Since the emerging moths usually damage the silk of their cocoons they are normally killed by heating the completed cocoon to a high temperature for a short time and the silk can then be unwound.

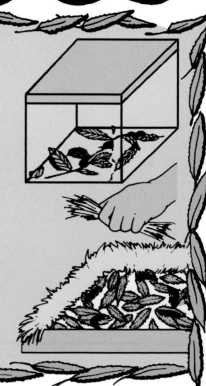

HOW TO TELL A BACTRIAN FROM A DROMEDARY

The two best known members of the camel family are easily distinguished – one has only one hump and the other, two. But which is which? Easy – the Dromedary is shaped like a letter "D" on its side, and the Bactrian like a letter "B".

How to avoid the evil eye

A very ancient belief, particularly strong in Mediterranean countries, attributes to some people the power to bring harm just by a look – one reason, perhaps, why few people like being stared at. To protect yourself from the malignant gaze you reflect the evil back upon the ill-wisher with the image of another eye. Paint it on your walls, as ancient Egyptians did, on the bows of your boat, as fishermen still do in many countries, or wear a glass eye amulet, like the blue ones popular among tourists to the Greek Cyclades. Those Greek eyes have blue irises, though blue beads, not necessarily made to look like eyes, will also give protection – hence all those blue faience beads on Egyptian mummies. Hang blue beads in your house, on your pets and livestock, and wear them on your body. Another effective amulet is the pattern of a hand – the Hand of Fatima, Muhammad's daughter, which you may paint around the doorway of your house. Again, a blue color strengthens its effect. A pair of horns set up on the roof also offer defiance to such unknown enemies and to distract them you may make, or wear the representation of, a powerful or obscene gesture, the horned hand or "cornuta" gesture of Italy and Malta, or the "fig" sign in which the thumb is squeezed between the fingers.

HOW TO TELL THE SEX OF AN EARWIG

Look at the pincers at its rear end. Those of the male (**a**) are curved, almost semi-circular; the female's are straight (**b**), just meeting at the tip.

a

b

How to make a camel dung cigarette lighter

Find a small, lidded tin (the kind that some throat lozenges come in is ideal), a piece of flint and a piece of ironstone. Fill your tin with dried camel dung, or horse dung or any fibrous type of animal dung. Use the raised lid of the tin to provide shelter from the wind, strike the flint upon the ironstone so that the sparks fall on the dung, blow gently – you should have a glowing patch of dung from which to light your cigarette. This type of lighter was used by soldiers during the North African desert campaigns of World War II.

How to cross the line

If you're sailing in a ship across the Equator for the first time you may find yourself on trial. You'll be brought before the court of Neptune, God of the Sea, for "trial." b You may be lathered and roughly shaved, and almost certainly ducked in the ship's swimming pool. It's all good-humored fun, but it used to be an occasion for some very rough horseplay. At the end of it all you'll get a certificate saying that you've "Crossed the Line."

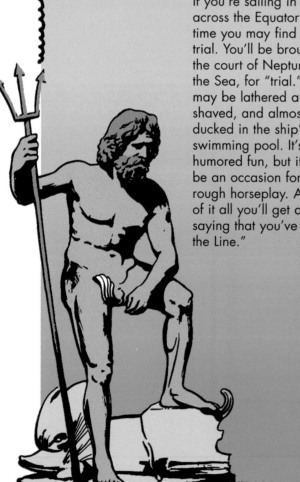

HOW TO RECOGNIZE A GREEK VASE

Greek vases were made in a number of basic shapes, each matched to its purpose so well that they were seldom varied.

1. The Krater:
A wide-mouthed container for mixing wine and water.
a) Column Krater
b) Volute Krater
c) Calyx Krater

2. The Amphora:
A large urn used for storing supplies. This might also have a pointed base for sticking into sand or soft earth.

3. The Hydria:
For carrying water, with two handles placed for easy lifting and with a third handle for pouring.

4. The Oenochoe:
A pitcher, the standard vessel for serving wine.

5. The Kylix:
A two-handled drinking cup.

6. The Lekythos:
An oil jar.

1a
1b
1c
2
3
4
5
6

HOW TO MAKE IT RAIN

If clouds pass overhead but do not release their moisture you can fly through them in an airplane and release silver-iodine smoke to "seed" them. This supercools and condenses water droplets in clouds, but is not always effective. Another method is to release water drops into clouds which collide and coalesce with the cloud's water droplets and so set off a rainfall pattern within the cloud. If no clouds appear you could try a rain dance. Throughout recorded time attempts have been made to influence rainfall. The snake dance of the Hopi Indians of North America, in which the dancers hold rattlesnakes in their mouths, is such a dance. The Omaha Indians, in periods of drought, would dance four times around a large pot of water. The leader would then fill his mouth with water and spit the water into the air to imitate rainfall. The pot would then be turned over and the valuable water allowed to spill on the ground. The dancers then attempted to drink the spilled water. The dance ended with all the dancers spitting water into the air.

HOW TO CLEAN RUSTY NEEDLES

Rusty needles or pins can be cleaned by sticking them several times into a pincushion stuffed with emery powder.

How to gain an indulgence

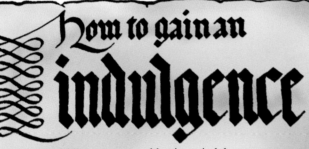

During the middle ages you could gain an indulgence, which would let you off time in purgatory by making a pilgrimage or going on a Crusade. The prayers and good works of the saints and of all holy lives and the merits of Christ gave a surplus of goodness which could be set against our sins and earn remission for the deserving. Careful inquiry would establish which shrine would offer the greatest sums of remission for a visit and the Church would sometimes announce special times of pilgrimage when a plenary indulgence could be obtained, remission of all penance due. If a person died before completing a pilgrimage they might still gain their indulgence. Others could undertake to make a pilgrimage to fulfill a vow made by someone who had died and gain indulgence for the deceased. With the Crusades it became possible to pay someone to go to fight on your behalf and eventually a system developed by which the Church accepted cash payments instead of the performance of physical penance – one of the key causes of the protestant reformation. However these indulgences would not have been truly effective without true repentance on the part of the sinner.

Today the attitude of the Roman Catholic Church is very clear. In 1967 Pope Paul VI restated the doctrine of the Treasury of the Church (the store of goodness) but made it clear that a penitent must be free of all attachment to sin, even venal sin, before a plenary indulgence can take effect, and they must make sacramental confession, take communion and pray for "the Pope's intentions" (that is, the whole Church on Earth). Remission is dependent on the spiritual state of the sinner, and the practice of attaching a length of time to partial indulgences has been abolished, since no one can compute the amount of remission gained. An approved collection of prayers and good works which would count towards the gaining of an indulgence is contained in *Enchiridion Indulgentiarum*, published in 1950.

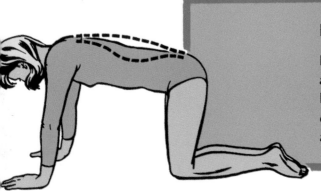

HOW TO EASE BACKACHE

Kneeling on all fours and alternately raising and hollowing your back is an excellent way of relieving the aches in your lower back.

How to play
AGON

Players Agon, or Queen's Guard, is an interesting board game for two. It can be played with counters on an improvised board. Players attempt to position pieces in the winning pattern.

The board is in the shape of a hexagon with 91 small hexagons in alternating light and dark bands.

Pieces There are two sets of pieces. Each set consists of one "queen" and six "guards"; the sets must be distinguishable from each other.

Objective The game is won when one player succeeds in positioning his queen on the center hexagon and his six guards on the hexagons immediately surrounding it.

Start of play There are two methods of starting play; either the pieces are positioned as shown, or each player positions his pieces in turn, one at a time, anywhere he likes on the board.

Moves Each player moves one piece in a turn. A piece may only be moved into a vacant hexagon. A player who touches one of his pieces must move that piece or forfeit his turn. Except when a piece is trapped between opposing pieces, it may be moved one hexagon sideways or toward the center of the board (**a**). If a guard is trapped between two opposing pieces (**b**) its owner must, in his next turn, move it to any hexagon in the outside band. If a queen is trapped between two opposing pieces (**c**), its owner must, in his next turn, move it to any vacant hexagon that his opponent requires. If more than one piece is trapped, the player must move them back one in each turn. Guards may be moved back in any order, but a queen must always be moved before a guard. Only a queen may be placed in the center hexagon. A player forfeits the game, if, when the center hexagon is empty, he positions all his six guards in the band immediately surrounding it.

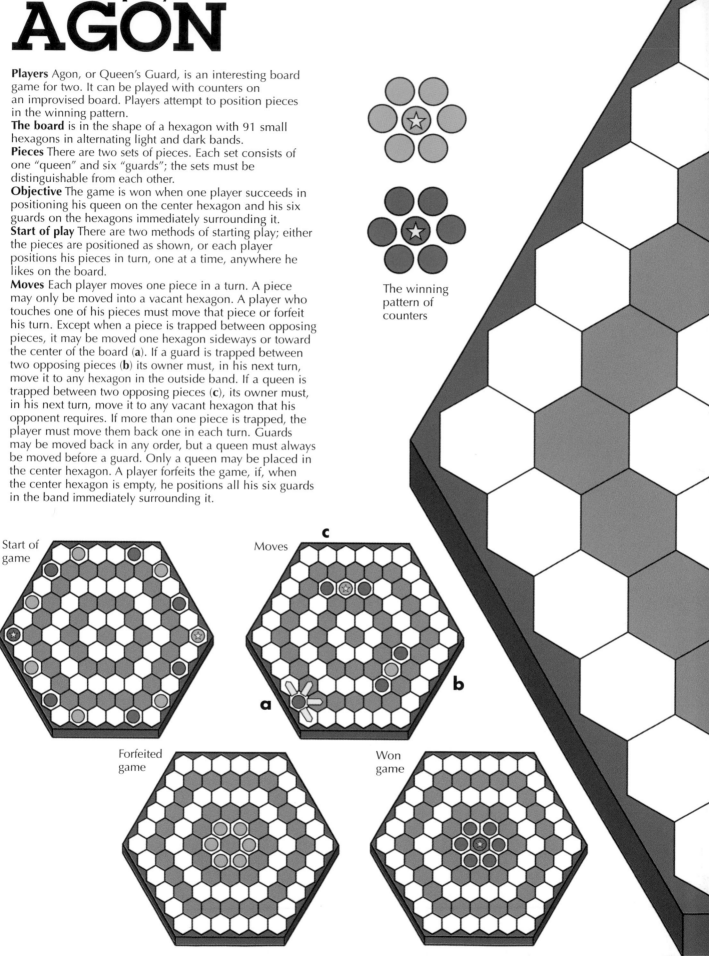

The winning pattern of counters

Start of game

Moves

Forfeited game

Won game

How to change from the dog to the dragon

The traditional Chinese calendar – which was also used by the Japanese – worked on a cycle of 60 years. Each year bore a name relating to the five elements wood, fire, earth, metal and water counted twice to form a cycle of 10, and an animal name corresponding to the twelve signs of the zodiac. For practical purposes the Chinese now use the Gregorian (western) calendar.

A Year
B Animal
C Sign of Zodiac
D Element

A	B	C	D
1981	Cock	Capricorn	Metal
1982	Dog	Aquarius	Water
1983	Boar	Pisces	Water
1984	Rat	Aries	Wood

1981 ⌐ ⌐ ⌐ ⌐ ⌐ ⌐ ⌐ ⌐ ⌐ ⌐ **19**

HOW TO POLISH STONE

Slate and marble can both be polished with an abrasive disk. Pour water onto the stone to act as a lubricant (**1**) and apply the disk in small circular movements (**2**). A slurry will form which should be washed off when the stone is polished sufficiently (**3**). Wax polish is then applied (**4**). Seal slate with a polyurethane varnish.

Brush marble occasionally with a mixture of shellac and methylated spirit.
An abrasive powder such as rouge should be used for polishing granite.
Alabaster should be polished with a furniture polish.

1   2   3   4

HOW TO BE A VALET
Mrs Beeton, the 19th Century English authority on domestic subjects, lists the following duties of the gentleman's valet:

1. To supervise the master's wardrobe and dressing room, look after all the clothes, seeing to cleaning and repairs, and even select what he will wear.

2. To air and heat the dressing room, and lay out the clothes in the morning. To sharpen the razor, and prepare hot water and soap for shaving.

3. To cut the master's hair, and trim his beard and moustache.

4. To hand the master his hat, gloves and cane and open the door when he goes out.

A	B	C	D	A	B	C	D
1985	Ox	Taurus	Wood	1993	Cock	Capricorn	Water
1986	Tiger	Gemini	Fire	1994	Dog	Aquarius	Wood
1987	Hare	Cancer	Fire	1995	Boar	Pisces	Wood
1988	Dragon	Leo	Earth	1996	Rat	Aries	Fire
1989	Serpent	Virgo	Earth	1997	Ox	Taurus	Fire
1990	Horse	Libra	Metal	1998	Tiger	Gemini	Earth
1991	Sheep	Scorpio	Metal	1999	Hare	Cancer	Earth
1992	Monkey	Sagittarius	Water	2000	Dragon	Leo	Metal

2000

How to measure the distances of stars and planets

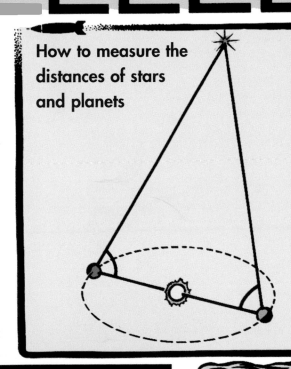

Measuring the distances of heavenly bodies is a simple problem in trigonometry. It's done by triangulation, just in the same way as surveyors calculate the heights of mountains. To measure the distance of an object in the solar system, such as the Sun, Moon or the planets, you take as long a baseline as possible on the Earth and take sightings of the planet concerned. These give you one side and two angles of a triangle. Using a table of sines, you can calculate the length of the other sides, which will give you the distance to the planet.

No baseline on the Earth is long enough for measuring the distance to the stars, so use as baseline the diameter of the Earth's orbit, 186,000,000 miles (299,000,000 km) – do this by taking your two sightings six months apart. For more distant stars astronomers use photometric readings, based on the luminosity of the stars.

©DIAGRAM

5. To pack the suitcases and make all the minor arrangements for a journey.
6. Perhaps act as a loader and carry the second gun when the master goes shooting.

How to make a hair rinse

"Queen, Queen Caroline, Washed her hair in turpentine" goes an old English song and, although turpentine is not recommended for your hair, many things have been used to rinse soap out of the hair when you wash it, including beer, vinegar, lemon water and numerous herbal infusions. Here is one suitable for blonde hair: Take a handful of camomile flowers and put them into about two cups of boiling water. Simmer for twenty minutes and cool. Add an equal quantity of boiled water and use as a final rinse.

HOW TO CALCULATE VOLUMES

1 The volume of a cube is the length of its base x the height x the length.
2 The volume of a pyramid is base x length x height, divided by three.
3 The volume of a cylinder is the length x radius squared x π
4 The volume of a cone is height x radius squared x π, divided by three.
5 The volume of a sphere is the radius cubed x π x four, divided by three.

π = 3.1415

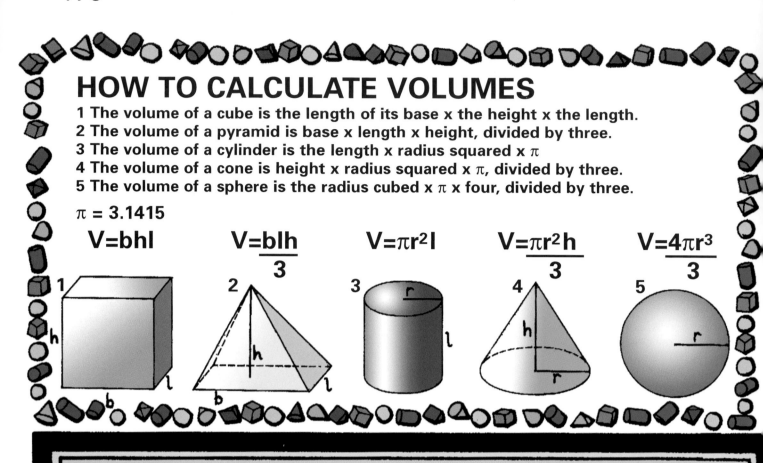

$V=bhl$ $V=\dfrac{blh}{3}$ $V=\pi r^2 l$ $V=\dfrac{\pi r^2 h}{3}$ $V=\dfrac{4\pi r^3}{3}$

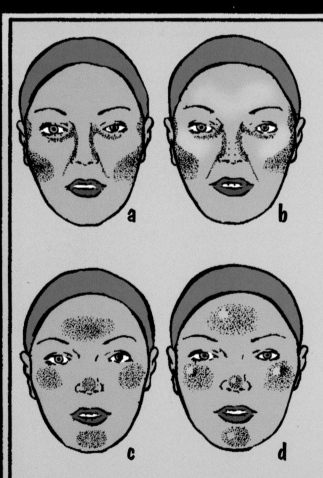

HOW TO LOOK FAT OR THIN

A perfectly ordinary looking person can be made to look fatter or thinner with carefully applied stage make-up. Basically you need one stick of dark make-up and one stick of light or white; cover your face with foundation before you start. For a lean face, put dark make-up in the hollows of the cheeks, the lines from nose to mouth, the lines under the eyes, the sides of the nose, and the hollows in front of the temples (a); add pale highlights to the cheek bones, the top of the nose and the brows (b). For a fat face, put a rosy glow of dark make-up on the cheeks, the chin, the tip of the nose and the forehead (c) and then highlight these with blobs of white; wear cotton pads inside the cheeks to complete the illusion (d).

HOW TO ROAST AN OX

You will need a huge open fireplace or a flat, clear, but sheltered area outdoors, away from trees and bushes that might catch fire. If outdoors dig a trench the length of your ox and about 2 feet (60cm) deep. Embed the upright members of your spit firmly beyond each end of the trench. If you have to improvise a spit you will need firm uprights with bearings to carry the spit shaft, a sturdy spit-shaft to which a cogged disk is welded or bolted and gearing to a smaller wheel which can be turned by an electric or gasoline motor. Have a handcrank on the end too, in case of breakdown, but hand-turning a 700 pound ox would demand several strong men working in rotation. Gear the shaft to turn very, very slowly. If you can make your spit-shaft in two pieces so that one fits over the other it will make getting the ox in position easier.

Get a wood fire going about 2 hours before you intend to start cooking; when you are nearly ready, beat it down to red-hot embers and pile on charcoal to come just above ground level. Skewer the carcass with the spit-shaft as close to the backbone as possible and fix it in position. You may want to wire the outside of the carcass to prevent pieces falling off. Hang a drip tray beneath it.

An average-size beast of perhaps 600 pounds (270kg) will take about 18 hours to cook. Keep the heat fierce to begin with to seal in the juices. If it starts cooking too slowly all the insides may begin to decompose before the process is completed. Do not worry if the outside gets charred, it's important that all the meat is cooked to avoid food poisoning. After a few hours you can open up the belly so that the middle can roast more quickly. Basting is not essential but will satisfy the onlookers' need to see some culinary activity. Reflectors and wind barriers on at least three sides will help cut down heat loss. Have plans for some sort of overhead shelter in case of rain and some fire buckets in case anything goes wrong. There must be a continual watch to supervise the cooking and keep off marauding dogs and humans. As an alternative you could use anthracite coal for the fire: it gives a steady, fierce, glowing heat, but it hasn't the attractive smell of wood smoke. If roasting an ox seems too ambitious, (and if you've ever done it, it is unlikely that you will want to do it again!) try a baron of beef instead (6–7 hours cooking) or a whole pig (8–9 hours), both of which are much easier to spit.

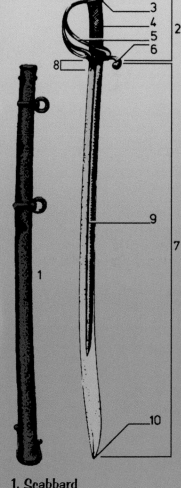

HOW TO NAME THE PARTS OF A SWORD

The sword was for centuries an important weapon and sumbol of status or power, and a special technology grew up around it. Here are the main parts named:

1. Scabbard
2. Hilt
3. Pommel
4. Grip
5. Guard
6. Quillon
7. Blade
8. Ricasso
9. Fuller (groove)
10. Point

©DIAGRAM

HOW TO IMPROVE YOUR POSTURE

STAND PERPENDICULAR TO A MIRROR AND ADJUST YOUR POSTURE SO THAT YOUR NECK, SHOULDERS, LOWER BACK, HIP JOINTS, KNEE JOINTS AND ANKLE JOINTS ARE ALIGNED VERTICALLY. THIS POSITION PUTS THE LEAST STRAIN ON THE JOINTS AND MUSCLES, AND SHOULD BE MAINTAINED WHENEVER POSSIBLE.

How to build an Arch

First build a simple wooden form or scaffold to support the arch while it is being constructed. Then take a series of wedge-shaped blocks of wood, stone or brick or other material, and set them flank to flank around the support. The keystone, which is larger and wedge-shaped to fit the space at the very top of the arch, is placed last; the arch should then be self-supporting and the supports can be removed. The blocks that make up the arch are called "voussoirs".

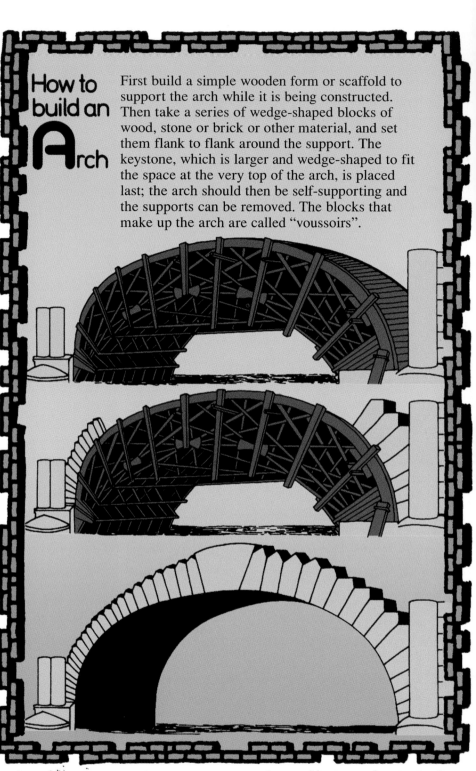

HOW TO MAKE A SQUARE KNOT OR REEF KNOT

Put the two ends of rope together and twist the first one over and under the second one as shown (a). Loop the second end above the knot, and twist the first end over and under it again (b). The knot is tightened by pulling both ends.

a

second end   first end

How to make invisible ink

There are several recipes for making invisible inks.

1 Dissolve 1 part of cobalt chloride and 1 part of gum arabic in 8 parts of water. Messages written in this ink show up in blue when the paper is heated.

2 Dissolve 10 grains of nickel chloride and 10 grains of cobalt chloride in 1 oz of water (metric equivalents – 0.65g of each of the chemicals in 29.5ml of water). This ink turns green when heated.

3 Use rice water as ink. The writing will show up when it is brushed over with tincture of iodine.

4 Write in milk. The writing will show up if you rub a dirty finger over it. This method has been used by prisoners to write messages between the lines of otherwise innocuous letters.

HOW TO REMOVE A DENT FROM A TABLE TENNIS BALL

Put it in hot water – you'll have to hold it down. The expansion of the air inside will gradually push the skin back into shape provided it is not actually cracked.

first end
second end

b

HOW TO CARRY OUT RESUSCITATION

Mouth-to-nose, or mouth-to-mouth, resuscitation is the easiest form of artificial respiration for the layman to apply and should be used in almost all circumstances except when there is severe injury to the face and mouth, when the casualty is pinned in a face-down position, or if vomiting occurs as breathing is re-established and interferes with resuscitation.

If a casualty is not breathing:

1 Make sure the air passages are not obstructed. Pull the head firmly back as far as it will go, bringing the lower jaw upward and forward until the front teeth meet. In this position the tongue cannot fall back and block the throat. Remove any solid or fluid blockage, scooping it out with the fingers if necessary and blotting up blood or vomit from the mouth with a handkerchief or tissue. This may be sufficient to restart breathing. This is a vital step, as without clearing the air passage there is no point going on to the next stage.

2 Place the mouth over the patient's nose, completely covering the nostrils. Close the patient's mouth and keep it closed by pressure on the jaw, which will also keep the head steady. Blow. Watch the patient's chest for movement. Remove your mouth, inhale, replace your mouth and blow again. Expel air deeply and slowly. Make sure that you have an airtight seal so that air does not escape as you blow.

3 If the chest does not rise and fall, check to make sure that the head position is correct (see diagram). If the nose is blocked, cover the patient's mouth with yours and pinch the nose to keep it closed as you exhale into the patient's mouth. With babies and young children cover both nose and mouth with your mouth. If you do not relish such close contact with the patient, place a clean handkerchief over the casualty's nose and mouth and breathe through it.

©DIAGRAM

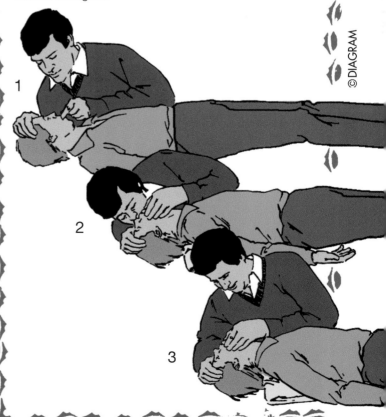

1

2

3

HOW TO DRILL FOR OIL

First, you need a geologist to tell you where oil is likely to be found. Then you bring a team of skilled and tough oilmen to the spot. They set up a derrick, up to 200 feet (60 m) high, from which the drill is operated. The drill bit is attached to a length of heavy steel pipe, about 30 feet (9 m) long. The pipe passes through a rotary table fixed in the floor of the derrick. An engine turns the table, and as the pipe is clamped to it, it also turns to operate the drill. The upper part of the pipe is attached by a swivel to a block and tackle hung from the top of the derrick. As soon as the first length of pipe is nearly into the ground, another is screwed onto it. As much as 10,000 feet (3,000 m) of pipe may be attached to reach a really deep source of oil. When the bit becomes worn, or a change of rock requires a different kind of bit, the pipe must be drawn – pulled up and unscrewed in lengths of several sections, which are stacked up inside the derrick.

To force the debris out of the hole, liquid mud is pumped down the pipe, so that the debris is carried up the space between the pipe and the shaft of the hole. The mud also helps to keep the drill bit cool. As drilling continues, the hole is lined with a bigger diameter steel pipe. When oil is struck the drill is drawn for the last time and a smaller pipe lowered down the hole to carry the oil to the surface. Some oilfields have natural gas or reservoirs of water that force the oil to the surface, but in others you may have to pump the oil out.

For drilling at sea a portable drilling platform that can be anchored to the seabed must be used.

How to be a lady's maid

A lady's maid served the mistress of the household in much the same way that a valet served the master (see "How to be a valet"). Mrs Beeton, the authority on household subjects in 19th-century England, listed these duties for a lady's maid:

1. In the morning, to bring the mistress a cup of tea, and prepare her bath.
2. To check and put away the clothes worn the day before, cleaning them as necessary.
3. To help the mistress dress.
4. To air the bedroom, clean it, and make the bed.
5. To prepare and lay out all changes of clothes required later that day.

In general, the lady's maid should be a capable dressmaker, hairdresser, and adviser on fashions. She would pack for the mistress, accompanying her and performing her usual duties on trips away from home.

PORT   STARBOARD

HOW TO TELL PORT FROM STARBOARD

MARINERS NEVER REFER TO "LEFT" AND "RIGHT". THE CORRECT SEAFARING TERMS ARE "PORT" AND "STARBOARD" RESPECTIVELY. IF YOU HAVE DIFFICULTY REMEMBERING WHICH IS WHICH, THINK IN TERMS OF THE ALPHABET:

L COMES BEFORE R

P COMES BEFORE S

HOW TO CLEAN STONE

Porous stone such as limestone develops a protective crust and if this is removed the stone may crumble. It is best cleaned with a strong jet of water and a stiff brush. Stains are removed by soaking blotting paper in white spirit or turpentine and applying it to the stain until the stain is absorbed by the blotting paper. Mildew is removed by soaking blotting paper in hot distilled water and applying. Non-porous stone such as granite is more robust and can be cleaned with a wire brush and detergent. White spirit removes oil stains. Clean marble with a solution of soap and water, and add half a cup of ammonia per bucket.

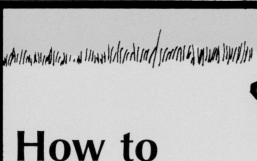

How to milk a goat

You will need a bucket and a small milking stool, which most people place at the side of the goat. If you milk from the rear, be prepared to step back quickly if the goat produces something other than milk! If you milk from the side, always make it the same side. Tie up the goat and wash its flank and udder with warm water. A proprietary udder cream should be wiped over the teats and your hands – it acts as both lubricant and antiseptic, and in winter will help to prevent chapped hands on you and chapped teats on the goat. Take one of the two teats in each hand, between your thumb and forefinger; gently squeeze thumb and forefinger together and then bring down the second, third and fourth fingers in rapid succession. Examine the first few squeezes of milk for evidence of mastitis, an unpleasant but easily curable complaint. If the milk is anything other than the expected creamy white, or if there are clots in it, the animal probably has mastitis and the milk should be thrown away. If the milk looks healthy, continue milking the animal gently and quietly, talking to it if you like, since goats enjoy having a fuss made of them.

How to determine the new year

New Year's Day is celebrated on January 1 in most parts of the world. Until 1582 the whole of Europe celebrated it on March 25, but then most countries adopted January 1 which the Romans had observed. England adopted it in 1752, when the English calendar was altered to come into step with the rest of Europe. Various religious groups observe different dates: the Jewish new year falls on the first day of the month Tishri, which varies between September 6 and October 5; the Chinese new year varies between January 20 and February 20; Muslims reckon time by a year of 354 or 355 days, so their new year is always changing.

How to play the knicky-knackers

The knicky-knackers were two pieces of the rib bone of an animal used as a percussion instrument by 19th-century minstrel bands. Rest one lightly on the finger tips of one hand, with the palm cupped to act as a resonator, and strike it with the other, held between the thumb and the first two fingers of the other hand.

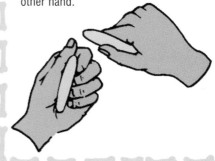

© DIAGRAM

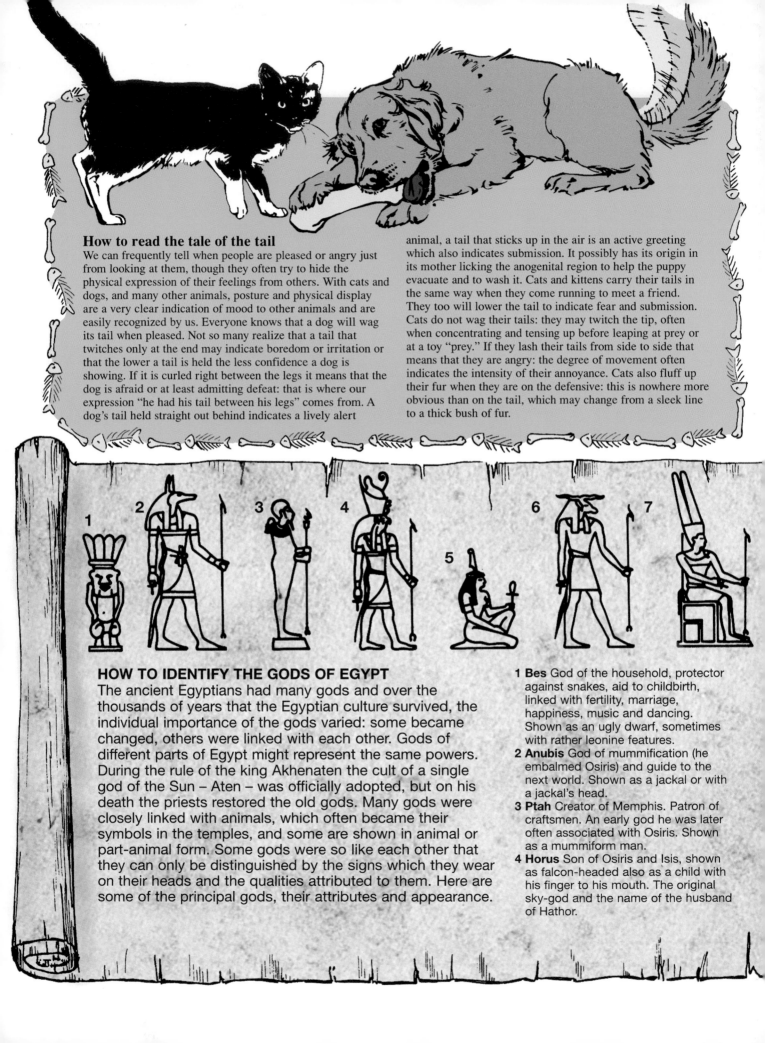

How to read the tale of the tail

We can frequently tell when people are pleased or angry just from looking at them, though they often try to hide the physical expression of their feelings from others. With cats and dogs, and many other animals, posture and physical display are a very clear indication of mood to other animals and are easily recognized by us. Everyone knows that a dog will wag its tail when pleased. Not so many realize that a tail that twitches only at the end may indicate boredom or irritation or that the lower a tail is held the less confidence a dog is showing. If it is curled right between the legs it means that the dog is afraid or at least admitting defeat: that is where our expression "he had his tail between his legs" comes from. A dog's tail held straight out behind indicates a lively alert animal, a tail that sticks up in the air is an active greeting which also indicates submission. It possibly has its origin in its mother licking the anogenital region to help the puppy evacuate and to wash it. Cats and kittens carry their tails in the same way when they come running to meet a friend. They too will lower the tail to indicate fear and submission. Cats do not wag their tails: they may twitch the tip, often when concentrating and tensing up before leaping at prey or at a toy "prey." If they lash their tails from side to side that means that they are angry: the degree of movement often indicates the intensity of their annoyance. Cats also fluff up their fur when they are on the defensive: this is nowhere more obvious than on the tail, which may change from a sleek line to a thick bush of fur.

HOW TO IDENTIFY THE GODS OF EGYPT

The ancient Egyptians had many gods and over the thousands of years that the Egyptian culture survived, the individual importance of the gods varied: some became changed, others were linked with each other. Gods of different parts of Egypt might represent the same powers. During the rule of the king Akhenaten the cult of a single god of the Sun – Aten – was officially adopted, but on his death the priests restored the old gods. Many gods were closely linked with animals, which often became their symbols in the temples, and some are shown in animal or part-animal form. Some gods were so like each other that they can only be distinguished by the signs which they wear on their heads and the qualities attributed to them. Here are some of the principal gods, their attributes and appearance.

1 **Bes** God of the household, protector against snakes, aid to childbirth, linked with fertility, marriage, happiness, music and dancing. Shown as an ugly dwarf, sometimes with rather leonine features.
2 **Anubis** God of mummification (he embalmed Osiris) and guide to the next world. Shown as a jackal or with a jackal's head.
3 **Ptah** Creator of Memphis. Patron of craftsmen. An early god he was later often associated with Osiris. Shown as a mummiform man.
4 **Horus** Son of Osiris and Isis, shown as falcon-headed also as a child with his finger to his mouth. The original sky-god and the name of the husband of Hathor.

HOW TO IMPROVISE A BUOYANCY AID

A TEMPORARY FLOTATION AID CAN BE IMPROVISED IN AN EMERGENCY FROM A PAIR OF PANTS. IF OPPORTUNITY ALLOWS, THE AID IS MORE EASILY MADE ON DRY LAND, BUT IT AS WELL TO PRACTICE TAKING YOUR PANTS OFF WHILE TREADING WATER.

1 KNOT THE END OF EACH LEG, AND FASTEN THE BUTTONS, OR ZIPPER, AT THE FLY.
2 HOLD THE PANTS BY THE WAISTBAND BEHIND YOUR HEAD.

3 SWING YOUR ARMS QUICKLY OVER AND DOWN INTO THE WATER IN ORDER TO TRAP THE MAXIMUM AMOUNT OF AIR INSIDE.
4 CLIMB BETWEEN THE INFLATED PANTS AS SHOWN. REINFLATE AS NECESSARY.

©DIAGRAM

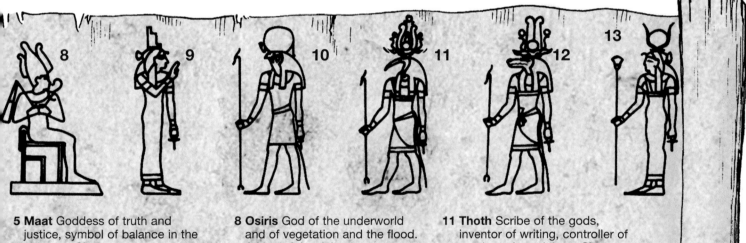

5 Maat Goddess of truth and justice, symbol of balance in the universe. Shown as a woman wearing an ostrich feather in her head.
6 Khnum Another creator god, from the Cataract region, said to have made man on his potter's wheel. Shown as a ram-headed man.
7 Amun (Amen, Amon) Tribal god of Thebes. When Theban princes gained the throne of Egypt, Amun became supreme deity. Shown as a man, sometimes with phallic emphasis, he was later identified with Re as Amun-Re. The ram and the goose are his sacred animals.

8 Osiris God of the underworld and of vegetation and the flood. A king of the delta, he was murdered by his brother Seth, but the pieces of his body were reunited by his wife. Shown as an enthroned king.
9 Isis Wife of Osiris; divine mother. Often shown with her son Horus sitting on her knee. Her cult became popular with the Romans.
10 Re (Ra) Sun god of Heliopolis, judge over all. Shown as falcon-headed. In one papyrus shown as a cat overcoming the serpent of night. Father of the gods and creator of mankind.

11 Thoth Scribe of the gods, inventor of writing, controller of magic and magicians. Shown with the head of an ibis.
12 Sobek Water god, associated with fertility. Shown as a crocodile-headed man.
13 Hathor Goddess of love, music and dancing, a sky goddess. Shown as a cow or as a woman with the head or horns of a cow. The Greeks identified her with Aphrodite.

How to identify the apostles and the evangelists

Paintings, carvings and stained glass portraits of the saints often identify them by incorporating a symbol linked with their life or death. This may be part of the design, on a shield or carried by the saint – like the keys of St. Peter, which commemorate that Christ gave him the name Peter (meaning rock) on which the church should be built and the keys of the kingdom of heaven. Here are the symbols of the most important saints: the apostles and the evangelists.

Christ Himself, called in the Bible, "the Lamb of God," is often depicted as a haloed lamb, usually white, holding a cross (see above).

The four evangelists were the writers of the four gospels; two of them, Matthew and John, were also apostles.

The evangelists
A **Matthew** angel
B **Mark** winged lion
C **Luke** winged ox
D **John** eagle

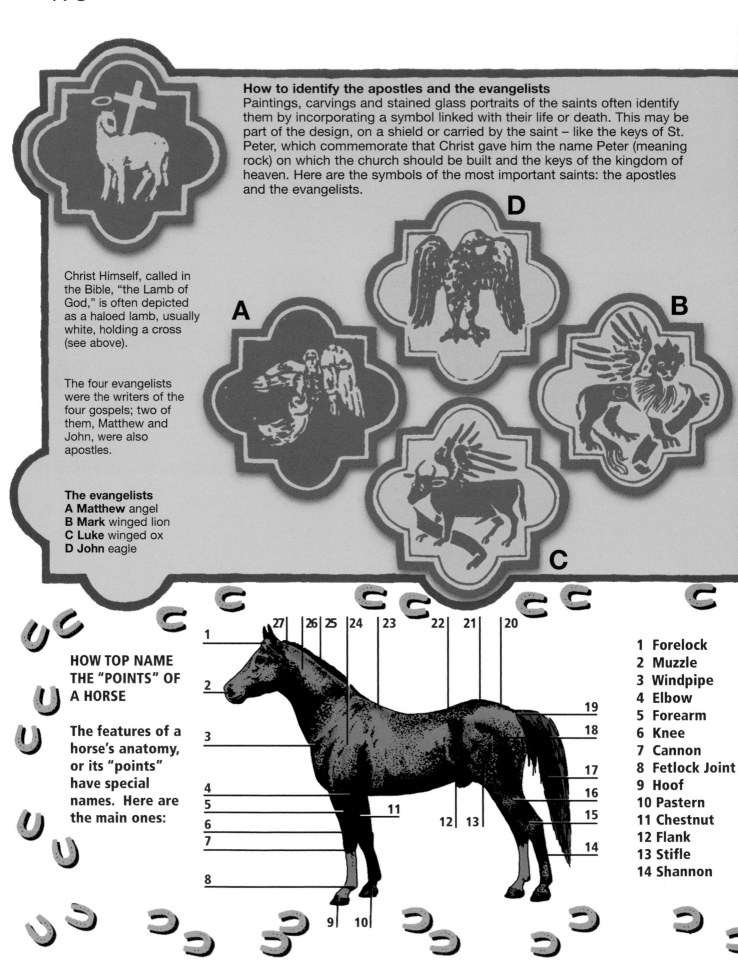

HOW TOP NAME THE "POINTS" OF A HORSE

The features of a horse's anatomy, or its "points" have special names. Here are the main ones:

1 Forelock
2 Muzzle
3 Windpipe
4 Elbow
5 Forearm
6 Knee
7 Cannon
8 Fetlock Joint
9 Hoof
10 Pastern
11 Chestnut
12 Flank
13 Stifle
14 Shannon

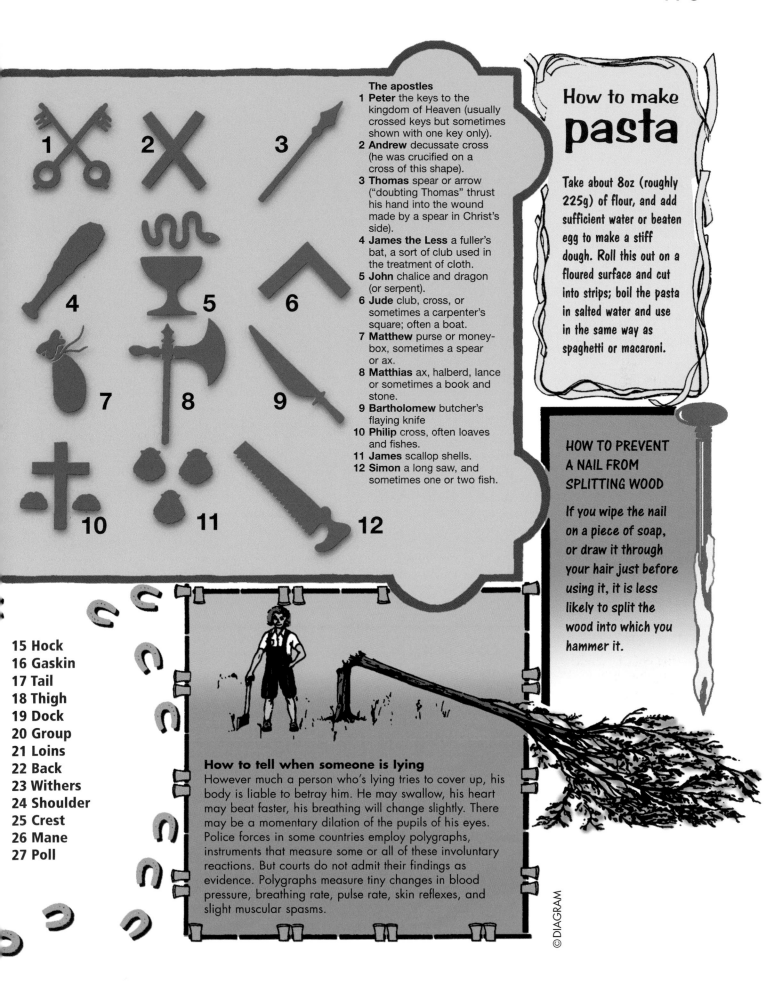

The apostles

1 **Peter** the keys to the kingdom of Heaven (usually crossed keys but sometimes shown with one key only).
2 **Andrew** decussate cross (he was crucified on a cross of this shape).
3 **Thomas** spear or arrow ("doubting Thomas" thrust his hand into the wound made by a spear in Christ's side).
4 **James the Less** a fuller's bat, a sort of club used in the treatment of cloth.
5 **John** chalice and dragon (or serpent).
6 **Jude** club, cross, or sometimes a carpenter's square; often a boat.
7 **Matthew** purse or money-box, sometimes a spear or ax.
8 **Matthias** ax, halberd, lance or sometimes a book and stone.
9 **Bartholomew** butcher's flaying knife
10 **Philip** cross, often loaves and fishes.
11 **James** scallop shells.
12 **Simon** a long saw, and sometimes one or two fish.

How to make pasta

Take about 8oz (roughly 225g) of flour, and add sufficient water or beaten egg to make a stiff dough. Roll this out on a floured surface and cut into strips; boil the pasta in salted water and use in the same way as spaghetti or macaroni.

HOW TO PREVENT A NAIL FROM SPLITTING WOOD

If you wipe the nail on a piece of soap, or draw it through your hair just before using it, it is less likely to split the wood into which you hammer it.

15 Hock
16 Gaskin
17 Tail
18 Thigh
19 Dock
20 Group
21 Loins
22 Back
23 Withers
24 Shoulder
25 Crest
26 Mane
27 Poll

How to tell when someone is lying

However much a person who's lying tries to cover up, his body is liable to betray him. He may swallow, his heart may beat faster, his breathing will change slightly. There may be a momentary dilation of the pupils of his eyes. Police forces in some countries employ polygraphs, instruments that measure some or all of these involuntary reactions. But courts do not admit their findings as evidence. Polygraphs measure tiny changes in blood pressure, breathing rate, pulse rate, skin reflexes, and slight muscular spasms.

HOW TO READ HEBREW NUMERALS

SHOWN HERE ARE THE HEBREW SYMBOLS FOR THE NUMBERS 1 TO 10 – THE SYMBOLS ARE ALSO LETTERS OF THE HEBREW ALPHABET.

1	2	3	4	5	6	7	8	9	10
א	ב	ג	ד	ה	ו	ז	ח	ט	י

HOW TO BE AVERAGE

If you want to meet the average statistics of a US adult, you will need to conform to the following measurements.

FOR A MAN:
Weight 162lb (73.5kg)
A Height 5ft 9in (1.753m)
B Chest 38³/₄in (98.5cm)
C Waist 31³/₄in (80.6cm)
D Hips 37³/₄in (95.5cm)

FOR A WOMAN:
Weight 135lb (61.2kg)
Height 5ft 3³/₄in (1.625m)
Bust 35¹/₂in (90.2 cm)
Waist 29¹/₄in (96.5cm)
Hips 38in (96.5cm)

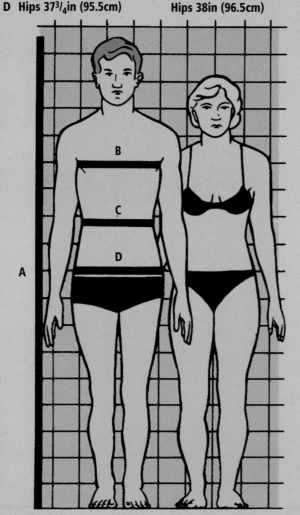

How to move around in space

Whether you are in a space capsule or outside in space, you will be in a condition of weightlessness due to the lack of gravity. Once you begin to move in any direction there will be nothing to slow you down or arrest your movement. In your capsule you must be careful not to bump into objects or touch instruments as you float around. It is preferable to control your movement by holding onto hand grips and guiding yourself around. Outside, much the same principle applies. Always tether yourself to your space craft so that if you float away you can haul yourself back. Guide yourself around by projections on the space vehicle. Pull yourself along your tether lines. By jerking on your tethering rope or pushing off from the craft surface you can initiate movement but you cannot control direction as you can in water or even as a sky-diver, for there is no medium against which to move yourself. As we gain more experience of maneuvering in space we may possibly use small retrorockets to propel us, just as, on a large scale, they propel our space vehicles.

Space is a hostile environment. Temperatures are extreme. There is no air to breathe. There is no atmosphere to give protection from radiation. Even weightlessness may have a long-term effect on the circulation and on balance mechanisms and cause problems of readaptation on return to Earth. You must take your own environment with you into space – that is, a spacecraft, or a spacesuit if you are going to leave the craft. This must supply oxygen at suitable pressure, water and carbon dioxide, a means of removing waste and contaminants, and temperature control.

How to interpret wine labels

The information on wine labels varies from country to country. Basically, every label tells you the country of origin and the amount in the bottle, and the type of wine. Other information you may find includes the vintage, or year of production.

France. The term *Appellation Contrôlée* is an official guarantee of where the wine comes from, how it is produced and the grapes used; *Château* refers to a particular estate or vineyard; *mise en bouteilles au château* means it was bottled at the vineyard and not shipped in bulk for bottling elsewhere; VDQS, standing for *Vins Délimites de Qualité Superieure*, is put on wines not up to Appellation standard; Vins de Pays are ordinary, local wines.

Germany. The information on the labels is a guarantee of actual quality. The best wine is *QmP* (*Qualitätswein mit Prädikat*); next comes *QbA* (*Qualitätswein bestimmter Anbaugebiete*); below that is *Tafelmein*, dinner-wine or ordinary "plonk". The best wines carry the name of the vineyard (*Einzellage*) or group of vineyards (*Grosslage*). *Erzeugerabfüllung* means bottled by the grower. The variety of grape (generally Riesling) may also be named.

Italy. The DOC (*Denominazione di Origine Controllata*) system is roughly equivalent to France's *Appellation Contrôlée*. The name of a wine may be the region where it is produced, a traditional name, or the kind of grape. *Classico* means the central part of the particular region.

Spain. *Reserva* is a good quality wine; *Rioja* is the best wine region; a *Bodega* is a firm producing wines; *Denominacon de origen* is an "official" wine region.

United States. Californian wines carry the brand name and the variety of grape used; similar information is found on labels from New York State.

England. The name of the vineyard and the variety of grape used are the main information.

Australia. Labels carry full details about the wines, but there are as yet no "official" standards of quality.

HOW TO KEEP FLAMINGOES PINK

Flamingoes in captivity may lack the natural environmental factors to maintain their pink color; if they show signs of fading, the inclusion of carrot juice in their diet will soon restore their rosiness.

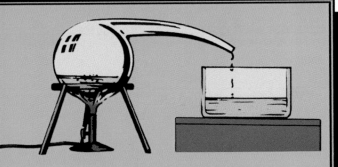

How to distill water
Distilled water is de-ionized water. To de-ionize the water, boil it and cool the steam: the condensed steam is distilled water. Alternatively scrape the ice from the sides of a freezer or the ice-making compartment of a refrigerator. When it melts, you've got distilled water.

HOW TO MAKE A ZEN GARDEN

A Japanese sand garden – or Zen garden – is sparse in design but rich in the contemplative space it offers the beholder. To sit and meditate upon it is to glimpse the layer structure of existence – is the garden a small sea, a wide ocean, cloudtops, a vast and undefined universe, or is it all of these things at the same time?

As a site for your garden, choose a small area relatively free from wind. Give the ground a slight slope to improve drainage. Pour in a concrete bed or cover the earth with a sheet of vinyl and punch holes in it where water can seep out. Don't leave the earth bare; mud will come to the surface after a rain and spoil the garden's appearance.

How to predict a volcanic eruption

1 Before you do anything else, investigate the prior history of the volcano. If its eruptions have occurred at regular intervals in the past and an eruption is long overdue, then the likelihood of an eruption occurring is great.

2 If the volcano is smoking, examine the gas being discharged. With some volcanoes, eruption is preceded by increases in the temperature, volume, and chloride content of the gas. But this is not true for all volcanoes, and weather conditions can also affect temperature and volume.

3 Magma (molten igneous rock) moving toward the surface heats the surrounding rock and reduces the intensity of its natural magnetism. You can determine whether magma is in motion by using a device called a magnetometer to measure the degree and direction of shift in the local magnetic field.

4 Aerial infrared photography may help you detect temperature changes as the hot magma comes to the surface.

5 Magma flowing underground can make the surrounding rock heave up or subside. Measure these changes with a tiltmeter, a device consisting of two vessels connected by a tube and partly filled with water. When the slope of the ground changes, liquid runs from one vessel to the other. Two tiltmeters placed on the ground at right angles to each other will give the direction and amount of change in the slope. As yet, however, no correlation has been made between the degree of tilt and the likelihood of eruption.

6 Eruptions are generally preceded by a prolonged series of small earth tremors. While none of these factors by itself can be used with certainty to predict an eruption, the presence of many of them is a clear sign that something unusual is happening. Notify your local authorities first if you think an eruption is imminent. Spreading panic among your neighbors is counter-productive and, should your alarm turn out to be false, lessens the willingness of others to respond should there later be a genuine emergency.

Spread crushed granite (not beach sand) over the bed to a depth of 2½ to 3 inches (6 to 8 cm). Add a large rock grouping in one corner or scatter smaller groupings seemingly at random through the garden. Avoid symmetry and keep your design simple. Rake in decorative wave or ripple patterns with a serrated piece of wood. Renew or change the pattern every week or so.

Add moss or tiny plantings around the bases of the rocks to soften their lines. Coniferous trees (pines, junipers, etc.) on the border of the garden provide a good color counterpoint throughout the year and make the mood a little less austere. Try not to use deciduous trees – their leaves will fall into the garden and crumble, and it will take hours to pick them out.

HOW TO WEAR THE SAREE

The traditional Indian saree is made from a rectangle of fabric about 6 yards (6m) long, and is worn over a close-fitting short-sleeved bodice. The fabric is wrapped once around the body, then most of the rest of the free end is folded back and forth in pleats (1) and tucked into the waist at the front (2). The last part of the fabric is wrapped around the body and over the left shoulder (3).

©DIAGRAM

HOW TO TRAP SLUGS

SINK A SAUCERFUL OF BEER LEVEL WITH THE SURFACE OF THE GARDEN SOIL. SLUGS WILL BE ATTRACTED TO THE BEER AND BECOME TRAPPED IN THE SAUCER. WITH LUCK, TOADS OR BIRDS WILL COME AND EAT THEM FOR YOU, OR YOU COULD FEED THEM TO YOUR AXOLOTL (SEE PAGE 118).

HOW TO PLAY
CHINESE DOMINOES

The civil series

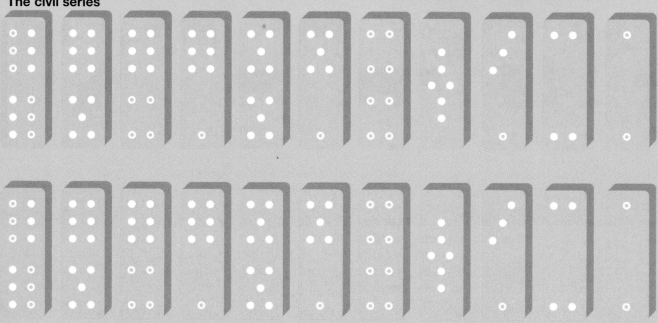

The dominoes Chinese dominoes are longer and narrower than Western dominoes – typically 3 inches x 7/8 inches x 3/8 inches (8cm x 2.5cm x 2cm). Spots on the dominoes are colored red or white – all 4s and 1s are red, double 6 is red and white, all others are white. There are no blanks.

One set consists of 32 dominoes, divided into two series: the civil and the military. Many games – like the one described here – require more than one set of dominoes.

The civil series comprises 22 dominoes, forming 11 identical pairs: all the doubles plus the 6:5,6:4,6:1, 5:1, and 3:1.

The military series comprises 10 dominoes: 6:3,6:2,5:4,5:3,5:2,4:3, 4:2,4:1,3:2,2:1.

The military series

The game described below – "k'ap t'ai shap" or "collecting tens" – is just one of many Chinese domino games. If you can't find any Chinese dominoes, you could improvise with Western dominoes or make card substitutes. Several sets are needed. The objective is to be the first to make up a complete hand, as described below. A forerunner of mah jongg, ktap t'ai shap is often played for very high stakes in the Orient.

A

B

C

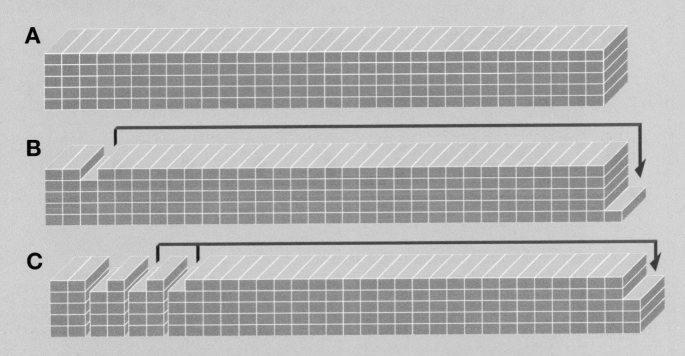

Start of play A long "woodpile" five dominoes high (**A**) is built down the center of the table, using several sets. Players join the game by placing equal stakes, and dice are thrown to decide who will have the first turn. The woodpile is then prepared for play by removing the top domino from the third stack from one end and placing it face down at the other end of the woodpile (**B**). The top domino is then taken from each alternate stack up to one less than the number of players, and these are also added in order to the far end of the woodpile (**C**). The first player then takes the end two stacks (with ten dominoes) and the other players in turn each take two stacks (with nine dominoes).

Turns If the first player does not have a winning hand, he starts play by discarding one domino and placing it face up on the table. Then each player in his turn:
1) may take any discarded domino to complete his hand – or to exchange it for one of his own dominoes; and
2) draws one domino from the end of the woodpile, which he may immediately discard or keep in place of another domino from his hand.
Result The game ends when one player completes his hand. This entitles him to the total staked (less the gambling house commission).

A complete hand consists of: (a) four pairs, each with a total spot count of 10 or a multiple of 10; and (b) any identical pair. An example is shown here.

a   b

HOW TO RECOGNIZE MYTHICAL BEASTS

1 Griffins were huge beasts, with the head and wings of an eagle, the ears of a horse and the body of a lion. They were often thought to guard a hoard of gold.

2 Unicorns were reputedly a lithe, powerful combination of a horse's body and head with an antelope's legs, a lion's tail and a fearsome spiral horn on the forehead. Only the virtue of a young maiden could tame a unicorn.

3 Cyclopes were man-eating hairy giants with only one eye, set centrally in the forehead. The biggest and most famous cyclops, polyphemus, lived in a cave and grazed sheep.

4 Satyrs had the torso and head of a man, but the horns and hindquarters of a goat. They were woodland creatures, associated with fertility.

5 Harpies were said to have the head and torso of a woman, pale, thin with dirty matted hair, but with the wings and feet of a vulture. They were immortal, although always on the point of starvation.

6 Centaurs had the upper body of a man combined with the body and legs of a horse. They were very civilized, being famous for their noble nature and knowledge of medicine.

5

6

How to grow a crystal garden

Make up a supersaturated solution of the substance you want to grow as crystals – common salt, alum and copper sulfate are good ones to experiment with. To make the solution, pour the substance into hot water and stir until it dissolves, and add more until no more will dissolve; then pour off the solution into another vessel.

Suspend a piece of thread in the middle of the solution and leave it undisturbed for several days. Crystals will build up on the thread. If you put a small crystal of the substance on the end of the thread, you'll get quicker results.

Another method is to drip isinglass, a very pure form of gelatine, into the water for the crystals to grow along. This produces more interesting shapes.

HOW TO MAKE A CAKE FOR BIRDS

FILL A SMALL BOWL WITH ANY MIXTURE OF MILLET, BIRDSEED, CHOPPED BACON RIND, SHELLED PEANUTS AND COCONUT, AND ADD ENOUGH SUET TO MAKE THE MIXTURE PLIABLE. PRESS IT DOWN HARD INTO THE BOWL, CHILL AND, WHEN IT IS FIRM, TURN THE "CAKE" OUT; THEN PUT IT ON A CAT-PROOF BIRD TABLE.

HOW TO HEAT A ROMAN VILLA

WHEN HEATING WAS REQUIRED IN ROMAN VILLAS, A SYSTEM KNOWN AS HYPOCAUST WAS INCORPORATED. COLUMNS OF BRICKS OR TILES SEPARATED THE FLOORS FROM THE FOUNDATIONS, AND WARM AIR FROM CENTRAL FIRES CIRCULATED THROUGH THE CAVITIES.

(in case you thought we had forgotten...)

©DIAGRAM

How to hold a crocodile

A small crocodile or cayman can be controlled by grasping it just behind the head with one hand, with your thumb on the opposite side of the head from your fingers, and using your other hand to restrain its hind legs and support its body. Remember even the tiniest crocodiles can bite so it is advisable to wear tough leather gloves. As it grows its lashing tail can injure too. Crocodiles grow rapidly. They soon become too big to be held in this way and are virtually impossible to keep as pets – so don't even think of keeping a young one.

A noose over the snout, pulled tight to keep the jaw shut, and ropes around the body and tail – with a number of people to help – are necessary to control an adult.

HOW TO RECOGNIZE A MEMBER OF THE DIAGRAM GROUP

1 Bruce Robertson
2 Ruth Midgley
3 Gail Lawther
4 David Heidenstam
5 Trevor Bounford
6 Wolfang Foges
7 Kathleen McDougall
8 Graham Rosewarne
9 Jane Morgan
10 Sean Gilbert
11 Cornelius Cardew
12 Richard Hummerstone
13 Howard Loxton
14 Cissie Myers
15 Bob Chapman
16 Brian Hewson
17 Stephen Clark
18 Janos Marffy
19 Mark Evans
20 David Harding

CONCEIVED AND
PRODUCED BY
THE DIAGRAM GROUP

WITH CONTRIBUTIONS FROM:
TREVOR BOUNFORD
CORNELIUS CARDEW
BOB CHAPMAN
JEAN COOKE
MEL COOPER
PETER GOODMAN
DAMIAN GRINT
NORMA JACK
ESTHER JAGGER
GREG JEFFRIES
RUTH MIDGLEY
BERNARD MOORE
THEO ROWLAND-ENTWISTLE
ALEC TINDAL

EDITED BY HOWARD LOXTON
WITH DAVID HARDING
MAUREEN CARTWRIGHT
JENNIFER JUSTICE
GAIL LAWTHER

ILLUSTRATIONS AND
DECORATIONS BY:
STEPHEN CLARK
SEAN GILBERT
STEPHEN GYAPAY
BRIAN HEWSON
RICHARD HUMMERSTONE
KATHLEEN MCDOUGALL
JANOS MARFFY
GRAHAM ROSEWARNE

ART EDITOR: MARK EVANS

The Diagram Group have enjoyed collecting the information in this book for your interest and amusement. They have included some very practical tips from their own experience, and ideas from wide ranging sources from different cultures and different centuries. Naturally they have not been able to test them all – it is not so easy to find a vampire or to gather the resources to build a pyramid and none of our editors was prepared to volunteer for mummification. We frankly don't believe that Aristotle ever succeeded in putting his method of measuring fleas' leaps into practice, and wonder whether the medieval herbalist gave the full instructions for using poppy seeds, so we are certainly not promising that all the ideas presented *really* work. We have included some of them because we thought you would find them fun to read about. So please be sensible and don't take needless risks. We share with you the information that we found, but cannot guarantee that you will have success, and can accept no responsibility for anything that may occur.